KNOWING WORDS

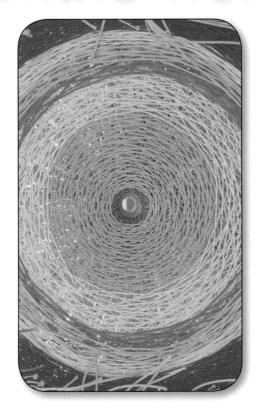

A GUIDE TO FIRST-YEAR WRITING & RHETORIC
2015-2016
12TH EDITION

Colorado
University of Colorado at Boulder ™

FOUNTAINHEAD
PRESS

Our green initiatives include:

Electronic Products
We deliver products in non-paper form whenever possible. This includes pdf down-loadables, flash drives, & CDs.

Electronic Samples
We use Xample, a new electronic sampling system. Instructor samples are sent via a personalized web page that links to pdf downloads.

FSC Certified Printers
All of our printers are certified by the Forest Service Council which promotes environmentally and socially responsible management of the world's forests. This program allows consumer groups, individual consumers, and businesses to work together hand-in-hand to promote responsible use of the world's forests as a re-newable and sustainable resource.

Recycled Paper
Most of our products are printed on a minimum of 30% post-consumer waste recycled paper.

Support of Green Causes
When we do print, we donate a portion of our revenue to green causes. Listed below are a few of the organizations that have received donations from Fountain-head Press. We welcome your feedback and suggestions for contributions, as we are always searching for worthy initiatives.
Rainforest 2 Reef
Environmental Working Group

Cover Photo: "Obsession with Death" by Dylan Gebbia-Richards

Copyright © 2015 Department of Writing and Rhetoric, University of Colorado Boulder

All rights reserved. No part of this book may be reproduced or utilized in any form or by any means, electronic or mechanical, including photocopying and recording, or by any informational storage and retrieval system without written permission from the publisher.

Books may be purchased for educational purposes.

For information, please call or write:

1-800-586-0330
Fountainhead Press
Southlake, TX 76092
Web Site: www.fountainheadpress.com
E-mail: customerservice@fountainheadpress.com

Twelfth Edition

ISBN: 978-1-68036-057-8

Printed in the United States of America

PWR Contact Information

The PWR main office is located on the lower level of Environmental Design in Room 1B60. Our office hours are 8–12 and 1–5, Monday through Friday. We are closed on regular university holidays.

Program website: http://www.colorado.edu/pwr/

Main office (drop/add, general questions), 303-492-8188

Program Director
John-Michael Rivera
303-735-5654

Associate Director of First-Year Writing
Lonni Pearce
303-492-4478

Associate Director of Sustainability and Residential Academic Programs
John Ackerman
303-492-8015

Associate Director of the Writing Center
Eric Klinger
303-492-1690

Associate Director of Service Learning and Outreach
Veronica House
303-735-4774

Coordinator for Information Literacy and Norlin Research
Michelle Albert
303-735-4673

Coordinator for Writing Technology/Digital Learning
Petgar Schaberg
303-736-4673

Coordinator for Conflict Resolution
Rebecca Dickson
303-735-4908

Table of Contents

Chapter 1

Introduction

Welcome to your writing class! And welcome to your textbook, *Knowing Words*! The book you hold in your hands is one of a series that has been published for the University of Colorado Boulder's Program for Writing and Rhetoric classes for over a decade. While this book is specifically written for students of WRTG 1150, it follows many of the conventions of the textbooks you'll read in other classes. This chapter, for instance, like the first chapter in many textbooks will introduce you to the main concepts that will be defined in more detail in other chapters. We will provide you with some more informal ideas about how writing can impact your life. We will discuss the relationship between writing and knowledge, identity, change, and community. Then, we'll introduce our understanding of the key processes that you'll explore in your course, continuing our argument for the importance of this requirement, and perhaps expanding your expectations for a writing class. We'll introduce the concepts of reading, research, and reflection not necessarily as "information" that you can "learn" but as complex processes that this class will ask you to experience.

Penultimately, this chapter will orient you to the Program for Writing and Rhetoric (PWR)—the administrative unit responsible for the teaching and promotion of writing studies on the CU Boulder campus—and to the ways that the faculty members of the PWR approach the teaching of the first-year writing course.

> The word "penultimate" is an interesting and very specific word meaning "second to last." We hope you'll be pleasantly surprised at how often you can impress your friends with this word!

Finally, introducing one of the features of all of the chapters in this book, we'll end with a series of reflective questions that will help you think about the ways that your personal experiences connect with the concepts in this chapter and how understanding those connections then prepare you for the following chapters.

Why Are You in this Class?

Throughout this text, we use the first person plural pronoun to signify the various authors and editors who have contributed to this text. We also use the second person plural pronoun to signify our readers. Consider the implications of using the words "we" and "you" like this: how would this text change if we used the first person and *I* wrote that *I* wanted *students* to think about why *students* are in this class?

The very first thing that we'd like you to think about—if you were to read this book from front to back, which is, of course, unlikely—is why you are here. The most basic answer is that you are here because you are required to be here. You cannot graduate without taking the required writing courses offered by the PWR. And these writing courses are required because a group of legislators called the "Colorado Commission on Higher Education" and the leaders of the statewide University of Colorado have decided that a student who graduates from this university ought to meet certain objectives.

Like almost every other topic we'll cover in this text, however, this requirement is not as straightforward as you might think. First, remember that regardless of the fact that this course is required and that your attendance is required, you are still continually choosing to be here. You could put this book down right now. You could walk out of the classroom, out of Boulder, and get on a slow boat to a South Pacific island. Even though a lot of your experience has been about meeting requirements, the only actually required human activities are limited to the central nervous system, i.e. we have to breathe, beat our hearts, blink, etc. Nearly everything else labeled "required" in human life is actually much more of a strong suggestion. You may feel like you "have to" go to work when you're scheduled, but the truth is that really, you are just being strongly and effectively persuaded to act in a certain way. It is your choice to be in this class, and in fact the study of rhetoric and writing is as much about discovering the ways that you are strongly (or weakly) persuaded to believe something is required as it is about developing into a "college level writer."

A deeper level of complexity exposes the difficulty in defining a college level writer. The CCHE has worked hard to define what it means to complete this course; they propose that your rhetorical awareness, sentence complexity, and research skills will define you as a college-level writer. But if you dig into research on college writing or academic writing or any kind of writing at all, you'll quickly discover that there is a lot of controversy about the definition of a "good writer" or "good writing" or even how to teach writing.

> We used a semi-colon in this paragraph. This is an often misused punctuation mark. Search for "semi-colon usage" online to learn about its rules.

So, we're going to take the liberty of answering the first question in this text for you and for the state and for the leaders of the university. You are here to explore. You are here to play. You are here to learn. And though we will provide you with boundaries, in some ways you get to explore what you want to and play how you want and learn about what you want. Of course, we hope that you focus on our curricula (we've spent a lot of time becoming experts!), but your instructors would agree that one of the most important and most fun aspects of this class is that its content can range with your own interests. And it should! You will have the opportunity to explore political topics, the potential majors you're considering, or almost anything that you have some curiosity about.

> "Curriculum" is a Latin word that means something like race track or race course. This idea of a course around which you lead people lent itself, in the 19th century, to being a metaphor for the way people teach, which is how we use it in this paragraph. "Curricula" is the Latin plural.

Literally anything you could want to explore, play with, or learn about requires language and rhetoric. You are in this class because it will help you build a perspective of rhetorical awareness and critical inquiry that in turn will only help you to make choices about how you want to spend your time at this university and on this planet.

What Is Writing?

Writing, as you are probably well aware, can take on many different forms and can mean different things to different people. In fact, you likely write all the time as a part of your personal, social life. However, many people don't consider what they do as part of their social lives to be writing. This is a mystery. The most basic definition of writing would describe the inscription of symbols whose particular combinations form words that then represent various things, concepts, actions, and relationships. When you compose a message for social media,

> If someone were to ask you what it was to learn to write 10 years ago, how would you have answered? What do you think it means to learn to write today?

3

or take and caption and send a photograph through an app, you are certainly representing something and you're doing so with combinations of symbols, including the alphabet. And yet, many people do not consider the composition of a social media post to be writing. And perhaps stranger still, the time we spend on social media doesn't seem to be reading either.

The revolution of networked and digital means of communication makes the job of a writing teacher—and therefore a book like this—much more complex. This complexity, however, is not entirely new. Scholars and thinkers in our educational tradition—which dates back to ancient Hellenic society—have been dealing with the challenges of writing instruction by exploring the different ways that people read and write. And even though the study of writing dates back thousands of years, those who study it continue to find more complexity.

> The adjective "Hellenic" refers to the era of classical Greece, the most popular depiction of which comes from *The Iliad* and *The Odyssey*, the plots of which pivot on the abduction of the famous beauty, Helen.

Put more simply, writing has a certain ineffable power. Writing can function as a snapshot of our minds, which then allows us to see what we're thinking from a different perspective. And a new perspective can expose us to thoughts we didn't even know we had. Writing can help us focus on the problems and questions whose answers will make the world a better place. Writing can help us to more fully understand our own responsibilities to the good of the global community. Writing can also bring us to that global community. Writing allows us to communicate with people whose disagreements with us may change our minds in unexpected ways or force us to better understand our own positions. And writing can do much, much more. It is a beautiful mystery, this creation and consumption of symbols, and without it life would be different indeed.

This course is meant to help you to continue to explore this mystery, to take on the perspective that the writing you do and the writing you read can be much more than sequences of symbols. To that end, we posit the following values as a way to orient you to this perspective, a perspective we believe will help you develop as students, as citizens, and as people.

Writing to Know

Knowledge is inseparable from words.

You've heard the old question, "If a tree falls in the forest, and no one is there to hear it, does it make a sound?" The question was first posed in 1710 by George Berkeley in his book *Concerning the principles of human knowledge,* which is concerned with the nature of reality itself. His question is meant to demonstrate that reality itself—the trees, rocks, and air of the world we all live in—is in some ways limited to our individual sensory experiences. If you're there to hear that tree fall, the question becomes ridiculous. Even if you're not, you might think the question is ridiculous because the vibrations in the atmosphere we interpret as sound are a physical by-product of the kinetic energy released by the falling of the tree. And yet, you can't really know the answer to this question, which is part of the reason that people have been asking it for 300 years.

> This idea and many like it have been seriously and continually critiqued over the centuries. A quick internet search for the philosophy of human subjectivity will demonstrate the breadth of this inquiry.

Regardless of how ridiculous the tree question might seem, think about the reality of dreams that we have but do not remember. Many scientists are convinced that most people have many dreams that we may not remember when we wake up. We experience these dreams just as surely as we do those that we remember, and yet that experience is more or less lost forever (psychologists and others disagree as to the function of dreaming—dreams we don't remember may in fact have lasting effects and thus not be "lost").

Consider, now, those thoughts that we've had that we may not have spoken aloud or written down. Many of you may have had the experience of having a great idea and then forgetting everything about it except how great it was. That means that we can't work to make that idea better, more feasible, more helpful, or more complex.

However, if you write an idea down, you have the benefit of time; you can come back to an idea you've written down and make it better. This is what we mean by writing to know: writing is the best way to explore the processes of thinking and re-thinking about a particular subject from multiple perspectives and for multiple uses. Writing is a way to remember the forgotten dream, to hear the silent tree-fall, to discover things about the world and about yourself that you didn't know that you knew.

Writing to Grow

Identity is inseparable from words.

As you continue at CU, you'll learn that a common academic perspective suggests that people are all constantly constructing their identities. No one is born as a snowboarder or gamer or ballroom dancer; we become those. You might even remember that first moment when you really felt, really really felt like you could claim a new identity. And you may even remember learning the vocabulary associated with that identity. One day you wake up not knowing what a three-sixty switch grab is; you go to the terrain park at a ski hill; you hear older kids talking about it and then doing it; you learn what it means and how to do it; you land it; and you go to bed as a "real snowboarder."

> You may guess that we, your editors, are not "real" snowboarders–Eds.

In a lot of ways, becoming a college graduate isn't much different. Of course, taking on the identity of an academic or a college graduate is a little more complicated; academics don't only have a specific vocabulary (though we do), but also take on different ways of looking at the world, what we call theories. Some neuroscientists believe the theory that human behavior is the result of a combination of brain chemistry and the ways that that chemistry interacts with the individual's history, while some sociologists see behavior as a result of a huge complex of human history and societal expectations.

> Notice the word "some," repeated twice, in this paragraph. This is a qualification and keeps us from having to defend a position–i.e. we know what *all* neuroscientists believe–that is clearly indefensible.

The upshot, here, is that writing is a good way to create a record of your development into a given identity. Even if you don't keep a journal or diary, you can always look back at your social media history and witness your own embrace of certain identities. You can see, for example, the way that you transitioned from a Pokemon to a One Direction fanatic. With writing then, you can more clearly recognize your development and then work to take more control of the ways that you come to inhabit those identities that you choose. Because writing allows you to slow down or even stop your thoughts at a given moment and then come back to them, it can also help you to understand who you were, who you are, and who you want to be.

Writing to Change the World

Change is inseparable from words.

Writers are people who have a reason to write. You may say that you write only when you have to—but most writers would say the same thing. That "have to" can take several different forms—an idea, an inspiration, an assignment—and it can come from a number of different sources—a teacher, a boss, or yourself. Writers write for any number of reasons: to express themselves, to think "out loud," to persuade and inform others, to enter conversations beyond the small circle of their direct experience. They write because writing is a way to make things happen, to change hearts and minds—including their own. As a writer, you write because it is one of the best ways not only to tell others what you think and feel, but to discover what you think and feel.

> Think about books that have certainly changed the world or how the coding that directed computers to the very first internet counts as writing.

And this, without exaggeration, can change the world. Although it is unspeakably rare for a writer to compose something that changes the whole world, it has certainly happened and will again. Changing the world does not have to be quite so dramatic, however. Changing the world can be as simple as giving someone a note reminding them of their personal strength, a note they may very well keep for the rest of their lives. Writing can change the small worlds that we all live in, the worlds of families, friends, even the worlds we create inside our own skulls.

Writing to Engage

Community is inseparable from words.

If someone asked you to picture a typical "writer," some of you would conjure up an image of a solitary figure, lost in a world of her own, hunched over a piece of paper, staring into space, or looking for enlightenment in the glare of a computer screen. What this lonely image forgets, however, is that writing never takes place in a vacuum. You write not only for a reason, but for an audience, and the choices you make as you write determine your relationship to that audience.

> An interesting development in writing conventions in the last 50 years is the recognition of the hidden sexism in basic writing conventions. Using the masculine pronoun "he" to signify any unknown person reveals our society's belief in the primacy of the masculine perspective. In this text, we will alternate between the masculine and feminine pronouns in recognition of the women who will read and hopefully identify with our perspective.

The recognition of the relationship between a writer and his audience will provide our first definition of "rhetoric": writing with an understanding of the choices you have available to you as a writer and how those choices are always shaped by the contexts in which you write—who will read what you write and why. Whether you have a lot of writing experience or a little, college likely represents a new writing context for you, one that brings with it a new set of challenges. The purpose of this course is to help you meet those challenges.

Entering college means you are bringing yourself into a classroom where new questions will challenge you to find deep, complex answers. The flurry of questions can obscure the fact that the answers begin with you—with the person who steps into a lecture hall or a workshop or a library, the person who takes notes, reads, discusses, and sits down at a computer. You bring to every question a reservoir of experiences, beliefs, motivations, and dreams, moved in mysterious ways by your genes, your desires, your culture, what you eat (and drink), and how much you sleep.

And the way that you're individually responsible for your performance in college can obscure the fact that you are a member of a community or more accurately a number of communities. We believe that it's important for you to recognize the ways that you communicate with, interact with, and persuade the communities that you already belong to as you enter what may be the novel community of the university.

To encourage the development of community in this course, we encourage writers to work with one another; the course is taught as a cross between a reading seminar and a writing workshop. Writing workshops will give you a chance to read your writing through others' eyes and to learn new strategies by seeing how other writers work, while class discussions will provide a forum to test your thinking, to practice listening to what others have to say, and to talk through your writing. And the community you create should not be confined to the classroom. The collaborative work you begin in class will spill over into your instructor's office hours, discussions over e-mail, and—we hope—talk in coffee shops and dorm rooms.

As you develop communities around and even outside of the university, you may notice that one of the central purposes of academic writing is to inform the civic discussions that shape our communities. First-Year Writing and Rhetoric challenges you to think academically, to engage in academic discussions with your teachers and peers, to recognize the audiences who can benefit from your education, and to convey your insights in forms of communication that are persuasive and productive. Your writing workshop is a short course in what it is to know yourself and to take your place as an informed, thoughtful member of your communities.

What Will Happen in this Class?

Although the above values do suggest, we think, something fundamental about writing, we also realize that this perspective is difficult to take on. One of the reasons you're in this class is to practice and experience writing in this way. To that end, we'd like to introduce you to three more concrete and recognizable activities you will undertake in this class: Reading, Research, and Reflection.

Reading

First-Year Writing and Rhetoric is grounded in reading: assigned readings, sources you find through your own research, and the texts written by other students in the class. Discussions and writing assignments will require you to read critically—to discern not just information but the author's reasoning, so that you can respond more thoughtfully with your own questions and insights. Where can you find holes or confusion in the argument? How does the text connect with your own experience? Your response might take the form of a class debate, an analysis of an article, a persuasive paper based on research, or an oral or written critique of the work of one of your peers. You'll also practice reading like a writer: When a piece of writing makes you feel something, how does it do it?

Research

Many assignments for First-Year Writing and Rhetoric will require research. The course introduces you to campus resources, methods of research, and criteria for determining the credibility and validity of your sources. Inquiry-driven research involves substantially more than compiling information. It requires cultivating curiosity.

Your experience may be a starting place for inquiry into the roots of your own values and perspectives. But curiosity will also take you into other times and places—other generations, cultures, religions, classes, levels of education, and areas of expertise. When you understand your own position and step back to examine it from other perspectives, you can reinforce or reshape your own views with more confidence and authority. And you'll come to understand a certain "academic conversation," which is a metaphor for the ways that academics share and critique and build on each others' ideas with their articles and books.

> Increasingly, academics use social media to interact and to have this "conversation." However, traditionally published print outlets continue to be the official medium of academics—even though many of these articles and books are accessed through academic databases as PDFs. Why do you think this is?

The questions you ask as you research are driven by the demands of the issue as well as your own curiosity. What is the current thinking on this issue? How rapidly does it change, and why? What are the competing points of view? Who has the expertise to speak with authority? What are the strengths and weaknesses in the arguments from each point of view? What topics have been left out of the debate? As you gain mastery in the process of reading, writing, and researching, you'll learn to ask deeper, more relevant questions, and you'll become more adept at answering them.

Reflection

Throughout the processes of reading, writing, and researching for this course, you will be asked to reflect on what you are doing. In class discussions, conferences with your instructor, journal entries, or short essays, you will cultivate the habit of thinking about the choices you make as a reader, a writer, and a researcher, so that you can become more conscious of those choices, more in control of how they work. Reflection will become a habit of mind.

The questions you ask as you read make you aware of how you are entering a conversation or dialogue with the text. How am I responding intellectually and emotionally? What about a text or a practice makes me feel like this? How does this connect to my own experience and observations? What is foreign and new? What confuses me? Why? What gives me new insight? How?

The questions you ask as you write help you understand your relationship to the subject you are exploring. On the deepest level, what do I think about this issue? Are my evidence and reasoning honest? Am I asking relevant questions? Am I using my own voice? What subjects and issues compel me enough to read, research, and write about them? How can I cultivate curiosity? What parts of this writing task am I resisting and why?

WHAT WILL WE LEARN?

Although the types of assignments you are given will vary according to your instructor, the PWR has set six learning goals for the course and therefore critical inquiry. These goals are woven into the homework, class activities, and writing assignments. Through your work this semester, these six goals will guide you as you ask questions, search for and then analyze information, and decide on your response. In other words, you'll be reading, writing, researching, and reflecting in order to know through words.

First-Year Writing and Rhetoric Goals

◆ To develop rhetorical knowledge, analyzing and making informed choices about purposes, audiences, and context as you read and compose texts.

Whether it's an academic article, a blog, or a newspaper editorial, all writing is a response to particular situation written from a particular perspective (the author's), for a particular purpose (or purposes), and using particular composing strategies. As a reader and a writer, you'll use rhetorical knowledge (the reflexive process of critical inquiry) for interpreting other people's writing as well as for composing your own work.

◆ To analyze texts in a variety of genres, understanding how content, style, structure and format vary across a range of reading and writing situations.

You'll study the strategies through which writers explore their subjects and express meaning by responding to a variety of texts, thus interacting with the text as a reader who shares responsibility with the author for a text's meanings and implications. You can think of this at least partially as an attempt to understand the choices and processes engaged by the authors of other texts, as an attempt to figure out the critical inquiry followed by the people you read.

◆ To refine and reflect on your writing process, using multiple strategies to generate ideas, draft, revise, and edit your writing across a variety of genres.

You'll write frequently, generating writing on a variety of subjects for different purposes and from different perspectives. You'll also have frequent opportunities to workshop writing in progress with your peers and to confer with your instructor in individual conferences. You may also be asked to write short reflective pieces about your writing—about your process and progress, breakthroughs and setbacks. Again, the reflective pieces will help make your learning more visible to you.

◆ To develop information literacy, making critical choices as you identify a specific research need, locate and evaluate information and sources, and draw connections among your own and others' ideas in your writing.

You'll learn how to formulate and pose a question, problem, or issue for research, how to explore what is already known about your subject, how to choose an appropriate method or strategy for your own research, how to analyze data and determine the credibility and validity of your sources, and how best to convey both the information and your own discoveries through writing intended to inform and persuade other readers.

♦ To construct effective and ethical arguments, using appropriate reasons and evidence to support your positions while responding to multiple points of view.

As discussed earlier in this chapter and in more detail in Chapter 6, an argument involves joining a conversation. As part of your writing class, you'll both analyze others' arguments and construct an argument about a topic of interest to you. You'll join the conversation about your topic by gathering research to help you develop an informed opinion you can support with clear reasons and credible evidence. As part of your argument, you'll also consider and respectfully respond to counterarguments.

♦ To understand and apply language conventions rhetorically, including grammar, spelling, punctuation and format.

What counts as "correct" grammar changes in different rhetorical situations. Because this is an academic course, in most of your major assignments you'll be expected to use a writing style and tone that is considered appropriate for a general academic audience. However, as part of the course you may also write in other genres imagining other audiences, so you'll need to think carefully about how to adapt your writing for the rhetorical situation at hand.

WHO TEACHES THIS CLASS?
About the PWR

The "About the PWR" section of this chapter comes from the official description of our program, available on our website. Did you notice the slight shift in tone and voice in this section?

The Program for Writing and Rhetoric at the University of Colorado at Boulder is an active community of teachers and scholars committed to making writing central to the undergraduate education of our students. We train students to think critically about reading and guide them to produce writing that effectively shapes and expresses ideas in any context—academic, civic, professional, or personal. Through small class sizes and intensive workshops that focus on substantive revision, our students refine and advance compositional and rhetorical skills that they will use inside and outside the classroom.

Teaching over 8,000 undergraduate students each year, the PWR is an autonomous unit in the College of Arts and Sciences and is responsible for campus-wide instruction in writing. The program coordinates and oversees all writing curricula and instruction intended to meet college and campus core requirements, including writing courses in specific disciplines and in targeted campus programs, such as CU's Residential Academic Programs.

Drawing on the complex intellectual tradition of rhetoric and composition, our program integrates current research and best practices to provide students with rigorous and engaging courses that help them understand and apply rhetorical skills in their academic, civic, and professional lives as writers and active thinkers.

Our Courses

Through workshop style classes limited to 19 students, PWR courses emphasize the recursive nature of writing, offering students multiple avenues to explore, enhance and reflect on their own writing strategies and processes. This course, First-Year Writing and Rhetoric, focuses on critical analysis, argument, inquiry, and information literacy. Students develop their rhetorical knowledge by analyzing texts from various genres, and then— through a variety of writing assignments—students apply this knowledge by adapting their writing to the specific rhetorical situation, whether it's writing a research–based essay with an academic audience or composing a multimodal text for a specific group of decision-makers. Students also develop their information literacy through our partnership with CU's libraries, learning through online tutorials and in library seminars strategies for finding and evaluating sources and then effectively and ethically integrating these materials into their own work.

As they continue their education at CU, students will also take one of our broad array of upper–division writing courses building on the rhetorical skills of this course. These advanced courses address writing in various disciplines, writing on interdisciplinary topics of special interest, and professional and technical writing. PWR upper–division courses help students link the disciplinary knowledge acquired in their majors to issues of broad public importance. These courses stress the advanced rhetorical skills needed to address specific disciplinary, professional, and civic audiences.

Our Writing Center

Our campus–wide Writing Center offers undergraduate and graduate students free one–hour consultations with our professional staff to support writing in all courses and for career preparation. The Writing Center also serves as the consulting arm of the PWR: we support faculty in various departments as they integrate writing into courses and curricula. Students can find the Writing Center website at: http://www.colorado.edu/pwr/writingcenter.html or by searching "CU Boulder Writing Center."

REFLECTION QUESTIONS

1. Think about the last writing class you took. When you think about that class, what is the first thing that comes to mind? Why do you think that thought came to mind even though you certainly had many complex experiences in the class? What did you learn in that class? How did you learn it?

> Reflection questions will end each chapter of this text. Whether your instructor directs you to answer these questions formally, in class, or perhaps not at all, thinking about the answers to these questions will help you make connections between your previous experiences, the experience of being in this class, and the experiences you will have as you continue your education.

2. Think about the writing you do in your personal life. How does that personal writing promote the values that underlie writing more generally: knowledge, identity, growth, and community? Why do you think that your personal writing often feels effortless while writing for school can be so difficult?

3. Think about what you expect from this class. What do you think is the main difference between writing for college contexts and what you've done for other writing classes? Why do you think this course is required? What do you think you'll learn from this class?

Chapter 2

Critical Inquiry

As we mentioned in the first chapter, even the most esteemed scholars of writing have difficulty agreeing about the content of a writing and rhetoric class. In astronomy you'll need to learn the distances between planets, stars, and galaxies and how those distances affect our perceptions of those bodies. In a sociology class, you'll learn specific methods for analyzing social trends. But there is no cohesive set of rules or procedures that you can learn that will help you write effectively every time, because every time you sit down to your computer, you're writing for a different audience with different values and expectations. While there are practices that scholars suggest can be more helpful to a writer in nearly any situation, there is no nor has there ever been consensus on what "good writing" is.

What we teachers of writing can all agree on, however, is that for college writing to be effective, it must take on the perspective of critical inquiry. You'll learn variations on this perspective as you write for your other courses as well as in the course of your personal life, but this class is designed to teach you the basics of academic or critical inquiry.

Critical Inquiry Defined

At its most simple, inquiry is the process of finding, asking, and answering questions. You do this constantly. You wake up on a beautiful, warm, sunny morning in Boulder in April, and you wonder what to wear. And then you remember the fall and strangely unpredictable weather of this valley. So you wonder about

> Even in this era of big data, weather prediction remains difficult for even the most sophisticated machines. In many ways, like critical inquiry, weather is reflexive in that it creates its own contexts and then acts based on these new contexts.

the weather forecast. You pick up your phone and learn that the sunshine will turn to snow. You throw your shorts in a pile on the floor and grab your winter coat. This example is a little boring. It's boring because inquiries such as these are so common that they become automatic—it doesn't feel like you are even making choices. Other inquiries may not be boring, though they still might not feel similar to the academic processes of researching for an essay. One of our arguments in this chapter is that though you are already capable and practiced with many of the processes of inquiry, a more intentional practice of inquiry will only yield better results.

Critical inquiry is the same process, but at each stage you pause, and perhaps write, but ask more and more questions, research those questions, and reflect on the answers you find. Then, you find more and more questions based on those answers, and the process continues. Academics use the word "critical" to signify an *unending* and *reflexive* process.

That critical inquiry is unending suggests that it is like solving a problem where the solution becomes a further problem and so on, *ad infinitum.*

> "Ad infinitum" is a Latin phrase that means "to infinity" and which is used to indicate that a list or conversation could continue without end. "Ad nauseam" is a similar Latin phrase that means that a list or conversation could continue until participants are physically sick. Both of these phrases are often used facetiously.

That critical inquiry is reflexive means that these unending questions don't necessarily lead you to other topics (though they can), but focus back on more and more subtle understandings of your original question and the answers you've found. And you may already realize that because this process is reflexive, it has the potential to become exponentially more complex.

This complexity is why the writing and revision process is so important. Finding new ideas will lead you to new answers which will necessitate revision which may lead you to new questions and

> The reflexivity of critical inquiry is also why you should ALWAYS save drafts and notes and everything you write.

so on. If you're engaged with critical inquiry, you'll never know where you'll end up nor what seemingly insignificant piece of information or insight will become important.

Going back to our boring inquiry about what to wear, if you were to ask this question critically (that is, with this perspective of critical inquiry) you may not ever get dressed. You'd wonder what to wear. And then you'd wonder about why you're wondering what to wear. You'd think about the social, economic, political, and cultural histories of the clothing in your closet. You'd think about the rhetorical efficacy of your clothing choice: do you want to appear professional? relaxed? like a skier? Why, you'd think, does a certain combination of fabrics, shapes, and colors signify so clearly the various identities you might inhabit? And then you'd start to think about the weather.

Critical inquiry, put simply, is never being satisfied with an answer. It is asking questions and then questions about those questions from every possible angle you can think of. This is why academics write entire books dedicated to esoteric and specific topics like clothing choice among teenagers.

> A quick search using Google Scholar for "teenage fashion" will reveal a host of academic work on this topic. Such a search could be a very good place to begin a critical inquiry!

This course is limited to what can be written and written well in fifteen weeks. This means, clearly, that you'll have to approach critical inquiry with efficiency in mind and that means that you might not get to fully critically engage with a given question— although if you'd like to write a book, we won't stop you! However, you'll get the feel for this perspective throughout the assignments you complete for this course, a perspective that you'll learn to turn on and off, but one that will make your experience of the world deeper and stronger.

Finding Questions

Finding questions appropriate for academic critical inquiry can be more difficult than finding questions in daily life. Academic questions should be something you are interested in, but something that academic scholars are interested in as well. If scholars are interested in the question, then you'll be able to more efficiently find academic scholarship on the question. However, you'll also need to again gauge your interest in the various ways that academics deal with the question and how you will be able to deal with their answers (notice the reflexivity already?). These questions, then, should be worded with care. The way that you phrase a question will generate certain assumptions. You can imagine that asking the question "what clothes should I wear today?" will lead to different answers than asking "why do I choose the clothes I do?" or "why are jeans so common in the USA?" or "what are the historical precedents for gendered fashion choices in youth culture?"

Asking academic questions academically can be challenging, especially for students who are new to university and academic culture. But this is why your teachers are here and one way that the Writing Center and the library can be very helpful indeed. And this is why you're taking this class.

Being interested

This may seem so obvious as not to bear re-statement, but effective inquiry processes begin with the interest of the writer. You have probably already had the frustrating experience of sitting in front of a computer trying to think of something to say about something that you don't care about at all. You have probably also had the experience of effortless writing, a kind of flow state in which your words can't keep up with your thoughts. The trick is to be able to find interest in topics that are appropriate for your work in this class and beyond. Even if you are a most enthusiastic student of Victorian Literature, there will be aspects of that subject that you find boring and have nothing to say about.

> The psychologist Mihaly Csikszentmihalyi has famously inquired about "flow" in areas as various as writing and basketball.

Clearly, much of the responsibility of finding interest in any topic rests in the individual asking the question. However, there are tricks. Here are some questions that if you ask them about any topic, you might be able to find an aspect of the topic that interests you:

◆ **People**: Who was involved? Why were they involved? What are their personal histories or relationships?

◆ **Time**: When did this happen? What else was happening at that point in history? Are there any connections between other events and this one?

◆ **Place**: Where did this happen? What else was happening there? Are there any connections between other places and this one?

◆ **Culture**: What culture did this happen in? Has this happened in other cultures? If this happened in other cultures, how was it different?

◆ **"Texts"**: What has been written or performed or spoken or painted or sculpted or filmed related to this? What do these different "writers" think? Why do they think differently?

Scholarly interest

As you progress in your education, you will come to learn about what scholars are interested in and you'll be able to guess what they are going to say about it. In the boring example of choosing clothes, for instance, someone with experience in academia might guess that gender roles and clothing or the sad economics of clothing production might be the best places to start. Academics know these are good places to start because we talk to each other, we read journals, and we have been on and around college campuses for years and years.

But you haven't. There are two easy ways to learn if scholars are interested in a topic or question that you are. The first is to inquire whether and how academics are talking about what you're interested in. You can look to your other class reading lists, or ask your instructor or a librarian or a Writing Center consultant.

The second is to do some preliminary research. And believe it or not, this is precisely where "popular" sources such as newspapers, magazines, or even Wikipedia can be helpful. If you are interested in a topic, use the internet while keeping a close eye out for clues of academic interest: does the article or listicle or blog post or wiki you found refer to studies? If so, then academics are probably interested.

> Once you've found one academic article on your topic, an easy and efficient way to find others is to try to find the works that article lists as references. This may seem like cheating, but it is a common way that academics do research.

You've also got to watch out for the kind of scholarly interest you find about a given topic. Some topics, while incredibly interesting, are the domain of scholars whose work is just plain too difficult for anyone but experts to understand. To go back to our boring example of choosing clothing for a spring day, you may be interested in how weather apps work, but unless you already have a working knowledge of a couple of programming languages, meteorological fluid dynamics, and whatever else goes into such apps, you'll probably find yourself frustratingly out of your depth.

Writing the Question

This may seem like the most automatic aspect of this process, but from a perspective of critical inquiry for academic audiences, in many ways it's the most important. Writing the question is itself a reflexive process. You may know that you are interested in contemporary USA clothing choices and the weather, but you'll need to further interrogate your own interest and the preliminary research you've done in order to word a question in the way that will be the most efficient and productive.

Of course, this process of writing a question is also reflexive, which means that as you continue down the path of critical inquiry, your question and the way that you word it will change. However, even at an early stage, think about wording your critical inquiry based on the kind of answers that your interested in. In a lot of ways, this is one of the key academic skills, one that will take you years to master.

However, this course will introduce you to some practices that make such question-asking more achievable. To continue with our example, you may start with "What clothes should I wear?" And you may start with a quick Google search that retrieves a huge amount of information from around the world that uses those words. However, these results take the forms of quizzes about personality and body type, and internet quizzes are not academic. If you move over to Google Scholar (which is a good place to find sources that are more academic, but which is not as good as the scholarly databases available from the CU Library) and type the same question, your results include a book from 1975 on dressing for success, and a book on teaching children vocabulary words. From our academic perspective, these results do not seem to lend themselves to critical inquiry without a big change of topic.

Part of the reason for this is that academic work is not organized with natural language but instead is "tagged" with keywords. In other words, while you can literally ask your phone a question, academic databases respond best to sequences of keywords. Going back to our example, a Google Scholar search for either the word "fashion" or "clothing" shows results that are much more promising for academic inquiry.

Because we are all members of cultures and we all experience social psychology, it's often easiest for new college students to read and cite work from these fields. Academic science writing is often too complex and requires too much knowledge to make for efficient academic research at this level.

And yet, you still don't quite have a question yet! When you do your preliminary Google Scholar search for "Clothing" you'll notice that a couple of results mention social psychology and culture, but some mention body temperature and seem quite medical and advanced. Of the results that mention culture and social psychology, you also notice the word "fashion."

Now, you've got some academic vocabulary you can use to begin building your question. You could ask, "How does my culture affect my fashion choices?" or "What does fashion mean in my culture?" or "What do other cultures think about fashion?"

Of course, this is just an example. This brief example illustrates one version of the process of developing a workable critical inquiry question, and we hope that you can understand the logic behind this sequence. However, we also realize that such a process will be different for different writers and for different topics. And this means that we also realize that this process can be difficult and frustrating. That's the bad news. The good news is that difficulty and frustration are often signs of good critical thinking!

> Even if you are not required to repeat this process in your particular section, we suggest that you quickly try it. You may find it helpful!

Research

Once you've got a question, you can go about answering it. Digital and information technologies might seem to make research easy and effortless. Research, though, is incredibly complex, especially when approached with the perspective of academic critical inquiry. That is why we've included an entire chapter on research or what we in the field of writing and rhetoric call "information literacy."

Writing

Then you write your paper! Writing is not just displaying your critical inquiry to your teacher, however. In addition to all the writing you've done for the other processes of critical inquiry (taking notes on the research you've found, writing an inquiry question, entering words into search engines, etc.), writing and revising drafts of an essay is an unending and reflexive process. Thus, we include chapters 5, 6, and 7 as a discussion of the different ways that you can conceptualize, write, and revise your papers.

Reflection and Reflexivity

Everything you do during the entire process of critical inquiry will affect and inform every other part of this process. This is what is meant by "reflexivity." The idea is that during critical inquiry you are constantly finding new information or thinking of new ideas or changing your argument based on other new information, ideas, or argument. To make a larger analogy, you might think of your own life: you may have thought that you were going in one direction, but things happen out of your control and you have to re-calibrate your expectations and your actions based on the new situation. Say you fell in love in high school, but you and your beloved ended up going to different universities and though you thought that your life was figured out, the challenges of a long distance relationship changed the nature of your relationship and your feelings. All of a sudden, your life plans have radically changed. Of course, this is a terrifying and awful feeling, and yet because you must go on, you do. At this point you don't know where you're going, but you should have faith that though you can't anticipate the path, you have (or will discover) the resources that will help you figure out a new path because you're already doing it for the last big change.

You'll notice a similar (although much less dramatic) experience in following your inquiry. You may start with the question "How does my culture affect my fashion choices?" but then you may become more interested in the way that a certain scholar writes about gender and power and fashion. You didn't know that you were moving in that direction, but now you're there, and you might have to re-research or re-write or re-revise. And completely unlike in your personal life, you can feel more confident in asking questions because you know that you can go back and change the question based on the answers you find.

Even though writing and life can seem terrifying and strange at times, writing is much, much easier than living. Writing, as we've argued elsewhere, gives you the opportunity to make wrong turns, think about why you made them, and start over. Or writing can allow you to follow this new path. Either way, this class is designed to help you develop strategies and perspectives that will allow your writing and your thoughts to adapt to finding answers that change the question and vice versa.

The educational term for this process is "reflection." Reflection is the process of looking back at the series of events, choices, and ideas that have gotten you to where you are in order to assess and learn from that series. In other words, to reflect is to hold a mirror to the entire process of critical inquiry in order to understand just what happened. Our poor, lovelorn example above may have thought that a long distance relationship would be easy before he realized the reality of college responsibilities changed the nature of his relationship. Upon reflection, upon looking back, this student realizes that his expectations of these types of relationships have changed. And this will affect the way he acts in the future. In a lot of ways, reflection can also be defined as the process of learning.

As we've talked about elsewhere, though, our choices are often invisible until we work to put them into words. This is especially true of a writing process. If you remember the last text message you wrote, can you clearly express the reason that you chose every space, letter, and emoji? Can you really describe why you chose to put one word in front of another? So much of language is automatic and natural that it is often nearly impossible to answer these questions.

Thus, your instructor may provide you with guidelines for your reflection. She may ask you to explore and describe why you chose one article over another for your research; she may ask what worked especially well for you during your inquiry or writing process or what didn't work at all. These seemingly simply questions, however, can help you to make what you did into what you learned. Additionally, reflective writing can help you orient yourself, your whole, private, daily self, with the expectations of writing for college and public audiences. Reflection can help you figure out—using the magical power of writing to slow down time—what you yourself really believe and assume and want to know, which in turn will help you figure out a strategy for a given task.

Frustratingly, like we've said, reflection is also reflexive. This means that as you reflect and learn about your writing and inquiry process those processes will change as a result of your reflection. Although this is certainly frustrating for those people who want strict, linear processes, we'd urge you to think of this reflexive reflection as the lifelong process of learning how to write well.

REFLECTION QUESTIONS

1. When you are interested in learning about something on your own, what do you do? Where do you go for information? How do you imagine this class will be different than learning about a topic on your own?

2. Can you think of times when you've followed the process of critical inquiry to solve problems or answer questions outside of school? How did you decide which college to go to, which dorm to request, or whether to bring your car from home?

3. Think of a decision that you've made in the past that turned out to be the wrong decision. When did you know it wasn't working? How did you know? What did you learn from this experience? How do you know you learned it?

4. What do you think will be the most challenging aspect of the critical inquiry process for you? What makes you think that? What do you think will be the easiest part of this process? Why?

Chapter 3

Information Literacy

We are drowning in information. Every day, we encounter enormous amounts of information in a wide variety of formats. Think back over the last few days. What sources of information have you encountered?

These days, you can easily find information about any subject—whether it's academic, professional or personal—in a matter of seconds. Have a question? Just Google it! Or jump on Wikipedia. Or crowdsource it: post a question on Facebook or Twitter and see what your friends and followers have to say. Getting information is easy. What's much more difficult, though, is distinguishing the useful information from the less useful. How do you know which sources are credible? How do you know if the content is accurate and valid? As scholars and citizens, we should approach information critically and cautiously so that we can choose how to best respond to what we find. To meet this challenge, we need information literacy.

Information Literacy: What Is It?

Information literacy can be described as the ability to:

Determine what kind of information you need
What questions do I have?
Where might I find the answers?

Access information efficiently
What is the best way to find the information? (Person, search engine, book, etc.)
How much time do I have to search?
Is there any place where I can seek help?

Evaluate information and sources critically
Can I trust this information?
Can I find better information?
Can I find confirmation or disagreement?
Should I search again?

Integrate information with what you already know
Have I changed my mind?
Do I agree or disagree?
How will this information shape what I say or do in response?

Use information effectively to accomplish a specific purpose
How will I synthesize the information with my own voice?
How will I present my response?

Understand the economic, legal, and social issues surrounding the use of information[1]
How do I give credit?
How do I cite?
Am I accurately presenting or responding to the information?

Beyond these specific skills, information literacy can also be described as a critical approach to all modes of information. You will continuously refine your information literacy over time in all areas of your life, not only in your academic work but in your personal and professional lives as well.

---

1 Adapted from the Association of College and Research Libraries' Information Literacy Competency Standards for Higher Education

Situation: Imagine you are having a dispute with your landlord about the return of your security deposit.

Information need: You need to know: What are your rights as a tenant? What is the best course of action? What help services are available to you?

Access: You consult family and friends.

Evaluate: One of your friends has experienced a similar situation in the past. She agrees that you are justified in your complaint and recommends that you search for legal or government assistance with the issue.

"Ultimately, information literate people are those who have learned how to learn. They know how to learn because they know how knowledge is organized, how to find information, and how to use information in such a way that others can learn from them. They are people prepared for lifelong learning, because they can always find the information needed for any task or decision at hand."

– American Library Association's Presidential Committee on Information Literacy, 1998.

Access: Through savvy searching, you locate the "Colorado Renter's Guide" published by the Colorado Department of Local Affairs. You also identify Boulder County's Mediation Services for landlord and tenant relationships.

Evaluate: The websites confirm your friend's opinion. And you are confident that they will be persuasive sources to your landlord.

Use: You compose a letter to your landlord requesting the return of your deposit. You suggest mediation if the landlord does not comply.

Understand: In the letter you reference and cite the government information that you found. Your deposit is promptly returned.

Information Literacy and Your Writing Class

If you remember, one of the six goals for the first-year writing class is to help you:

Develop your information literacy, making critical choices as you identify a specific research need, locate and evaluate information and sources, and draw connections among your own and others' ideas in your writing.

In your first-year writing class, you will develop your information literacy by pursuing a research project that will require you to assess the specific demands of your research situation.

You will begin with an issue or question that engages you. You may begin with little prior knowledge of your topic, but through your research, you will explore the conversation, draw connections, pose new questions, and locate more information as needed.

As part of your research, you will investigate a variety of information sources to identify:

- the conversation around your issue or question
- the social and cultural context
- the voices represented
- the competing views
- the problems and controversies
- the key events, people, places

> *"You come late. When you arrive, others have long preceded you, and they are engaged in a heated discussion, a discussion too heated for them to pause and tell you exactly what it is about. ... You listen for a while, until you decide that you have caught the tenor of the argument; then you put in your oar. Someone answers; you answer him; another comes to your defense; another aligns himself against you, to either the embarrassment or gratification of your opponent, depending upon the quality of your ally's assistance. However, the discussion is interminable. The hour grows late, you must depart. And you do depart, with the discussion still vigorously in progress."*
>
> – Kenneth Burke, *The Philosophy of Literary Form.*

Your goal is not to gather sources in order to echo others' voices, but to actively engage in the conversation. As you analyze the texts and works of others, you will establish allegiance with writers whose ideas you wish to embrace. You will also discover writers who present counterarguments or ideas you wish to refute. Additionally, your research may reshape your initial ideas, and you may begin to ask new and more refined questions. Research is a time-consuming and complex intellectual process, one which sparks new knowledge and new questions but is also rich with curiosity and learning.

Your research is intricately tied to your writing; researching will help you understand your question or issue as you analyze and interpret sources. The sources you choose to incorporate in your writing may provide context, support your claim, enhance your rhetorical appeals, establish credibility, or point to precedence for your readers, among other possibilities.

As you develop your knowledge through research and enter the conversation with other writers, you will begin to develop your own identity as a student-scholar and researcher.

RIOT & the Library Community:
http://ucblibraries.colorado.edu/pwr/index.htm

RIOT: Research Instruction Online

RIOT, Research Instruction Online Tutorial, is an online tutorial that you will complete as a component of your first year writing course. The tutorial will help you to think critically about your topic, your search strategies, your sources, and your own ideas. The tutorial will also encourage you to reflect on your research process and the implications of your choices as you engage in conversation with other writers and scholars.

The tutorial is composed of five modules. The modules simulate steps in the research process and introduce many of the research tools available from the University Libraries. The module's goals are briefly outlined below:

Module 1: Think

Goals:

◆ To recognize assignment requirements (information context)
◆ To choose a topic
◆ To brainstorm
◆ To locate background information
◆ To determine specific information needs in order to expand one's knowledge
◆ To begin research question formulation

Module 2: Find

Goals:

◆ To distinguish between information sources
◆ To judge appropriateness of sources to match your need
◆ To generate search strategies

Module 3: Tools

Goals:

◆ To become familiar with CU research sources

Module 4: Evaluate

Goals:

◆ To understand need for critical evaluation
◆ To become familiar with some evaluation criteria
  • Purpose
  • Credibility
  • Validity
  • Relevance

Module 5: Cite

Goals:

◆ To understand citing
◆ To understand academic integrity
◆ To understand pragmatics of citing"

Each module concludes with a graded quiz. You will have one opportunity to complete the quiz.

The tutorial also includes two optional modules. *Module 6, My Research*, provides a summary of links to resources and tools that will help with your research.

The final module, *My Research Reflection*, provides a space for you to reflect and assess your strategies. The module invites you to answer questions like: *What do I think? What is foreign and what is new to me? What do I need to know more about? What gives me new insight? Am I asking relevant questions? Am I using my own voice?*

To learn more, go to:
http://ucblibraries.colorado.edu/pwr/index.htm

Library Seminar

You will also attend an in-person library seminar which will be scheduled during your regularly scheduled class time. You will work with a librarian to:

◆ explore the tutorial goals in more detail
◆ research your topic
◆ investigate other library resources and tools

Librarians

The University Libraries employs a number of research librarians who are available to help you with your research at any stage. You may contact a librarian in several ways, including: in-person, chat, email, phone, or virtual meeting.

http://ucblibraries.colorado.edu/askus/index.htm

If you wish you can schedule an individualized research consultation to expand on the seminar and tutorial. For more information, go to: http://ucblibraries.colorado.edu/reference/researchconsultation.htm

Situation: You are assigned an "Inquiry Project" in your first-year writing class. This project requires you to write a seven- to eight-page researched essay that incorporates a variety of scholarly and popular sources. You decide that you want to write your essay about the prevalence of zombies and the zombie apocalypse in contemporary popular culture.

Inquiry questions: You need to pose challenging research (i.e., "inquiry") questions to guide your research and writing. You want to know: Why does so much of our popular media these days feature zombies and the zombie apocalypse? What is it about our society, including environmental, political, and technological conditions, that makes the zombie the perfect monster for our times? How do zombies reflect our current cultural anxieties?

Information need: You need to find a variety of sources to help you answer your inquiry questions, including: recent examples of movies, tv shows, and video games that feature zombies; reviews and critiques of zombie-themed media in magazines, newspapers, websites, and blogs; documentary films or videos made about the zombie phenomenon; books that explain the history of the zombie in literature and other media; articles and maybe even books written by scholars who analyze the zombie trend from various perspectives, including sociological, cultural, and literary.

Access: You choose a set of keywords and phrases, including "zombies," "zombies and popular culture," and "zombies in literature and film." You conduct searches with those keywords and phrases using Google, YouTube, Chinook (CU's library catalog), and Academic Search Premier (one of the library databases).

Evaluate: You find more sources than you could ever read in a lifetime, so you assess some of the most interesting sources for their credibility, validity, and relevance. You choose the best sources from a variety of places (scholarly, non-scholarly, print, digital, etc.), and begin to read/view them and take notes.

Use: You draft your essay, synthesizing the information you learned from sources with your own ideas and insights. As you write, you discover more questions that you need to answer, especially about the relationship between contemporary environmental concerns and zombie literature/film.

Access: You do a more targeted search using Academic Search Premier and find two or three more articles that address these questions. You also schedule an appointment with your teacher for your Environmental Issues class to find out whether she can help you answer your newly discovered questions. You use this new information to strengthen your essay.

Understand: You've now written a researched essay that you're proud of, and you also have a deeper understanding of zombies that will make you even better appreciate the next episode of *The Walking Dead!*"

REFLECTION QUESTIONS

1. When you are curious about something, what sources do you turn to for information? What are some benefits/disadvantages of these sources?

2. After reading this chapter, how would you define "information literacy"?

3. How comfortable do you feel searching for information: For personal purposes? For academic research purposes? What's different about searching for personal or academic research purposes?

4. Can you recall a moment when you were NOT able to find information you needed? Describe. Where did you turn for help?

5. Can you recall a moment when you were very successful finding information? Describe. What made your search successful?

6. How do you know when you have found the information you need? How do you decide what information to trust?

Chapter 4

Rhetoric and Rhetorical Analysis–Words (and More) at Work

In this chapter, you'll read about rhetoric. Not the empty kind of inflated or misguiding language that we sometimes associate with politicians, but both the practice and study of how people communicate in order to achieve their specific purposes. After all, rhetoric puts the "R" in PWR, so it's important to understand what it is and how it works.

What Is Rhetoric?

People tend to use the word rhetoric pejoratively. It is often preceded by adjectives like *empty* or *hollow*. If someone other than a classmate or your instructor in this class makes a comment about your rhetoric, chances are he or she is not giving you a compliment. Politicians use the word *rhetoric* a lot. When they criticize their opponents' speeches, they almost inevitably use the word *rhetoric* to describe what they consider shallow, insincere, or manipulative language. For example, during the 2012 presidential campaign, the Obama campaign criticized Mitt Romney's views on foreign policy, noting, "This is somebody who leads with chest-pounding rhetoric." Similarly, Republican Vice Presidential candidate Paul Ryan told members of the conservative Heritage Foundation, "The president has opted for divisive rhetoric and the broken politics of the past." The assumption in both of these cases is that rhetoric is something misleading, irrelevant, and disconnected from reality.

But is rhetoric always such a bad thing? Should this course be re-titled First-Year Writing and Insincere Manipulation? Or can we use rhetoric to mean something else, something more practical and worthwhile? In the academic world and in everyday life, the answer is a resounding yes.

So what is rhetoric? Rhetoric is the art of persuasion. In this sense, it has a rich history that dates back to the ancient Greeks. For Aristotle, rhetoric involved identifying and using "the available means of persuasion" in a given situation. In his day, rhetoric referred to speeches, not written texts. Today, even when we have more means of persuasion available to us—including written texts and various forms of technology—we can still think of rhetoric as the art of persuasion.

But what does "the art of persuasion" mean? Basically it means that if you want to persuade people to change their views or take action, you need to adjust your language to suit the occasion. Whether you're writing an academic essay or an e-mail, a cover letter or a love letter, the choices you make about language will depend on your rhetorical situation—your

> "Rhetoric is the art, practice, and study of human communication."
>
> – Andrea Lunsford

purpose, audience, and context. Every rhetorical situation is unique, so you can't rely on simple formulas. You can, however, pay attention to the rhetorical conventions of particular genres. These conventions are ways of composing—sometimes called moves or gestures—that audiences have come to expect in certain circumstances. Usually it's wise to follow these conventions. If you don't, your audience may consider you naïve and dismiss your argument. If you were to write an academic essay using the conventions of a love letter—informal language, personal anecdotes, and a very personal tone, for example—you would probably not have much luck persuading your instructor or wider audience of your argument. And if you were to write a love letter using a distant, objective tone with a works cited full of scholarly sources, your significant other would probably think you were strange. The art of persuasion, therefore, demands that you respond to each rhetorical situation differently. Every time you speak or write, the degree to which you are successful depends on your attendance to the rhetorical situation, that is, the extent to which you account for purpose, audience, and context.

Purpose

Whether you're writing a grocery list or an annotated bibliography, you always have a purpose. Often writers have more than one purpose. Consider, for example, the website Best Food Nation (www.bestfoodnation.com). Created in 2006 (and since gone dark) by a group of associations including the American Meat Institute and the Cattlemen's Beef Board, the website summarized its purpose on the homepage:

BestFoodNation.com offers the facts about the U.S. food supply, which is among the safest, most affordable and most abundant food supplies in the world. The food and hospitality industries have joined together to tell our story; the positive impact made by each participant along the chain, to separate fact from fiction, and to set the record straight about Best Food Nation.

Here we see multiple purposes—to provide "facts," "to tell our story," and "to set the record straight." These purposes overlap, creating a fairly complex picture of what the website is trying to accomplish. On the one hand, a central purpose seems to be to defend the American food industry from criticism and misrepresentation. On the other hand, the site seeks to present the industry in a positive light without sounding defensive. The website's tagline makes clear its emphasis on the positive: "A Celebration of Our Safe, Abundant, Affordable Food System." Of course, some visitors to the site may find this approach reassuring and persuasive, while others may find it dubious and unconvincing. This leads us to another key element of any rhetorical situation—audience.

Audience

To whom are you writing? This question lies at the heart of rhetoric, and the answer is not always straightforward. To understand an audience, you often need to consider factors such as age, gender, race, class, political affiliation, and educational level. The best writers adjust their writing according to an audience. Often writing assignments come with specific guidelines regarding audience, as your writing instructor may have you adapt your rhetoric for a range of possible audiences. If you're writing a letter to the editor of the *CU Independent*, your audience is other University of Colorado students, staff, and faculty. If you're composing a report on the social psychology experiment you've conducted, your audience is the psychology scholarly community. For both of these examples, you'll make different style choices through word choice, tone, sentence structure, and sentence length, as well as different substantive choices through the arguments, examples, and supporting evidence you choose.

> *"[Rhetoric] is concerned primarily with a creative process that includes all of the choices a writer makes from his earliest tentative explorations of a problem . . . through choices in arrangement and strategy for a particular audience, to the final editing of a final draft."*
>
> – Richard E. Young, Alton L. Becker, and Kenneth L. Pike

If your PWR instructor doesn't specify an audience for a particular writing assignment, this is a great question to ask!

Among composition scholars, there's controversy about where in the writing process (brainstorming? researching? drafting? revising?) considerations of audience should be introduced. Most scholars agree that thinking about the audience should start early in the writing process. However, composition scholar Peter Elbow argues that some student writers are so focused on a potentially judgmental audience (such as an intimidating instructor!) that they shut down. As a solution, particularly in the early stages of writing, Elbow advocates freewriting—writing nonstop whatever comes to mind about the subject at hand, free of judgmental filters from oneself or others. Freewriting or fastwriting are useful tools—many students don't realize how productive and generative they can be—but considering your audience is best introduced as early as possible into the writing process.

Digital Media allows for sophisticated ways to interact with an audience. For example, the Blue Marbles Project created by Wallace J. Nichols, a marine biologist, asks visitors to the site to give away blue marbles as signs of gratitude (www.wallacejnichols. org/130/blue-marbles.html). The goal is to have a blue marble pass through every hand on earth! Nichols contends that the project, with its message of gratitude for our "beautiful, fragile, planet" will make participants in the game more aware of, and supportive of, conservation efforts. While environmentalism can often be a divisive issue, the website's design attempts to undermine partisanship. Dozens of portraits greet visitors to the site, showing people from all over the world, of all different ages, holding up their tokens of gratitude. Nichols explains that he debated using a more elaborate website—with maps tracking GPS-equipped marbles—but opted instead to create a forum for participants to share their stories. Rhetorically, Nichols does not cater his message to a specific audience, but invites us to join an ever-expanding audience—a community of participants—by playing the game.

Context

Every act of persuasion has a context. That is, it exists within a particular set of social, cultural, historical, and political circumstances, not in a vacuum. These circumstances inform an argument and influence its reception. For the Best Food Nation site, one of the main elements of context, alluded to in the site's very title, is investigative journalist Eric Schlosser's best-selling book *Fast Food Nation: The Dark Side of the American Meal*, the paperback version of which came out in 2005. In his book, Schlosser criticizes the fast-food industry for failing to protect consumers from dangers such as E. coli. "Again and again," he writes, "efforts to prevent the sale of tainted ground beef have been thwarted by meat industry lobbyists and their allies in Congress. The federal government has the legal authority to recall a defective toaster oven or stuffed animal—but still lacks the power to recall tons of contaminated, potentially lethal meat" (Schlosser, *Fast Food* 9). *Fast Food Nation* was not the only popular critique of fast food and the U.S. food industry that serves as context for Best Food Nation's rhetoric. Morgan Spurlock's critically and commercially successful 2004 documentary, *Supersize Me!*, chronicled his thirty-day McDonald's-only diet. Given this specific cultural and historical landscape, or context, the creators of the Best Food Nation website presumably felt the need to take action, to assuage public fears and to reassure consumers.

The medium of writing represents of significant part of the rhetorical context. We discussed how the Blue Marbles Project uses the internet to reach a global audience, but chose to keep the actual web interface as simple as possible. In contrast, The Johnny Cash Project (www.thejohnnycashproject.com) uses a complex interface only available through digital media. However, it does so for the same purpose—to engage the audience in active participation. Johnny Cash was a legendary country singer and cultural icon. Shortly after his death, his record label released the song "Ain't No Grave" and collaborated with digital designers to allow Cash's fans to create the video. They released images for the video on line at a much slower frame rate than usual. Fans from around the world animated the gaps with their own images of what the song (and Cash's life and music) evoked for them. Everyone who contributed to the animation was able to post a reflection on Cash in tribute to his memory. The resulting video is remarkable for its effectiveness. Even if we didn't know the way it was created, it would stand on its own as a haunting, elegiac visual companion to the song. But understanding the context of the video (the website engaged a worldwide audience in the creative process) allows us to see this as a genuinely amazing feat of both technology and rhetoric.

Whatever you think of the sites' visual appeal, purposes, and contexts, they also use what ancient rhetoricians like Aristotle called rhetorical appeals.

Rhetorical Appeals

Ethos

Ethos refers to the credibility and character of the writer. Although it is called the ethical appeal, ethos doesn't refer to ethics per se. Rather, it has to do with how credible the writer appears to be in the eyes (or ears) of the audience. Ethos often depends on the writer's relationship to the topic—does the writer have academic or professional expertise that relates to the topic? Does he have personal experience with the topic? Is she somehow involved in an organization that researches the topic? Is he being paid to espouse a particular viewpoint on the topic? A key question to ask when you are considering ethos is, "What do I know about the person or group that produced this text and how does this affect the way I view it?"

For an academic essay, your ethos as the writer often depends greatly on the credibility of your sources. If your evidence consists of random blog posts and personal websites that you found by conducting a simple Google search, readers will probably not find your argument as persuasive as they would if you cited scholarly sources written by acknowledged experts.

Above, we discussed the Blue Marbles Project and its attempt to create space for a remarkably broad audience (literally everyone on Earth). Of course, some visitors might be skeptical of the project, finding it too sentimental or gimmicky. Nichols attempts to preempt such reactions by evoking the authority of science: "Born one day in 2009, the wildly popular, absurdly simple, neuroscience-based initiative of marine biologist Dr. Wallace J. Nichols, has shared blue marbles around the world with millions of people." What might seem like a sentimental gimmick is in fact based on neuroscience and started by a biologist, lending rational credibility to the game. But it doesn't stop there. The website complements the photos of participants with a list of the many professions and famous individuals who have participated in the game: "Rock stars, presidents, kids, scientists, artists, explorers, eco-celebrities, teachers, business leaders...even the Dalai Lama and the Pope have received blue marbles and gotten their Blue Mind on!" The site relies on the authority of science and an already-established group of participants to strengthen its ethos.

Careless mistakes can wreck an otherwise solid ethos. When you apply for a job, for example, make sure that your cover letter is flawless, because busy employers will often toss your application if they find so much as a typo or a misspelled name. The same is true, more or less, with academic writing. Even if poor grammar doesn't interfere with your instructor's ability to comprehend your writing, it still hurts your ethos and therefore the overall strength of your argument. To some readers, the misused semicolon in the quotation from www. bestfoodnation.com would be enough to make them suspect incompetence and dismiss the site altogether ("The food and hospitality industries have joined together to tell our story; the positive impact made by each participant along the chain, to separate fact from fiction, and to set the record straight about Best Food Nation"). Such visitors might think, "If I can't even trust these people to use punctuation correctly, how can I trust what they have to say?"

Other visitors might balk at the site's inclusion of a press release by the American Council on Science and Health, a prestigious- and independent-sounding organization that, according to Source Watch (www.sourcewatch.org), "has taken a strong public position against the dangers of tobacco" but that "takes a generally apologetic stance regarding virtually every other health and environmental hazard produced by modern industry, accepting corporate funding from Coca-Cola, Kellogg, General Mills, Pepsico, and the American Beverage Association, among others."

> **Three Rhetorical Appeals**
>
> *Ethos*: appeal to character
>
> *Pathos*: appeal to emotions
>
> *Logos*: appeal to reason

Pathos

Pathos is the author's appeal to an audience's emotions, beliefs, or values. Known as the emotional appeal, pathos can include anything from a moving personal narrative, to a particular poetic rhythm, to the invocation of a deeply held cultural value. If you were to write an essay arguing in favor of increased funding for stem-cell research, you could appeal to readers' emotions by focusing on specific examples of children, respected celebrities, or even your own loved ones who are affected by diseases that scientists hope stem-cell research may one day cure.

When we think of pathos in texts that involve more than written language, we might think of a person's sympathetic tone of voice, the use of humor, a piece of sentimental music, or a powerful image that holds us under its spell. Both the Blue Marbles Project and The Johnny Cash Project evoke pathos in very straightforward ways. Nichols explicitly asserts the importance of gratitude in motivating people to become engaged in environmental conservation. The Johnny Cash Project provides an outlet for Cash's fans to express grief and admiration.

As it turns out, Best Food Nation used several of these elements in appealing to visitors' emotions. For example, it included a collection of multimedia profiles of people involved in the food industry—people whom the site referred to as "Friendly Faces." Short videos featured of likeable ranchers, farmers, and other workers talking about their kids, their "agricultural heritage," and their commitment to food safety, animal welfare, and nutrition. These narratives about family values and family farms help viewers identify with and sympathize with these individuals.

Rhetorically, this emphasis on individuals and their families not only appeals to viewers' emotions but also serves to divert attention from systematic critiques of U.S. food production. The website's use of pathos seems like an attempt to humanize the food industry in the eyes of an increasingly skeptical public, to shift the focus from corporations to individuals. Taken as a whole, the video profiles seem to say, "You may have read or heard some bad things about the food industry, but we *are* the food industry." The implication is that if you criticize the industry, you criticize the people behind the industry—a highly questionable assumption. As Schlosser commented in a speech at Princeton University in 2006, "It's not like there are half a dozen bad guys, and if we deal with them everything's going to be all right." Referring to the head of McDonald's Corporate Social Responsibility, Schlosser remarked, "He may be a *really* nice guy. He may be a really nice guy, but it's not about him. It's about a system that rewards cheapness, efficiency and speed that has a very narrow measure of what's efficient and that allows companies like his to impose their business costs on the rest of us" (Schlosser, "Moving Beyond"). Whether you consider the website's emotional appeals endearing or cunning, there is no doubt that they are rhetorically powerful.

Logos

Logos, also called the logical appeal, refers to the use of logic and reasoning in order to persuade. If you write an essay arguing that television is not the mind-numbing waste of time that critics dismiss it as, you would need to explain your reasoning. *New Yorker* writer Malcolm Gladwell does this well in a review of Stephen Johnson's book *Everything Bad Is Good for You*. To make the point that TV has become more intellectually demanding over the years, Gladwell writes:

> A typical episode of "Starsky and Hutch," in the nineteen-seventies, followed an essentially linear path: two characters, engaged in a single story line, moving

toward a decisive conclusion. To watch an episode of "Dallas" today is to be stunned by its glacial pace—by the arduous attempts to establish social relationships, by the excruciating simplicity of the plotline, by how obvious it was. A single episode of "The Sopranos," by contrast, might follow five narrative threads, involving a dozen characters who weave in and out of the plot. Modern television also requires the viewer to do a lot of what Johnson calls "filling in," as in a "Seinfeld" episode that subtly parodies the Kennedy assassination conspiracists, or a typical "Simpsons" episode, which may contain numerous allusions to politics or cinema or pop culture. The extraordinary amount of money now being made in the television aftermarket—DVD sales and syndication—means that the creators of television shows now have an incentive to make programming that can sustain two or three or four viewings.

Notice that the reasoning in this quotation doesn't rely on statistics. Sometimes people assume that only "hard facts" will persuade an audience, but logos need not include numbers to be rhetorically successful.

However, particularly in academic writing, "the facts" are often invoked as a form of logical persuasion. (It's helpful to remember that facts and statistics can be presented in a number of different ways—which may result in very different interpretations.) An appeal to logos might also include offering a persuasive definition of a particular word or phrase, making a comparison, or using a "cause and effect" approach to explaining the topic. Logos was Aristotle's favorite rhetorical appeal, and he studied its effects through both inductive and deductive reasoning. These are just a few strategies for appealing to an audience through logic.

Overlapping Appeals and Rhetorical Strategies

Ethos, pathos, and logos often overlap in different combinations. Both The Blue Marbles Project and The Johnny Cash Project rely on pathos and ethos, and they overlap fairly clearly. The Blue Marbles Project evokes gratitude and relies on the ethos of scientists to argue for the significance of the game. And it does so to inspire people to become informed, to seek out the logos. Nichols goes so far as to claim that emotions and scientific knowledge should go hand-in-hand. He complained in a tweet, "Young scientists are told to leave their emotions at the door. As older scientists, we're letting them in."

The connection of logos to ethos and pathos plays a less polemical role in The Johnny Cash Project. But we can look at the project itself as a kind of evidence: The global reach of Cash's music attests to his life. The video itself, created by fans, confirms the spiritual undertones of the song's lyrics about living after death. "There ain't no grave that can hold my body down." The project makes this true by allowing a community of fans to keep Cash's spirit alive.

Don't be surprised, then, if your instructor discourages you from structuring a rhetorical analysis essay by devoting one section to each appeal, giving the false impression that each exists independently. Rather, consider how ethos, pathos, and logos work together to create a successful (or unsuccessful) rhetorical strategy. Similarly, if you're writing an argumentative essay, you may find it more helpful to think about rhetorical strategies rather than appeals. Specific strategies, after all, will inevitably include rhetorical appeals, often in skillful combination.

Getting Started on Rhetorical Analysis: Why?

So if we have a general understanding of what rhetoric is, then how do we analyze it? And, perhaps more importantly, why analyze rhetoric? One answer to this question might be that we are surrounded by rhetoric every day—advertisements, news media, blogs, works of art, textbooks—all of these are examples of rhetoric. Scholar Sonja Foss asserted that rhetoric "is the process by which our reality or our world comes into being" (6). This seems like a large claim—does rhetoric really shape reality? While there may be a variety of answers to this question, it seems clear that we are—at the very least—influenced daily by rhetoric (and we also use rhetoric to influence others). In fact, rhetorician Kenneth Burke famously suggested that our very nature as rhetorical beings makes us human. Burke defined rhetoric as "a symbolic means of inducing cooperation in beings that by nature respond to symbols" (43). Because everyone is both influenced by and influences others through rhetoric, when we talk about rhetoric, then, we are talking about a form of power.

Rhetorical analysis is one way to better understand how power functions in our society. To some degree, people think, feel, believe, and act based on the persuasive power of rhetoric, so when we ask questions about rhetoric, we learn more about why certain laws are passed (or not passed), why certain attitudes are popular, why particular products sell better—in other words, we learn more about how the world works.

We can also use rhetorical analysis to closely examine a particular text (or texts) for the specific ways that rhetoric is at work. For example, we might examine a commercial for the ways that it relies on humor as an emotional appeal to persuade us to purchase the product. We might analyze President Obama's speech to Congress to ask questions about audience—is his primary audience the members of Congress or the American public watching on TV? Or we might read a series of blog entries to examine how people argue in a technologically-mediated environment.

The word *rhetor* refers to the person or group that produces the text–whether it's someone giving a public speech, a grassroots organization that produces a website to advocate for a cause, a writer producing an essay, or a person composing a Twitter update.

But, you might think, *this is a writing class—how does rhetorical analysis help me as a writer?* If you think about it, you're already a skilled user of rhetoric. When you communicate with different people (such as a professor, your mother, or a friend), you make adjustments to things like the specific vocabulary and tone that you use. Rhetorical analysis allows you as a writer—whether in an academic, civic, professional or social setting—to more deliberately and effectively choose the appropriate language and other symbols (for example, images, sound, or design) that will help you communicate with your audiences. Whether it's a lab report or a job application email, improving your knowledge of and skill with rhetoric gives you a better chance of successfully reaching your audiences.

How to Rhetorically Analyze. . . Anything

You can rhetorically analyze texts, objects, events, or practices. Going about rhetorical analysis is similar to any other form of analysis—it starts with questions. There are many questions that you might ask, including:

◆ *Who is speaking?* Or writing or sculpting, etc.? Is the text produced by a single rhetor or a group? What's the rhetor's relationship to the topic—is she a credentialed expert? Someone with personal experience? An interested observer? Is he representing a particular social or political viewpoint?

◆ *To whom is the rhetor speaking?* Who's the audience? Is there more than one? What's the relationship between the rhetor and the audience?

◆ *When did the text appear?* It's important to remember that the rhetorical significance of texts can change over time. For example, Lincoln's "Gettysburg Address" is interpreted differently now than when he originally gave the speech in 1863.

◆ *Where did the text appear?* Was it published in a newspaper, spraypainted on a building, designed as a website, spoken to a large crowd, aired during the Super Bowl, texted to a friend?

> In this class, your instructor may define the word *text* as any example of rhetoric–not only books and articles, but films, websites, speeches, and works of art, just to name a few. A text, then, is an act of communication designed to convey meaning(s) through rhetorical symbols (words, images, sounds, color, etc.).

◆ *What does the text say?* Yes, as in most analyses, there is some summary involved in rhetorical analysis. It's important to understand the major ideas—the content—of a text.

◆ *Why was the text produced?* While we can't read a rhetor's mind, we can look at the text and the context for evidence of the rhetor's purposes.

◆ *How is rhetoric at work in the details of the text?* How did the rhetor choose specific rhetorical strategies to appeal to the audiences in specific ways? Which appeals—pathos, logos, and ethos—are used and how? This can include everything from strategies such as the types of evidence that are used, to document design, certain "hotbutton" words or phrases, or the use of symbols other than language—images, color, etc.

◆ *With what consequences?* In other words, what are the effects of this rhetoric? Asking this question also raises the question of ethics—are there ways that rhetoric is being used ethically and/or unethically?

While this list of questions will help you look at rhetoric in action, it's important to understand that a sophisticated rhetorical analysis will also look at the relationships among these elements—for example, how does understanding who the audience is also help you understand the appeals and strategies that are used? And how does the relationship between audience and appeals affect ethical considerations?

For examples of rhetorical analyses written by students, see Chapter 7.

If you're thinking that this seems like a lot to do, you're right. Because you can rarely talk about all the elements of rhetoric in a particular text, it's up to you to choose which elements are the most significant, interesting, or powerful for your purposes. But wherever you choose to focus, at the end of the day, your rhetorical analysis should help you explore how language and other symbols exercise power in our culture.

Fallacies of Argument

Fallacies of argument are strategies that people use (knowingly and unknowingly) to persuade. Fallacies may mislead, distract, misrepresent, or make dubious connections between ideas. They weaken an argument by weakening credibility—when they are detected.   Identifying a fallacy doesn't always mean that the argument is false, but it does mean that the conclusions aren't necessarily guaranteed by the premises.

As with most systems of categorization, the boundaries between these types of fallacies are fuzzy—a particular fallacy may appear to be both an ad hominem and a straw man fallacy, for example—so labeling a particular fallacy with a specific name is perhaps less important than developing an overall awareness that not all arguments are equal. When you are doing rhetorical analysis, it's helpful to think carefully about the ways that rhetoric may lead an audience down a path of flawed reasoning. You may find yourself agreeing with an argument, but disagreeing with the way that rhetoric is used to make that argument because of fallacious reasoning.

One key question to ask when you are thinking about fallacies involves the relationship between effectiveness and ethics: Is it unethical to use fallacies, even when they are effective?

The following are some frequently used fallacies:

- ◆ **Ad hominem** – attacks someone's character to distract from the issue being debated. For example: "You can't believe what Candidate A says about economic policy because she cheated on her taxes two years ago."

- ◆ **Ad ignoratium** – assumes that something is true because it hasn't currently been proven false. For example: "God exists because it hasn't been proven that God does not exist."

- ◆ **Appeal to antiquity/tradition or novelty/modernity** – two sides of the same coin: appeals to antiquity or tradition assume that older ideas are better merely because they are older, while appeals to novelty or modernity assume that new ideas are better merely because they are new. For example:

"This is the way we've always done it; therefore, it's the right way to do it" or "This is the latest development; therefore, it's obviously better."

♦ **Appeal to authority** – argues that an idea is true either because someone famous endorses it or because an expert endorses it. (Often, we must rely on the opinion of experts, but experts can make mistakes.) For example: ads that use celebrities to promote a product. The underlying message is "because Taylor Lautner wears this brand of jeans, you should too."

♦ **Appeal to force or fear** – attempts to persuade by threats or fear—in other words, scare tactics. For example: "If you don't do your homework, you'll be very sorry."

♦ **Bandwagon or ad populum** – argues that—because a sizable number of people do or believe something—it must be acceptable. For example: "Everybody's doing it." Sometimes statistics are used to support this kind of fallacy: "Our product is number one in sales; therefore, it's the best."

♦ **Begging the question** – uses as one of the premises a restatement of the conclusion. For example: "Naturally growing plants should not be restricted; therefore, marijuana should be legalized."

♦ **Equivocation** – depends on the ambiguity or double meaning of a key word or phrase. For example: "Mr. A has been accused of sexual harassment; however, he shouldn't be punished because he didn't do anything sexual. He only made comments about her appearance." The meaning of the word "sexual" is unclear here.

♦ **Euphemism** – substitutes a more palatable term for a word or phrase that evokes strong negative emotions. For example: calling the death of innocent bystanders *collateral damage.*

♦ **False analogy** – attempts to persuade by making a comparison between two different objects. For example: "GMOs should be banned; look at the negative effects of pesticides." (Of course all analogies compare two different objects, so it's up to the analyst to determine whether the comparison is valid or not.)

♦ **False dichotomy** – argues that there are only two options. For example: "Abortion is either wrong or right—there's no middle ground"—or "You're either with us or against us."

◆ **Guilt by association** – attacks an individual or group based on an association with another individual or group. For example: "Osama bin Laden is a terrorist and a Muslim; therefore, most Muslims must be terrorists."

◆ **Hasty or sweeping generalization** – a hasty generalization makes conclusions based on incomplete evidence, while a sweeping generalization applies one rule to all objects in a class. For example: "Based on a survey of students who attended the pro-legalization rally, students on campus overwhelmingly support legalization of marijuana" or "All Christians are. . . " or "Women always. . . ."

◆ **Non sequitor** – uses premises that do not support the conclusion. For example: "You support gun control? Well, you also support marijuana legalization, so you're obviously wrong about gun control."

◆ **Poisoning the well** – uses emotionally-laden rhetoric to stir negative feelings in the audience. For example, "anti-abortionists are heartless fanatics."

◆ **Post hoc, ergo propter hoc** – confuses correlation for causation. For example: "Since President Obama took office, the economy has become a disaster—therefore the financial crisis is his fault."

◆ **Red herring** – suggests an irrelevant premise to divert attention from the central issue. For example, "No, we shouldn't continue to bail out failing businesses—there's too much going on in Afghanistan."

◆ **Slippery slope** – exaggerates the future consequences of a situation or action. For example: "If we don't stop the emission of greenhouse gasses, eventually all life on planet Earth will be destroyed."

◆ **Straw Man** – deliberately mischaracterizes the opposition's argument to make it appear weak or misguided. For example: "Proponents of physician-assisted suicide just want to get rid of the weak and the sick."

Rhetoric and Ethics

There's an old saying: "With great power comes great responsibility." If rhetoric is a form of power, then thinking about its relationship to ethics is important—both when you're analyzing someone else's rhetoric, as well as when you're producing rhetoric. While people

For other resources on rhetoric and fallacies, see the list of online writing and research resources on the PWR website at http://www.colorado.edu/pwr/resources.html. Click on "Writing and Research Links."

have various ideas about ethics, there are some concepts that seem to be common in discussions about rhetoric and ethics. Honesty, use of sound evidence, avoidance of manipulation (and fallacies)—these are some common commitments towards ethical rhetoric. (Even so, there is wide disagreement about how to define the terms in a discussion of ethical rhetoric. For example, is there a difference between *persuasion* and *propaganda*?) Or even more trickily, is it ethical to use scare tactics and lies to manipulate an audience into doing good? And who gets to decide what is "good"?

What's your definition of *ethical rhetoric*? As a reader, you will need to decide how to define the ethical use of rhetoric, and then evaluate texts based on your definition. As a writer, you will need to make choices about your own use of rhetoric—will you follow your definition of what's ethical and what's not?

REFLECTION QUESTIONS

1. If we define rhetoric like Kenneth Burke does, as using symbols to induce cooperation, can you think of any human interaction that is not rhetorical? The last time you changed your mind about something, was it because you were influenced by rhetoric or something else? Think of a specific example of a time you changed your mind about a belief, social or political issue or idea, and describe how and why you changed your mind.

2. At the beginning of this chapter, the book defines rhetoric as "the art of persuasion." However, there are many different definitions of the word "rhetoric." Look up five different definitions of this term. (Be sure to also write down your sources for these definitions.) In what ways are some of the definitions you find similar? Different? Based on all of these definitions, what's your definition of rhetoric?

3. What are some reasons that it's important to be able to accurately and effectively analyze the rhetoric in a text? Describe two or three situations (either inside or outside the classroom) where rhetorical analysis might be useful for you.

4. Think back to a piece of writing you've composed in the last year or so. Of the appeals presented (ethos, pathos, logos), is there a particular appeal you used more than others? How could your writing be improved by paying more attention to audience, purpose, and context?

5. The end of this chapter suggests that rhetoric is linked to ethics. When writing instructors create rubrics for evaluating student work, should they consider ethics, along with the more common criteria of style and arguments? How might you define "ethical rhetoric" and can you think of a specific example (a speech, a book, a song, an ad, etc.) of ethical rhetoric?

Works Cited

"Best Food Nation." *Source Watch.org*. The Center for Media and Democracy. 20 Mar. 2007. Web. 25 May 2014.

Burke, Kenneth. *Rhetoric of Motives*. Berkeley: University of California Press. 1969. Print.

Elbow, Peter. "Closing My Eyes as I Speak: An Argument for Ignoring Audience." *College English* 49.1 (Jan. 1987): 50-69. Print.

Foss, Sonja K. Rhetorical Criticism: *Exploration and Practice*. 2nd ed. Prospect Heights,IL: Waveland, 1996. 6. Print.

Gladwell, Malcolm. "Brain Candy: Is Pop Culture Dumbing Us down or Smartening Us Up?" *The New Yorker*. 16 May 2005. 88-89. Print.

The Johnny Cash Project. *www.thejohnnycashproject.com*. N.p. n.d. Web. 25 May 2014.

Krug, Steve. *Don't Make Me Think: A Common Sense Approach to Web Usability*. Berkeley: New Riders, 2000. Print.

Nichols, Wallace J. Blue Marbles Project. *www.wallacejnichols.org*. N.p. n.d. Web. 25 May 2014.

Schlosser, Eric. *Fast Food Nation: The Dark Side of the American Meal*. New York: Perennial, 2002. Print.

—. "Moving Beyond Fast Food Nation." *Food, Ethics, and the Environment Conference*. Princeton University. 16 Nov. 2006. Web. 20 April 2009.

Chapter 5

Genre

Genre

When you write, you are always writing "something." Selecting the best genre for your message is one of the many rhetorical choices you will make in order to communicate effectively.

What is genre?

We group texts by their characteristics and call those groups of similar texts "genres." But when we try to define genre, we immediately encounter a paradox. The word "genre" has its roots in the Latin word *genus,* which means "kind" or "class," and the Greek word *genos,* which means a social group. From its earliest use, there has been debate whether genre refers to form or function. In fact, genre is both **what** we write or create (form) and **why** we use that particular genre (function).

At its most basic level, a genre is a category, and a category is simply grouping things by similarities. Take, for example, Tweets and lab reports. Both have structures that are instantly recognizable, and those distinct, identifiable forms tell the audience what is coming. Two Tweets serve the same basic function, as do two lab reports. Both genres have typical authors, typical audiences, and typical purposes that can be defined. Tweets are often used by a younger, technology-savvy crowd that wants to stay connected. Lab reports are used by scientists and engineers to formally record experiments. Although Tweets and lab reports can be written and read by the same person, they are very different genres and the content of two Tweets or two lab reports can be vastly different.

This leads us to another paradox about genre. No two examples of a genre are ever exactly alike. Think about a Tweet you send to several friends: each recipient is a different audience, with potentially different interpretations and reactions. Nevertheless, the documents that we group into genres are similar enough that we recognize the genre, and we expect the individual texts to do similar things.

Genres—categories or forms of texts—occur in every field of study, every business, every hobby. When we think of genres, we often begin with literary forms: fiction, non-fiction, sci fi, mystery, romance. But genres also exist outside of literature. We have genres in film: chick flick, horror, comedy, drama, action. We have genres in music: punk, rap, blues, classical, hip hop, R & B, country. We have genres in business: annual reports, forms, business letters, PowerPoint presentations. The medical community has genres that only it uses: medical charts, intake forms, prescription bottle labels. We have genres in law: legal memoranda, briefs, judicial opinions. We have genres in academia: essays, research articles, annotated bibliographies, literature reviews, conference posters, syllabi, transcripts.

But looking at genre as just forms or categories is too limiting for the work you will be doing as a writer because good writing requires more than just form, style, or subject matter. Effective communication requires using the form or genre that works best for the rhetorical situation—your audience and your purpose. This is the rhetorical approach to genre, and it means that individual examples of a genre share a similar purpose, a similar audience, and do similar work in recurring rhetorical situations.

You might think of genre as code. Members of the community using that genre know the code. When I say "essay" or "grocery store receipt" or "blog," you know what I mean. You know that essays do not look like receipts, but blogs can look a lot like essays. You know that the same person can use all three genres, but that each genre can be used by or connect with very different audiences. What this means is that the naming of a genre creates certain expectations about form, content, the relationship between the audience and author, the community that uses this genre, and even expectations about what actions that genre will require of the reader.

> A rhetorical definition of genre: genre is a typified response to a recurring rhetorical need.

Rhetorician Carolyn Miller defined genre as social action: communities or groups create or borrow genres that they use to do their work, and genres reflect what is going on inside a community. By examining the genres that a group of people use, we can learn how that group sees itself and how that group sees people outside of it.

Thinking about the relationship between groups and the genres they use reveals another of the paradoxes about genres. Genres are how groups meet outsiders—you might call them the "front porch" of the community where they meet and greet people. But genres are also how communities exclude people from their communities. If you belong to a community, you know the "secret handshake"— you speak the language of the community and use its genres well.[1]

For example, when you go to the doctor, you'll frequently (and often repeatedly) fill out a patient examination or intake form. The form is a point of contact between you, your doctor, and the larger medical community. On the one hand, the language on the form is easily understandable ("Do you smoke?" "Does anyone in your family have heart disease?"). On the other hand, the doctor will put your intake form into a medical chart or file for you that contains notes and diagnostic forms. If you read your medical chart, it might not make much sense to you because of the specialized vocabulary and abbreviations, and because you are not the primary audience for these documents. In this way medical charts can keep non-medical people at a distance, and they help create an exclusive community not easily accessed by non-members. Medical charts help do the work of the medical community—medical charts aren't used in the automotive industry because the two communities have different needs.

Finally, there is the idea that in order to do the work of a community, genres talk to each other and work together. Think about college. Before you came to CU, you filled out an application, wrote personal essays, and asked people for letters of recommendation. CU responded with a letter (or email) of acceptance and an admissions packet. And then you had to go online and confirm that you wanted to come to CU. These documents—both print and digital—worked together to get you to CU. Genre scholars call groups of documents that talk to each other *genre sets* or *genre systems* or *genre ecologies*. By studying how these genres interact, scholars learn more about how communities function and what these groups value.

Using Genres

You will read and write a variety of genres throughout your academic, professional and civic life. Often we don't have a choice of genre—we are told what we need to write.

♦ *Write a twenty–page* **paper** *on the life of a tee shirt, emphasizing the economic and social implications as the shirt begins as cotton fiber, moves through production and packaging, and on to marketing.*

♦ *Write a six-page* **lab report** *describing the methods and results of your biochemistry experiment.*

♦ *Send me a* **memo** *on the status of the parking ramp project.*

♦ *Write a* **grant proposal** *so that we can fund our homeless shelter for another six months.*

When this happens, you will need a way to figure out how to write these possibly unfamiliar genres effectively. You have the name of a genre but you may not know what that code word means.

Sometimes we are told what to do—what is needed—but the genre is less specific.

> *We need new computers in the human resources department. Should we go with Macs or PCs? And should we buy laptops, desktops, or tablets for everyone? Send me an email.*

In this situation, is "email" the genre or really just the method of transmission? "Email" is pretty non-specific, and the kind of email you send to your BFF probably isn't going to be what your boss wants to get from you. So, you will need to identify the genre— or genres—you will be writing before you begin. "Email" is what rhetorician Peter Medway might call a "baggy genre." Emails are containers for all kinds of content and forms. This is an example of genre blending or mixing. So, if this were my assignment from my boss, I would first write a report, and then either copy it into the body of the email or attach it as a separate file.

You already have some of the tools you need to make decisions about genres because you know what questions to ask when analyzing a text rhetorically. When doing a rhetorical analysis, we are usually looking at a single text and its author and purpose. When we talk about genre, we expand our analysis to look at more than one sample. We ask whether a specific text is a good representation of other texts in that genre. And we begin to look at the author as a representative and member of the community that uses this genre. The complexity of genre is that while we may begin with its format—what it looks like on the page—format is often the least important information about a genre. To use a genre well, we need to understand its moves—how it is used by the community and how it, in turn, works to create that community.

Analyzing genres

To analyze a genre, first find several examples of that genre. Start your analysis with a list of common features. Which features seem to be essential, usually present, or optional?[2] Once you have an idea of the basic features of that genre, you can begin asking questions similar to those for rhetorical analysis that will help you dig deeper into how this particular genre works, and how you can use the genre with some credibility within this community.

Some of the questions you might ask include:

◆   ***What is the name of this genre?*** The name you assign to your text will determine the answers to the questions that follow. An analysis may require you to look at the author's moves in organizing her evidence while a reflection might just be what you think of a piece and why.

◆   ***What is the purpose of this genre?*** To understand genre, you need to look at the individual text you are creating and at how this group of texts function in its community.

> ***Micro . . .*** Why are you writing this genre this time? How are you going to use it? What is the exigence (need/ occasion) for this genre at this time and place? Do you intend to follow the conventions of the genre closely or stray from them?

> ***Macro . . .*** How does the community generally use this genre? What tends to be the exigence within the community for writing it? What actions does the genre make possible or difficult?

◆   ***Who are the audiences for this genre?*** Who uses the genre? Who reads this kind of text? Is there more than one type of reader for this genre? What roles do the readers/audiences perform? What characteristics do the readers/audiences of this genre possess? Under what circumstances (when) do readers read the genre (e.g., at their leisure, on the run, in waiting rooms)? How does the intended audience typically read this genre (scan and skip around, read slowly and sequentially)? What features does the audience expect to find? And how will readers react if certain features are absent or changed?

◆ ***Who is the author of this genre?*** Who normally writes the texts in this genre? Are multiple writers possible? (Texts in the workplace are often collaborative works without named authors.) What roles do the individual authors perform? Under what circumstances do writers write the genre (e.g., in teams, on a computer, in a rush)?

> Although we often begin with what a genre looks like, the format is often the least important aspect of the genre. When we go back to the format after we talk about audience, purpose and community, we can begin to see why the genre looks and sounds, and is built the way it is.

◆ ***What are the physical requirements of the genre?*** How would you reproduce this genre? What features recur in samples of this genre? How does it look on a page or screen? What kind of vocabulary does your audience expect you to use? How much "wiggle room" is there to stray from the formal conventions?

1. What is the typical ***content***? What topics, issues, ideas, questions does the genre address? How is the content treated (respectfully, flippantly, with self-importance)? How much content is usual? What content is considered most important? What topics or details are ignored?

2. What counts as ***evidence***? Does this genre use personal testimony or facts or hypotheticals? What sorts of examples are used? How much evidence is typical?

3. Does the genre call for any specific ***strategies***? Profiles use narration; lab reports explain processes.

4. What ***rhetorical appeals*** are used? What appeals to logos, pathos, and ethos appear?

5. How are texts in the genres ***structured***? What are their parts, and how are they organized?

6. What type of ***citation*** does this genre use? Formal academic systems—MLA, APA? Only signals? How much information goes into a signal? Only informal references?

7. In what ***medium*** are texts of this genre presented? Print, electronic, text, visual or a combination?

8. Does the genre have specific ***design requirements***? What format, layout or appearance is common? Does the

genre use paragraphs, lists, typeface, call outs, textboxes, images?

9. What's the typical **organization** of the genre? How **long** is a typical text in this genre? Are there **headings** or sections? What's the layout on the page or screen?

10. What types of **sentences** do texts in the genre typically use? How long are they? Are they simple or complex, passive or active? Are the sentences varied? Do they share a certain style?

11. How would you describe the writer's **voice**? Is the tone formal or informal? Is the writing formulaic?

12. What **diction** (types of words) is most common? Is a type of jargon or specialized vocabulary used? Is slang used?

Why genre?

While all these questions you can ask about genre may seem overwhelming, remember that you already use all kinds of genres every day. From a daily news feed, to text messages, to academic essays and blogs and movies, you actively use genres all the time. Remember, too, that genre is a rhetorical choice. Asking questions about how genres work will help you use them more effectively in the future. Picking the most appropriate, interesting, or powerful genre for your purpose helps you communicate with your audience. The right genre will build your credibility as an author. It signals to your audience that you know what you are doing and that you are thinking about its needs.

A glimpse ahead

As you continue to study at CU, you will be asked to write in the genres of your discipline or in the genres of a community that has formed around an issue. When you first use a genre, you'll focus primarily on its form. To become an expert and full member of a community,

> If you belong to a community, you know the "secret handshake"—you speak the language of the community and use its genres well.

you will move beyond the form to understanding how genres do the work of that community. That understanding will help you write those genres better, and will demonstrate your membership in the community.

You will continue to ask the basic rhetorical questions about a genre. But as you become a more sophisticated writer, you will also need to analyze the community you are participating in as an author. Genre gives us insight into what a community thinks, how it uses language, what it values, and how it functions. That awareness will help you communicate more effectively. Some of the questions that will help you understand the relationship between genres and your community are:

◆ ***Place in the community***. What sort of genres does this community use? What other genres does this genre talk to? Is this genre part of a genre set? Did the community create this genre or do you think it modified one borrowed from another group? What are its antecedent genres and do the earlier forms give you any insight into this genre?

◆ ***Power***. Who can use and cannot use this genre? How is one invited into or excluded from the genre? By what means are they invited or excluded? What roles for writers and readers does it encourage or discourage? Who can break or bend the rules of this genre?

◆ ***Knowledge and beliefs.*** How does this community build or acquire or use knowledge? What genres do this work? What kind of information does this community value? Which genres showcase this information? How does this community attribute the knowledge that it acquires? Are there political and ethical implications when you use this genre?

REFLECTION QUESTIONS

1. What genres do you use every day? Make a list of all the genres you read or write in a 24-hour period.

2. What genres do you use as the member of a community of some kind? Think about your school work and your hobbies. Select one of those genres, and use the questions in this chapter to analyze it. Based on your answers, how might you write that genre differently in the future?

3. Think back to an unfamiliar genre that you wrote in the past year or so. How might you have produced that genre better by asking the questions in this chapter?

4. Name three of four genres that you think are particularly powerful or influential in our culture right now. What are some of the characteristics of these genres? Why do you think they are powerful?

Works Cited

Medway, Peter. "Fuzzy Genres and Community Identities: The Case of Architecture Students' Sketchbooks" *The Rhetoric and Ideology of Genre.* Eds. Richard M. Coe, Lorelei Lingard & Tatiana Teslenko. Cresskill: Hampton Press, 2001. 132-153. Print.

Miller, Carolyn R. "Genre as Social Action," *Quarterly Journal of Speech* 70: 151-167 (1984). Print.

Endnotes

1. Pieplow, Kathryn. *"Rhetorical Literacy: Transferability of Genre Analysis Strategies Across Disciplines and into the Workplace."* Genre 2012: Rethinking Genre 20 Years Later, an International Conference on Genre Carleton College, Ottawa, Canada (June 2012). Conference Presentation.

2. Deans, Thomas. "Genre Analysis and the Community Writing Course." *reflections* Vol. 1 & 2 (Spring 2006). 7-25. Print. See also Amy Devitt, Mary Jo Reiff, and Anis Bawarshi. *Scenes of Writing.* New York: Pearson Longman (2004).

Chapter 6

Argument–Presenting Your Views

Argument as Process...and Progress

In the process of critical inquiry, argument follows research and analysis. After exploring a topic through reading texts, listening to speakers, visiting museums or attending cultural events, interviewing people, and analyzing various sources of information, you have probably developed an opinion about the topic. But merely stating your opinion is not enough to convince anyone else to share your view. You need to compose an argument.

As we mentioned in the second chapter, the word *argument* may make us think of two people shouting at each other. But the term has a much deeper, richer history. The classical Greeks considered argument to be a form of public and collaborative decision-making. Over the centuries, the art of constructing and presenting arguments was considered central to a well-rounded education. In this more formal sense, the meaning of *argument* is similar to the definition presented earlier in this book: *argument* is "a process aimed at advancing the discussion." So arguments are actually very useful things—in one form or another, they provide opportunities for us to present our views, to listen to others' views, and to change minds—both our own and others'. Arguments also result in other kinds of changes—laws, consumer buying habits, funding for scientific research, the fall lineup of new TV shows—all of these are largely the results of successful arguments. An effective argument can truly change the world...or at least a part of it.

Think, for example, of an argument we mentioned in the last chapter. By writing the book *Fast Food Nation*, Eric Schlosser presented the claim that fast food may, in fact, be more harmful to our health than we know. He presented reasons and evidence that supported this claim, including scientific research, interviews with workers in the slaughterhouse industry, and photographs of Ronald McDonald. Schlosser's book has been very influential, in persuading many people to stop eating—or at least reduce their intake of—fast food. In turn, some fast food chains have responded by offering healthier alternatives. Schlosser's argument has had a significant impact on our culture.

Building Your Own Argument

It's important to note that arguments rarely take place in a vacuum—that is, a text (whether a book, a film, a speech, an advertisement, or website) presenting an argument is generally a response to a conversation already circulating in society. While some texts are more influential than others, generally our views are shaped by multiple texts that present varying perspectives on an issue. In other words, we are influenced on a daily basis by many arguments that address the same (or similar) topics. In the same way, when we compose an argument, we need to consider how it fits into the ongoing conversation.

In the last chapter, you learned about how other writers (and speakers and artists and web designers, just to name a few) use rhetorical appeals and strategies to compose a text (an article, a song, a website) that presents an argument. You also learned how to recognize—and hopefully avoid—the use of *fallacies of argument.*

In this chapter, you'll learn how to construct your own argument. As with most pieces you'll write, an effective argument needs a clear structure. Although you have many choices when it comes to organizing your argument, it's helpful to begin with an understanding of your purpose, your audience, and the context. In other words, you should spend some time thinking about the *rhetorical situation* before you begin to write.

One place to start might be to go back to your research to consider the *context* of this argument, to look at how and where this topic is being discussed.

◆ What's the current conversation?

◆ Who's talking about this topic?

◆ What are the key questions and controversies?

◆ What's the evidence that's been presented by various groups in support of their positions?

After looking at what others are saying, it's important to examine your own assumptions, or your underlying beliefs about your topic. These assumptions are probably why you became interested in your topic to begin with and have probably come from a variety of sources. For example,

> For more information on rhetoric, see Chapter 4.

perhaps you have seen recent news coverage regarding the increased use and abuse of prescription medications and also read a magazine story about a cancer patient who became addicted to her pain medication, which led you to the following assumption: prescription drug use is out of control in our society.

When you think about your *purposes* for writing an argument, what comes to mind? One way to answer this question would be to say, "I want to prove..." But the word "prove" implies that you can definitively demonstrate your claim is true. This is rarely the case in most arguments—mostly because the topics

> Your assumptions do not have to be directly stated in your argument, although sometimes it's helpful to acknowledge them in order to clarify your position for your audience.

we deal with are frequently matters of judgment rather than "fact." More importantly, when we argue we are engaging with an *audience* that may or may not be persuaded. When you write an argument, your *general purpose* is to offer to your audience the best case you can by providing a clear claim, solid reasons and credible evidence. Your *specific purpose* may be to attempt to persuade your audience to become more informed about a topic, to change their minds about a political or social issue, or to take action (for example, change their buying habits, contact a governmental official, reduce their consumption, or donate time or money to a nonprofit organization). Once you've presented your argument, the audience then has the responsibility to read your argument, evaluate your case, and decide how to respond.

How do you know how your audience will respond? The short answer is, you don't. But there are strategies you can use to build a strong argument, such as

◆ understanding the assumptions and beliefs your audience brings to this topic

◆ offering reasons and evidence that draw on your audience's assumptions and beliefs

◆ using specific rhetorical strategies that will appeal to your audience.

63

For example, to get back to our example about prescription pain medication, if you're writing an argument addressed to doctors schooled in traditional western medicine, you can assume that your audience is generally supportive of the use of prescription medications and that they will want to see scientific data about the relationship between these medications and certain harmful effects. In addition, you would most likely write your argument in a fairly formal style in order to gain credibility with your specific audience.

> "The aim of argument, or of discussion, should not be victory, but progress."
>
> –Joseph Joubert

The structure of your argument might then look something like this:

1. **Establish a relationship with the audience by introducing the topic, providing the necessary background, and showing an initial understanding of your audience's assumptions and views.**

   In our example, you might review some of the current mainstream media coverage of the abuse of prescription pain medication but also—given that your audience is doctors—review the information that suggests ways that pain medication has made many people who are suffering with unbearable pain more comfortable.

2. **Present your claim.**

   The central element of an argument is the *claim*—the debatable point you want to present. In making a claim, you need to be sure that your position is specific and debatable. For example, the claim that "excessive drug use is bad" is most likely a statement that a majority of people would already agree with, so it's not debatable. In addition, this claim is extremely vague. What kind of drug use are you including in this statement? Illegal drugs? Prescription drugs? Is alcohol included in your definition of a drug? If you were to revise this claim in order to make it more specific and debatable, you might come up with the following tentative thesis for your essay:

   Claim: *Prescription pain medications should be more closely regulated.*

   Now your claim is much more specific, as you have defined the drugs you will examine and the specific change you hope to see take place.

3. Support your claim with reasons and evidence.

A claim on its own probably will not convince your audience. You also need to support your claim with *reasons* and *evidence*.

Reasons are the specific points that support your claim. In other words, they are your "because" statements. One way to find your reasons is to add "because" to the end of your claim.

> The use of reasons and evidence separates an argument from an opinion.

For example:

◆ Prescription medication should be more closely regulated because...

◆ We should "buy local" because...

◆ The deadline for this essay should be extended because...

As you can see from these examples (particularly the last one), your reasons will need to be convincing for your specific audience.

In our example, the following reason would support our claim:

Excessive use of prescription pain medication can lead to additional health complications, addiction, and in some cases overdose and even death.

This reason ties the overuse of pain medication to specific harmful consequences, something that doctors would particularly want to prevent.

But even a clearly articulated claim with solid reasons is not enough to persuade most audiences. In addition to your reasons, you must provide *evidence* that roots your reasons and claim in human knowledge and experience—through logic, emotion, or credibility. In other words, evidence is where you show why your reasons and, therefore, your claim make sense.

In rhetorical terms, evidence may be based on any of the three appeals: logic *(logos)*, emotion or beliefs and values *(pathos)*, or credibility *(ethos)*.

For example, evidence that presents a logical appeal might involve the use of facts and expert opinion. In order to adequately support the claim in our example, you might want to research medical studies to explore whether excessive use of pain medication negatively impacts overall health. To find logical evidence for our example, a good place to start would be professional medical journals, including the *New England Journal of Medicine* and the *Journal of the American Medical Association,* both of which can be found in the Medicine and Health subject area databases of CU's online library resources. You might also research leading psychology journals found through the psychology subject area databases.

> For more information on *logos*, *pathos* and *ethos*, see Chapter 4.

To find evidence that offers the *credibility* of first-hand experiences, look for personal interviews or stories from people who use prescription medications, doctors, or psychologists.

> For help on finding information, see Chapter 3.

Evidence presented through interviews and personal anecdotes might also offer an *emotional* appeal and would grab your readers' attention and make them interested in your argument. Often, visuals such as photographs can also be a powerful form of evidence that carries an emotional appeal.

The key to offering effective evidence is knowing where to look for the right kind of information to support your reasons. While you might have quite a bit of evidence taken from the research you've already done, you may discover that you need to find additional information to provide effective evidence for your reasons.

But what happens if you find evidence that contradicts your claim or your reasons? When this happens, you will need to decide how to adjust your argument to allow for the evidence. Depending on the significance of the evidence, you might:

◆ Revise your claim altogether

◆ Revise one of your reasons

◆ Integrate this contradictory evidence into your argument by using the strategies in step 4.

4.   Acknowledge and respond to other views.

Think for a moment about verbal arguments you have previously engaged in. You probably didn't take the time to stop and consider opposing points of view. Similarly, when you were first taught to write an argument essay, you probably weren't asked to address the opposing side. And if, during your research, you found evidence that supported an opposing point of view, you likely ignored it. Now that you are expected to write more formal academic arguments, you can no longer ignore *counterargument.* In an effective argument, you need to address the counterarguments—views that differ from your own. In fact, addressing counterargument will help you to present your claim. There are several strategies you can use for acknowledging and responding to counterarguments.

Refuting: When you present opposing points of view and then show that these counterarguments are weak, you are *refuting* the opposing viewpoints and thus providing additional support for your own point of view. For example, one counterargument to our example claim that pain medications should be more closely regulated could include the point that prescription pain medications provide relief for millions of patients in the US. A refutation to this counterargument could include evidence that other forms of pain management, including physical therapy, acupuncture, over-the-counter medications, and exercise have also been shown to provide significant pain relief without the negative side effects of prescription pain medications.

It's important to note that any approach to argument is very culturally determined. In US society, we are used to arguments where the claim is presented right away, whereas in other cultures it's more typical to lead gradually into the argument by providing background, reasons and evidence before you present the claim. Even in US culture, the direct approach is not always the best choice–if your audience is very resistant to your argument, you may want to take more time to introduce the topic and offer some reasons and evidence before you present your claim.

Conceding: Sometimes, in addition to refuting a counterargument, you will find you need to *concede* certain opposing viewpoints, admitting that a particular counterargument has validity. For example, consider the following counterargument: Prescription pain medication may be the only logical option for some patients, including post-surgical patients and those who are terminally ill. This is a valid counterargument that you might have to concede. Conceding is an important part of engaging in argument as progress—it's a way of finding some common ground where various groups can agree.

Acknowledging limitations and offering qualifiers: Another method of engaging different views is to acknowledge the limitations of your own argument.

> "When I'm getting ready to reason with a man, I spend one-third of my time thinking about myself and what I am going to say–and two-thirds thinking about him and what he is going to say."
>
> —Abraham Lincoln

In other words, whether the opposition has raised the point or not, if you find that your argument has a weak spot, you should state the *limitation* and use a *qualifier* to demonstrate you understand the limitation and can offer a response. For example, if you're arguing for additional regulation of pain medication and your audience is doctors, most likely they will be the ones who will deal with the additional paperwork and bureaucracy of regulation. This is a limitation of your argument. But you might offer the qualifier that the additional paperwork is in the best interest of the patient and so the regulation is still needed.

5. **Close your argument by reiterating your claim and—if you haven't already—present the specific response you hope to elicit from your audience.**

   In an argument, the closing is important—it's your last opportunity to reiterate key ideas and to ensure that your audience clearly understands how you want them to respond.

   In our example argument for increased regulation of pain medication, most likely you will be asking doctors to support and advocate for legislation. Doctor support for your claim would probably be crucial. In your closing, you'll need to reiterate the benefits of increased regulation and connect again with your audience's assumptions and beliefs—that patient well-being must always come first.

When it comes to composing and structuring arguments, the important questions to remember are:

◆ **What is your *specific purpose?*** Beyond presenting a strong case, what's the specific and debatable claim you want to present and how do you want the audience to respond?

◆ **Who is your *audience?*** What are their assumptions and beliefs about this topic? What do they already know?

◆ **What kinds of *choices* can you make** in content, structure, and style in order to reach the audience? What kinds of reasons and evidence will be persuasive for them? What style should you use to reach your audience? Which rhetorical appeals and strategies will be effective?

> The last chapter raised the question of the relationship between rhetoric and ethics. This is also a key question for this chapter—when you are presenting an argument, you are necessarily trying to persuade your audience. In other words, you are exercising power.

◆ **What are your ethical *obligations*** to your audience? So how do you define an ethical argument? To what extent should you discuss the counterargument? How do you avoid fallacies of argument?

Based on your answers to these questions, you can begin to build an argument that presents a strong case for your claim and provides the audience with the information that they need to respond. While there's no guarantee that

> To see how other students have constructed their arguments, see the sample argument essays in Chapter 7.

your audience will respond in the way you hope, by presenting an effective and ethical argument, you will contribute to the conversation and, just maybe, change the world a little.

REFLECTION QUESTIONS

1. What kinds of arguments do you encounter every day? What makes an argument effective or not effective?

2. What are some arguments that are currently important in our society? What are the various ways we learn about these arguments?

3. How would you define ethical argument?

4. What effect does writing style have on an argument?

Chapter 7

Workshops and Revision

Workshops and revision are two important, closely related activities. For workshops to succeed, you'll need to be able to offer—and be willing to receive—constructive criticism. Revision is an ongoing process that involves a lot more than running a spell-check and fixing those pesky grammatical errors. This section explains common myths about workshopping and revision, and it offers advice about what you can do to make both of these crucial processes effective.

Workshop Guidelines

Workshops will play a key role in the course, so you'll want to know how to make the most of them. Whether your instructor asks you to discuss your writing in pairs, in small groups, or as a whole class—or uses a combination of these approaches—workshops will give you a good idea of what's working well in your writing, as well as what you need to rethink and revise.

Just as importantly, workshops will help you refine your skills as a critical reader. By learning to help your classmates improve their writing, you'll become a better reader of your own work, which will in turn make you a more confident and successful writer.

First let's consider two common myths about workshops. If you go into a workshop with a negative attitude based on one of these myths, you might miss a great opportunity to improve your writing and help your peers improve theirs.

Common Myths about Workshops

Myth #1: *I'm not qualified to comment on someone else's draft.*
You might think, "I'm no expert when it comes to writing, so who am I to criticize someone else's draft?" The assumption here is that you

have to be a superb writer yourself, or at least highly trained in the craft of writing, to have something valuable to say. This just isn't the case. In fact, as a general, educated reader, you can give invaluable feedback.

Tip: *Trust your instincts as a reader.* Just because you're not a published writer or a writing instructor doesn't mean that your thoughts and suggestions don't matter. Everyone writes for an audience, and as a reader you're a legitimate member of one. When reading someone's draft, don't waste too much time correcting grammatical errors. Focus instead on more important issues, such as how persuasive you find the writer's argument, how effective the supporting evidence is, and how compelling the organization is.

Myth #2: *Our opinions don't matter anyway, because our instructor will be the one who grades our essays.* Although it's true that your instructor will grade your essays, that doesn't mean that you and your peers can't help one another improve your writing. Chances are, if you find a classmate's argument unclear, so will your instructor. Likewise, if a peer thinks that your draft is poorly organized, don't be surprised if your instructor agrees.

Tip: *Have confidence in your ability to help your classmates improve their writing, and respect their constructive criticism.* Of course, you might not end up using every suggestion you get. After all, one person might love your title and appreciate its sense of humor, while another might find it unprofessional and inappropriate. Rather than throw up your hands in frustration when you get conflicting advice, think about each disputed issue and decide for yourself whose advice to follow. Finally, keep in mind that your instructor probably won't be able to read and respond to every draft you write, so you'll often need to rely on the advice of your peers.

By keeping this advice in mind, you can make a huge difference in the dynamics of your class throughout the semester. Will you be the person who reads a draft and says things like "It's good. You just need to fix a few commas"? Or will you be the person who genuinely tries to help your classmates by saying things like "The organization is clear overall, but you could use a stronger transition between the second and third paragraphs"? Will you talk about last weekend's big game, or will you talk about the need to address credible counterarguments? When it comes right down to it, your attitude and effort will make or break your workshops. So why not help make them positive learning experiences for yourself and your classmates?

Revision

So you've just spent two weeks—or four or six or 13—working on a piece of writing. You've done your research, you've workshopped drafts in class, you've conferenced with your instructor. And on top of that, all five of your roommates read your paper and told you it's great. You're done. Right?

Well, maybe not. Your instructor is telling you that you still need to revise your paper. Whether you're at the end of a long drafting process or at the beginning, you can expect to revise your writing many times along the way. To some writers, this sounds tedious and frustrating—but hold on! Instead of thinking of revision as a chore, think of it as a golden opportunity to make your writing better. You now have the chance to reread and reflect on what you've written, think about what you really want to say, and make whatever changes are necessary to improve your original work.

What Is Revision?

Revision literally means to re-envision, to see again. When you revise a piece of writing, you step back from your work and look at it again through new eyes. Now is the time to think about how readers will experience your writing, how other people will respond to your words and ideas.

Common Myths about Revision

Myth #1: *Revision means fixing the mistakes.* Many writers mistake "revising" for proofreading—in other words, running a spell-check on your computer or skimming your paper to look for typos or grammatical errors in the last few minutes before you turn your paper in for a grade. But revision is much more than that. Proofreading is one part of the revising process, but a successful revision can be anything from a change in the word choice or sentence structure to a radical change in content to a complete overhaul of the organization of your essay—among many other options.

Tip: *Keep an open mind as you revise.* Believe it or not, you may even benefit from doing more freewriting to generate new ideas. Some people even write entirely new essays, inspired by one key idea they had in their original essay. Revision is the process of re-thinking your essay, top to bottom, and choosing what elements of your writing you want to improve. Every time you look at a piece of writing, you'll probably come up with new ideas!

Myth #2: *Revision is always the last thing you do after you've completely finished a piece of writing.* Many writers think that revision comes only at the very end of the writing process, but really, you begin to revise almost as soon as you put the first few words on the page. You may write your first few sentences, decide they don't really say what you mean, and go back and rewrite those same sentences.

In addition to resources that your instructor and the library staff provide, you can find a list of online writing and research resources on the PWR website at http://www.colorado.edu/pwr/resources.html. Click on "Writing and Research Links."

Tip: *Remember that writing is a recursive and generative process, meaning you use writing to figure out what you're thinking about a topic.* As you write, you often sharpen your thinking and develop new ideas or new ways of seeing old ideas. Then you put those new ideas on paper, which in turn generate even newer ones. So really, revision is writing; writing is revision.

Myth #3: *Good writers don't need to revise because they get it right the first time.* Some students see revision as a sort of punishment, as if the teacher is telling them to revise because they're not good enough and they need to work harder than the "good" students. The truth is, all writers revise. No, let's amend (er, revise) that: all good writers revise. Writers know that their first ideas are just the beginning. No first draft ever sees the light of day. Writing is a long process that takes time and effort and lots of thinking and rethinking.

Tip: *Take heart in the fact that each time you write, you become a better writer.* So each time you revisit a piece, you are revisiting it as a better writer than you were when you wrote the previous draft. The more you practice, the better you get—and the more skills and insight you can bring to successive drafts of your writing.

What Makes a Good Workshop?

Positive Attitude

"A good workshop is when people bring their writing and are open and willing to have discussion about it. People have to be willing to accept, or at least acknowledge, criticism. That's the only way people are going to get better at writing, by accepting critical help."
— Mike Ramsey, WRTG 1100

Preparation

"In my opinion, a good workshop means that everyone in the class comes prepared. If there are only a few people who are wanting to workshop, then it won't be fun and you will not get the proper feedback."
— Kristen Hanson, WRTG 1100

Honesty

"In the past, I've always had workshops or small groups where they only tell you good things about your paper for fear of hurting each other's feelings. This year, however, I received good criticism on my papers because it was honest. In order for this method to work, you have to be open-minded and willing to accept someone else's thoughts or opinions."
—Casey Stokely, WRTG 1150

Specific Criticism

"Constructive criticism is the best way to collect other people's opinions on your paper, and vice versa. Be sure to give specific examples of what you liked, disliked, and what could be improved. It's more helpful to know what you did wrong when revising and editing."
—Tiffany Valdez, WRTG 1150

Focus

"I really dislike it when people constantly get off subject. It's great to hear discussion, but only if it involves a critical discussion of the person's paper; otherwise it seems pretty pointless."
—Emily Lumia, WRTG 1150

Balance of Praise and Criticism

"The workshops that were most helpful were the ones where I received comments about the strengths and weaknesses of my paper."
—Johnny Laychaypha, WRTG 1150

What Students Say About Revision

"Revising a piece of writing is the chance to do the 'coulda, shoulda, woulda' that you wish you had the time or thoughts for. I almost always find something I wish I had done differently, either just at the time I turn the paper in or in rereading it after the paper is graded and returned. Revising is your second chance to get it just the way you want it to be."

— Jean Rice, WRTG 1100

"Revision is a unique process for me. My final draft is completely transformed from my original draft. During the revision process, I come up with new ideas, and abandon old ones. After I have organized my thoughts, the last step in the process is to check for grammatical errors."

— Steve Bonner, WRTG 1150

"Revising takes raw ideas and turns them into coherent ideas."

— Bo Dodd, WRTG 1100

"Revising is when you clean up your thoughts on paper. The first draft is a conversation with yourself, the other drafts are for other people. I revise a lot because I always get new ideas and have a new outlook every time I reread a paper."

— Kaitlin Bernstein, WRTG 1100

REFLECTION QUESTIONS

1. Have you used workshops before in a writing class? If so, describe them—what kinds of activities and questions did you use in the workshops? If you haven't used workshops before, describe two or three specific things you hope to learn in a workshop for this class.

2. Either based on previous writing workshops or on reading this chapter, what kinds of comments on your work do you think will be most helpful for improving your writing? What kinds of comments seem least useful? (It's a good idea to keep this in mind when you are reading your classmates' work.)

3. Look at the revision checklist at the end of this chapter. Which three or four items do you most want to work on as you revise

your writing? What are two or three specific strategies you can use to improve in these areas?

4. What might you learn about your own writing from reading and commenting on the work of your classmates?

Are You a Writer or an Editor? Both!

At professional publications such as newspapers and magazines, multiple people contribute to every piece published. A story may have only one byline, but really, it has been produced by a team. Here's an example of how writers and editors may work collaboratively to produce a story:

◆ **Writer**: When the writer first comes up with an idea or gets an assignment, she pairs up with an editor to brainstorm ideas and figure out what sources to turn to for information.

◆ **Content Editor:** After the writer produces a draft, an editor will review it and send it back to the writer, asking her to make significant content changes, such as adding more information or rewriting entire sections. Often the writer and editor will work through several (or several dozen) drafts together.

◆ **Copy Editor**: When the writer and editor are confident that the content of the story is as good as it can be, the story goes to a copy editor, who reviews it for clarity, cohesion, flow, and wording. The copy editor will often consult with the writer to clarify ideas or sentences that may be confusing.

◆ **Proofreader**: Finally, the piece of writing goes to a proofreader, who reads it for correctness, making sure the grammar, spelling, and punctuation are perfect.

By the time the story is printed, it has usually been read and commented on by four people—and revised too many times to count!

In the same way, you play these different roles when you revise your writing. Although you'll work with other people—your instructor, other students in your class, friends—to revise your work, ultimately, you serve as your own content editor, copy editor, and proofreader.

Revision Checklist

Here are some questions to consider as you think about what elements of your essay you want to revise.

Rhetorical Situation

Purpose

- ☐ Do I have a strong purpose for writing this essay?
- ☐ Is the relationship among audience, purpose, and content appropriate and effective?

Appealing to Readers

- ☐ Do I effectively engage my readers?
- ☐ Do I appeal to my readers' logic and emotions?
- ☐ Do I establish my ethos as a writer?

Voice and Style

- ☐ Is the voice in the writing appropriate for the subject, purpose, and audience of this piece?
- ☐ Is the style of my writing appropriate for the subject, purpose, and audience of this piece?

Content

Ideas

- ☐ What do I really want to say in this paper? Do I say it?
- ☐ Is anything missing?
- ☐ Do I make enough points? Give enough examples?
- ☐ Could I go back and do any more research? Are there any other stories from my personal experience that I might include?
- ☐ Could I add more description or concrete, sensory details?

Meaning

- ☐ Does this essay have a strong sense of significance?
- ☐ Is there enough evidence to support the thesis (or controlling idea) of this essay?
- ☐ Is my reasoning sound, accurate, and convincing?

Focus

- ☐ Is my thesis (or controlling idea) clear, strong, specific, and sophisticated?
- ☐ Does all the information work to develop and support the controlling idea?
- ☐ Overall, is the writing thorough and compelling?
- ☐ Is all the information here relevant? Is anything superfluous or irrelevant or redundant?

Organization and Clarity

Introduction and Conclusion

☐ Could the introduction do anything more to engage the reader, establish the tone, and set up the controlling idea of the paper?

☐ Does the conclusion bring a satisfying sense of closure?

Structure

☐ Do I, as a writer, deliberately lead the reader through the essay in a clear, logical way?

☐ Is the information presented in the best possible order?

☐ Is there any redundancy of words, phrases, sentences, or ideas?

Paragraphs and Transitions

☐ Does each paragraph focus on one main topic? Is that topic relevant to the thesis of the paper?

☐ Are the transitions between paragraphs clear and logical?

☐ Does each sentence connect to the one that came before it and the one that follows?

Style

☐ Is the prose lively, engaging, and sophisticated?

☐ Is the voice consistent throughout the essay?

☐ Are all the words I've chosen accurate and clear? Are my vocabulary and diction appropriate and effective?

Conventions of Language

Sentence structure

☐ Does each sentence make sense?

☐ Are sentences well-constructed, effective, and varied?

☐ Are there too many short, choppy sentences? Too many long, wordy sentences?

Mechanics and Grammar

☐ Are the punctuation and spelling correct?

☐ Are there any grammatical errors?

Citation of Sources

☐ If the essay refers to outside sources, are they cited correctly in the text?

☐ Is the Works Cited or bibliography properly formatted?

Chapter 8

Student Writing

The following collection of essays shows how important student writing is for all first-year PWR courses. As you read the samples, you'll see how these student writers situated themselves, first and foremost, as writers. In your class, you'll experience different types of and occasions for writing, and you'll often use your own and your peers' essays in an ongoing discussion about writing and writing topics. Each piece that follows is very different from the others, with the focus and approach varying according to the purpose of the essay. A common thread in each is something you will likely encounter in all good writing: clarity, conciseness, and a strong sense of the writer behind the ideas and words.

We selected the following essays according to six categories—personal narrative, analysis, inquiry, argument, persuasion and rhetorical analysis, and reflection—because you will often encounter these forms of writing in your courses. Understand that these categories are not strict boundaries but rather genres that often bump up against one another depending on the purpose and occasion for writing. The most imaginative student writing often weaves something of each category to meet the demands of the subject and audience. Each essay presents a good opportunity to engage the writer and the many occasions for writing.

Becoming Changing Woman

Kimberly Preston

Personal Narrative: Sample Essay 1

WRTG 1150

Instructor: James Walker

In "Becoming Changing Woman," Kimberly Preston utilizes a confident, descriptive style and a dialectical narrative structure to reflect upon her coming-of-age ceremony. Her use of significant sensory details "shows" (rather than "tells")—helping place us in the scene. Distinguishing personal narrative from "story" however, the brief text never loses sight of its theme, commenting maturely upon a moment of personal transformation and the power of solidarity.

As I took off running to the east, the first beams of sunlight peaked above the horizon, transforming the sky into a million shades of pink. Although I had been awake all night, I felt alert and energized as I ran in the thick woven wool dress and turquoise jewelry. My heavy necklace bounced against my chest as the chill air whipped my face and my newly washed hair flew behind me. My moccasins felt light on my feet despite being bound in huge layers of buckskin around my calves. As the sun began to rise higher, I started hearing the sounds of my family and friends running behind me in support. As I came to a stop on top of a tall rock ledge and looked out over the vast desert landscape, I felt different. I knew that when I returned to everyone I would be seen as an adult instead of the small middle schooler I was.

Growing up, I visited my family on the reservation often, sitting quietly in small hogans[1] and trailers, listening as my family babbled away in Navajo. "Yá'át'ééh[2] child", they would say as they shook my small little hands. They would sit and talk for hours, intermixing English and Navajo words in each sentence. When I was lucky, I could escape out into the dry red dirt and play with my cousins until the stray dogs came around looking for food. We would wander down dusty dirt roads until we could look out across the edge of the mesa. Or, we would ride in the back of a pickup, out to my parent's hogan that has a clear view of the San Francisco Peaks, one of the four sacred mountains.

> Seeing all the people standing around waiting, waiting for me, was intimidating, but I knew I now possessed the strength to push past my shyness and be introduced to my community.

I was always the "cousin from California," the one kid that didn't look native, the one kid with colored eyes and lighter hair. My skin wasn't as dark, and I either wasn't as tall, or wasn't as round as the other kids. I hadn't lived in a trailer on the reservation my whole life, wasn't learning Navajo in school, and I hadn't grown up in the harsh desert climate. I was somewhat of an outsider and although everyone knew I was different, I was still family and had still grown up with an understanding of the traditional beliefs.

Once I got older, everyone would ask my parents, "when will you have her kinaaldá[3]?" "Where will it be?" "Better start preparing now." Much like in the Jewish tradition, the Navajo perform a coming of age ceremony for girls when they reach puberty, but instead of one large service, the kinaaldá is a few days long.

I had been looking forward to mine for years, with nervousness and anticipation. The ceremony would transition me into adulthood and demonstrate my strength in front of an entire community. In some ways, I was surprised at how many people wanted to help me into this new stage in my life. From the cooking to the nightlong prayers, every member of the family was involved. Family friends from around the country, who had seen me grow up, came and even people I had never met were there to support me and celebrate the traditional and ancient ceremony that would bring another Diné[4] woman into the community. All these people stayed up with me

---

1 **Hogan** *(HO-gahn):* eight-sided building that is a traditional Navajo home. Usually has a dirt floor with a smoke hole in the roof to draft a central fire. Also used for traditional ceremonies.

2 **Yá'át'ééh** *(ya-at-eh):* Navajo greeting used for "Hello". Literally translates to, "It is good."

3 **Kinaaldá** *(kee-nahl-DAH):* Traditional coming-of-age ceremony for Navajo girls.

4 **Diné** *(dee-NEH):* Navajo word meaning "The People," which Navajos use to describe themselves.

throughout the nights of prayers, and they spent the days keeping me awake and giving me advice. The medicine man and his wife sat with me for hours during the day, talking to me about my new responsibilities as a woman and how to respect myself, and others, and continue to work hard in everything I do to make an impact on the world.

For an entire day, I sat in the sweltering hogan, grinding corn with a grinding stone for the alkaad, which is a large cake baked during the last part of the ceremony. The circular cake, which spanned a few feet in diameter, was placed in the ground lined by cornhusks and buried. A large fire was built on top and tended to throughout the night by my uncle Roy, brother Bob, and other male family members. While I grinded corn, a sheep was slaughtered and traditionally skinned by the women to prepare for a large meal the next day. I took a break, and watched in astonishment as my grandma dug though a large bowl of sheep intestines, preparing a traditional dish of intestines coiled around strips of fat and grilled. In addition to the cake preparation, I was required to run in the four directions at dawn, noon, and dusk, to show my endurance and strength. The ceremony was grueling, and when I wasn't working on grinding corn or running, I was struggling to stay awake from being up all night in prayer.

The warmth and support that surrounded me was amazing. "You're doing great," everyone said. "If only your father was here; he would be so proud to see you doing this," my tiny frail grandmother said to me one morning. I knew that although he wasn't there to support me physically, he was thinking about me and staying up all night in prayer as well.

Coming into the ceremony, I was still a girl. A girl who loved her culture and was eager to be brought into the world as a young woman in such a special and spiritual way. The story of Changing Woman, the daughter of First Man and First Woman, had been told to me as a young child and depicts the first kinaaldá. She created the plan for the Earth and from her skin she created the initial four clans, one of which, Tó díchʼíinii, or Bitter Water Clan, is mine. Just like Changing Woman, I ran for the last time, starting before the sun had risen on the last day. My hair had been freshly washed with yucca[5] root and tied back in a Tsiiʼyeel[6] by my mother as the

---

5 **Yucca**: An evergreen plant in the agave family, with stiff, spiked leaves and clusters of white flowers. The root squeezed in water makes a soapy liquid. Leaves can be beaten and the fibers woven into baskets or rope. Native Americans also use the plant for several medicinal purposes.

6 **Tsiiʼyeel** (SEET-yeel): Traditional hair bun of a Navajo woman. Tied at the back of her head and tied with white buckskin or white yarn, it signifies that she is a woman.

fire above the corn cake died down outside. A lot relied on the cake. A good cake meant a good future, cooked all the way through without any burns. When I returned from the run, the sun had risen all the way, and even more people had arrived for the end of the ceremony. Seeing all the people standing around waiting, waiting for me, was intimidating, but I knew I now possessed the strength to push past my shyness and be introduced to my community.

> Often, I had felt like I couldn't relate to my cousins or other women in my family because I had not grown up the same way as them and hadn't lived in an entire community of Native peoples my whole life.

They had all come to be blessed. Not by the medicine man. But by me. In the Navajo culture, women are the leaders and are sacred for their ability to bear children and to nurture. When people hear about a kinaaldá taking place, they come from all around to be blessed by the new woman. As over a hundred people formed a line, I lay down on a rug outside and my closest female family members began to touch my arms and legs, symbolically molding me into a woman. After, each person approached and asked me to bless and mold them. Many asked me to touch their back to heal pain or their head to clear their minds of any bad thoughts. Although it felt strange to be seen as a healer, the feelings of maturity began to come to me. I was now the center of attention and focus of everyone's prayers in a community that I was only able to visit a couple times a year and had often felt separate from. Often, I had felt like I couldn't relate to my cousins or other women in my family because I had not grown up the same way as them and hadn't lived in an entire community of Native peoples my whole life. I had always been proud of my heritage and was grateful I was able to experience traditional ceremonies my whole life, but I had never felt so accepted into my community until then. As the ceremony ended, and the women in my family greeted me, I realized I had been accepted and initiated into a group of strong and spiritual women who understood the significance of the traditional ways and teachings and who would continue to teach me the ways of my people.

Cultural Chameleon

Jocelyn Liipfert

Personal Narrative: Sample Essay 2

WRTG 1250

Instructor: Rolf Norgaard

With the informal theme for the class being "Culture and Identity," Jocelyn Liipfert developed a personal narrative that drew on her years of experience living in Hong Kong. By analyzing her own experience and extending it to a set of experiences shared by so-called "third-culture kids," Jocelyn explores the tensions that surround the process of growing up in an increasingly multicultural world, thereby linking her personal experience to a larger social issue.

For me, being late to school meant chasing down taxis at 7:15 a.m. and hurriedly telling the driver, in broken Cantonese, to please hurry. A day of shopping meant searching the Hong Kong market streets for a pair of shoes larger than a size 7 and bargaining for thirty minutes with the shopkeeper to bring the price down to less than ten dollars. Lunch with a friend was being the only white girl in a small noodle house tainted by the smell of the ducks and chickens hanging in the window, my voice drowned out by music blaring through Cantonese speakers. Sometime in the five years I had lived in Hong Kong, between speaking a little Cantonese and knowing the downtown streets like the back of my hand, I was promoted from my status as a typical American blonde to a true Hong Kong kid. When I moved away the summer after my sophomore year in high school, I was leaving home and going somewhere completely foreign.

Texas.

I will always remember the first day of public school. My mom dropped me off at the front of the school, as kids sped by us in their huge SUVs to viciously snag a parking space. Inside, I was met with a swarm of Abercrombie-clad blondes and brunettes in every hall and at every corner. My thoughts were drowned out by singing of the latest songs on the radio, gossip, and laughter. Seeing as these were people who spoke the same native language as me, who looked the same and sounded the same, you would think that I would finally feel at home and relieved. But I had never felt so *foreign* in my life.

This American culture that my parents called their own did not at all feel like something that was mine. I was confused by the fact that I felt more at home and at ease in a culture where I stuck out as blatantly different than in one where I blended in completely. It was this challenge and these feelings that established me as what is commonly referred to as one of the world's "Third Culture Kids." In their book so titled, David C. Pollock and Ruth E. Van Reken describe in detail the concept of what it means to grow up in a culture other than that of your own native culture, and the challenges and emotions that are often met. My mom had given me a copy of this book a couple days after that horrific first day, and I found myself intrigued by the challenges it described. It surprised me that there was actually a name for my experience, and that the descriptions in the book matched exactly what I was experiencing at that particular moment in time. Pollock and Van Reken define a Third Culture Kid (TCK) as

> a person who has spent a significant part of [his or her] developmental years outside the parents' culture. The TCK builds relationships to all of the cultures, while not having full ownership to any. Although elements from each culture are assimilated into the TCK's life experience, the sense of belonging is in relationship to others of similar background. (19)

Children of businessmen, "military brats," and study-abroad students all fit this profile and, upon return to their home country, are confronted by both the benefits and challenges wrought by their experience. They find themselves deeply affected by "this weaving together of [their] two dominant realities" (78).

I could strongly relate to the benefits and challenges described by Pollock and Van Reken, including an expanded worldview met by confused loyalties, a three-dimensional take on the world met by a painful view of reality, cross-cultural enrichment met by ignorance of the home culture, adaptability met by a desperate attempt to define differences between cultures, and knowledge of the "outside world" accompanied by sheer arrogance.

Although TCKs often benefit from the expanded worldview they gain from spending time in a foreign country, they also simultaneously gain a set of confused loyalties. I found that because of my experience attending an international school in Hong Kong, I encountered a huge blend of people from various backgrounds. My best friend was Dutch South African and would often talk about her family being evacuated due to rioting rebels. A Chilean classmate would take an extra month off school during winter to go home for her summer. I became accustomed to the religious practices of my Hindu, Muslim, and Buddhist friends. While in context it seemed normal, I look back now and realize how living in such an international setting made me more open-minded and perceptive not only to other cultures but to the various beliefs and philosophies people of my own culture possess. Harboring this open-mindedness also brought on a strange sense of confusion.

Being one of few Americans at my international school, my habits and subconscious rituals, accent and appearance labeled me as an American to my peers. Wearing this label also came with a responsibility. Every time my president was criticized, or some catastrophic event occurred in the US, I always felt obligated to explain or defend my country, regardless of whether I really believed or supported the circumstances. I felt like it was my responsibility to educate people as to why my country did something this way, or to justify our actions. When the US would involve itself in the conflict of another country, I would often find myself in heated debate as to why my country was doing what it was doing. While personally I didn't always advocate or support US actions, I felt I had to at least force these people who were criticizing the US to entertain another possibility, another reason that led to such actions. I felt as though their criticisms of Bill Clinton or George Bush were criticisms of *me.*

However, when I moved to Texas, my position was quite different. I didn't feel *at all* American, and I felt instead a representative of the perspectives of the rest of the world. I was entirely offended when someone assumed that Hong Kong was part of Japan or asked me if I rode in a rickshaw to school. It was so frustrating—I felt like I was an American in China, yet Chinese in America. Pollock and Reken describe this feeling as a "confusion of loyalty" that many

TCKs experience, and "can make them unwelcome citizens in their own countries" (83). I think in my frustration with Texas, I failed to realize that here I was preaching about the rest of the world's perspectives and how Americans need to be more open-minded, yet was at the same time being completely close-minded toward my own country. It *was* hard trying to assimilate back into my own culture, and frustrating to deal with my classmates' ignorance of the world. Yet over time I realized how hypocritical and unsympathetic I was being, and how I had alienated myself and made it even more difficult to add onto and grow from my experience. Once I became more aware of how I was being perceived by others, I made an effort to be more understanding, receptive, and patient to the people of the culture I call my own.

Aside from confronting a quality of acceptance and a quality of frustration, TCKs also develop a different kind of perspective of the world. In addition to witnessing cultural differences, TCKs see the world in a way that "is impossible to do through reading books, seeing movies or watching nightly newscasts" (83). Because of the things TCKs experience—sights, smells, and feelings in regard to situations they are put in—watching the news or a movie can bring back these senses in the form of a "3-D panoramic picture show" (84).

> While TCKs gain knowledge and understanding of the various cultures outside theirs, they are often found to have a profound ignorance toward their native culture.

Daily news topics become more real and visually stimulating to TCKs than to their non-TCK peers. This same ability also brings on a more painful sense of reality. Pollock and Reken describe a painful reality that a TCK may experience in watching the news: Because of their "heightened senses," TCKs realize that behind the screen are real, living, breathing people. Watching the news can often seem redundant to people who have lived in their native country their entire lives. The pictures of suffering Middle Eastern women have recently been pervasive throughout the news and magazines. Their abundance has caused many viewers to become desensitized to their reality. To someone who has never been to the Middle East, these faces are often surreal and exist as though they are a removed reality. However, a TCK who had lived in the Middle East sees a real woman, in real pain, in a place that is familiar. The women they see on the flat screen resemble the women they saw in everyday life, in shops and markets. They resemble the faces of their maids, a friend, or a waitress from their favorite restaurant. To them, bombs are more real than scenes in a movie and are more meaningful than the statistics run off on the nightly news (85).

While TCKs gain knowledge and understanding of the various cultures outside theirs, they are often found to have a profound ignorance toward their native culture. I could give an in-depth breakdown on the history of politics and government in China; however, I could not begin to speak with any shred of knowledge in regard to US politics. I remember one particular experience when I had first moved to Texas and was having dinner with a few friends. One girl was also a TCK and had lived in Shanghai for a number of years, and the other two girls were Texas born and bred. My Shanghai friend and I were joking around about how one of the Texas girls thought the capital of China was Hong Kong. That was *crazy* to me that someone could not know the capital of the most heavily populated country in the world, not to mention that China reigns as a world power. But then the girls turned around and asked me if I knew the capital of Texas, and in all honesty, I couldn't say. At the time, it seemed to me inconsequential information, as Texas represents only a small fraction of the US, and was far less relevant than a major country's capital. But it was, nonetheless, the state I was living in, and my ignorance toward my own country became obvious (87).

It was at this point, or soon after, that I realized that it wasn't that America was the *only* ignorant place in the whole world and everybody else was ever-knowing and completely understanding. I realized that ignorance exists in every culture but manifests itself in different ways. I finally saw that people know mostly only what is relevant to their own lives, and the fact that I was lucky enough to be a part of multiple cultures has given me a perspective and understanding that is rare. This understanding led me to another, perhaps more important realization: The people I meet throughout my life can benefit from my experience, and as a TCK it is my responsibility to *share* my stories.

Moving between various cultures, and gaining an understanding from each, leads to another main issue Pollock and Reken address— the TCK sense of cultural identity. They divide cultural identity into four main categories: foreigner, mirror, adopted, and hidden immigrant (52). The descriptions of the foreigner and the hidden immigrant I found especially relevant to the lifestyles I have been a part of. In Hong Kong, I exhibited the characteristics of a foreigner: I looked different, and I thought differently (in a cultural sense). Yet when I moved back to the US, I became a hidden immigrant; I looked the same yet had completely different worldviews. Pollock and Reken discuss the complexity a hidden immigrant faces as a foreigner in another culture, and as a foreigner in a different sense when they are confronted with blending in and trying to set themselves apart (94–95).

According to Pollock and Reken, foreigners feel a sense of obligation to blend in and become a part of their new culture. I experienced this when I became apart of the international subculture of Hong Kong. Having been strongly influenced during its time as a British colony, the majority of English writing and speaking found in Hong Kong is British. Not really intending to, I developed a British accent, began referring to trash as "rubbish," erasers as "rubbers," lines as "queues," and so on. Because of my swift change of environments, I had become what Pollock and Reken like to call a "cultural chameleon," and blended into my surroundings (95). While this developed my adaptability to change, it created a challenge for me coming back to my home culture.

When I came back to the states, like many TCKs, everyone seemed to me to be the same. Everyone wore this, everyone listened to that, and everyone wanted to drive this car and watch that TV show. I felt that it so greatly contradicted the eclectic lifestyle I was accustomed to, and the fact that I looked and pretty much talked like these people that seemed so mundane to me was all the more frustrating and upsetting. I felt like I *had* to stand out and prove to everyone that I was different and that I wasn't like *them*. Pollock and Reken define these types of feelings as an "anti-identity": an inadvertent attempt by "hidden immigrants" to preserve what they view as their "true identity" (97). I look back now and see that I was trying so hard to be different that I wasn't really preserving who I really was. Trying so desperately to separate myself led to only more frustration with trying to come to terms with my cultural identity—American, Chinese, International, or some strange combination of the three. I abandoned my "anti-identity" when I finally came to terms with the fact that I wasn't just one, I was all three.

Behind the desire to acquire an "anti-identity" lies a great, often unrealized characteristic of TCKs that often leads to frustration and angst: their *arrogance*. Pollock reflects,

> It seems the very awareness which helps TCKs view a situation from multiple perspectives can also make TCKs impatient or arrogant with others who only see things from their own perspective—particularly people from their own culture. (103)

This arrogance occurs unknowingly for a number of reasons, the most important being that often TCKs don't realize the value of their experience and how much it has actually changed their perspective. TCKs often relate better to those with similar backgrounds—and all too often get together and talk about the ignorance of their native culture. One of my closest friends, for example, had just moved to Texas from Cairo for her senior year in high school. Not having wanted to leave Egypt, her bitterness toward Texas was especially strong. We would talk a lot about how difficult it was to come back "home," and the frustration in trying to be patient with ignorance was often overwhelming. She was often asked if she rode camels to school or had to wear traditional Muslim attire. These questions seemed a nuisance, as she expected everyone to be as knowledgeable about the rest of the world as she was. Ironically, my friend, like many other TCKs, unknowingly was doing the exact thing she hated having done unto her: "equating ignorance with stupidity" (104). I feel as though my arrogance was quite strong initially, but as I came to understand American culture and develop patience with people who came from different backgrounds, I became more aware of how I was acting, and almost disgusted that I had acted so condescendingly.

I can vividly remember the day we left Hong Kong. I had to force myself to choke on the resentment I had toward my parents for making me leave—to go to Texas, of all places. I couldn't believe they would do this to me. The resentment lasted for several months afterward—through my horrific first day in American public high school, through the "do you speak Japanese?"'s, and most especially through my insatiable desire to go "home." Yet now that I have graduated and can look back on my moving experience with a little more maturity than I had going in, I can confidently say that leaving for Texas when we did was the best thing my parents ever did for me. While I hated it at the time, I thought that the rest of my life could never measure up to my five years in Hong Kong, and feared that I would lose my international status, I find myself more international and understanding now than I ever was before. My uncomfortable confrontation with confused loyalties, painful views of reality, and ignorance toward my home culture challenged me to become a more adaptable and wiser person. My success in dealing with these challenges has made me no less of a TCK than I was before I moved to Texas, but has become another part of me. International. Third culture kid. Chinese. And now I can finally say, American.

Works Cited

Pollock, David C., and Ruth E. Van Reken. *Third Culture Kids.* London. Nicholas Brealey, 2001. Print.

Learning to Read

Erma Sampson

Personal Narrative: Sample Essay 4

WRTG 1150

Instructor: Tobin von der Nuell

The purpose of the assignment that prompted Erma's essay was to explore an experience that changed the writer's perspective on a particular subject. The writer was asked to focus on specifics—a specific time, person, or situation. The assignment called for reflective writing that drew upon concrete examples to discuss the significance of an event or concept. In this essay, Erma links her experiences with and feelings about reading to the complexity of moving from childhood to being "grown up."

I can't read. Numerous times I've tried, and somehow I just can't do it. Growing up I was a marvelous reader and I was recognized for being such by most of my teachers. However, these days I will do anything to avoid it. I'd love to be cultured and educated in literacy, but my lack of interpretative skills has kept me from being much of a book worm. The discovery of *Cliffs Notes* in high school saved my life, because the idea of having to sit down for an extended length of time *reading* made me want to kill myself. However, for some reason, I still envy those who rush home to "curl up with a good book" and can truly exclaim that the book was "far better" than the movie. The desire that some people have to read is mysteriously appealing to me.

It's not that I hate books; I've loved many books I've forced myself to read. It's just the process of actually *reading* them that I can't bring

95

myself to actually enjoy. I blame it all on my mother. I was such a spoiled little girl. With my mom, I never had to read anything. She read all of the greatest books, emphasized the most exciting parts, and even added voices to every character. My mom reading to me as a child was a seemingly brilliant idea—a surefire way of not only expanding my mind, but enhancing my own personal need for different literature in my life. Unfortunately, her bedtime stories did nothing but increase my need for more of her attention, love, and readings of *Charlotte's Web*.

I didn't always have such an incredibly short attention span. When I was young, my mom would read to my brothers and me every night, and I'd pay perfect attention, especially since she would often quiz us on what had happened in the story the following night. I think she did this because she really wanted us to remember all of the little details of the story, and thus all of the little details of our childhood. And, I do; I remember every phrase Charlotte scribbled into her web about Wilbur, and I can clearly recall every stop made while touring Willy Wonka's factory. Maybe it's the fact that these books were meant to be read by and for children, and I've just had a difficult time embracing the fact that I am no longer a child. Or maybe it's because I had no knowledge of any of the literary terms that I would grow to hate for complicating my reading ventures. I don't know, but whatever *it* is, it's keeping me from experiencing the joy that is reading a "grown-up" book, and liking it.

My mom is not the only one to blame here. If it weren't for Mr. Epstein, I'd never even have such thirst for reading. When I passed his class junior year with flying colors, despite its reputation of being brutal, he encouraged me to join his AP American Literature class senior year. I hesitated for about five minutes before I notified my advisor of my new class selection. I think his personal approach to my education gave me a feeling of superiority over many of my classmates, but nonetheless I immediately regretted my decision. I was fully aware of what I had gotten myself into. I was going to have to read, and I was going to have to read a lot. This wasn't going to be some kind of "cake" class, and I wasn't going to be able to pass it without actually reading the books. I was worried, but I didn't drop the class. That damn desire to go from completely inept to completely immersed had screwed me again.

I'm intrigued when some people say that books have changed their lives. I liked *Stuart Little,* but it certainly wasn't the *book* that changed my life. It was the moment, the experience, the way my mom looked like such a rock star in my eyes, just for reading me a story. In the eighth grade, I read *The Catcher in the Rye,* and I loved it. To feel such love for a seemingly inanimate object was oddly thrilling, and I couldn't wait to feel it again. It took an additional four years for that to happen and it left me wondering why it took me so long. I read 25 books during my senior year, all required for the AP class, and all without the help of *Cliffs Notes.* However, I still couldn't bring myself to walk into an actual bookstore and buy a book. Some of the books in class were dreadful, like *The Sound and Fury,* because I simply did not understand them. Other books were immensely boring like *Oedipus Rex* because I couldn't make sense of why he continued to talk *after* his eyes had been gouged out. Yet, as I reminisce about all of the crap he made us read, I'm reminded of the number of books and plays that were anything but crap. *The Stranger, Death of a Salesman,* and *Slaughterhouse Five* have all found a place in my heart, and on my bookshelf. I found these books to be captivating and realistic in a way I never imagined a book could be. They weren't particularly "easy" books to read, but they seemed to capture me. The angst, the struggle of the human spirit, all things that I could in some way relate to. I saw myself in those books. I was Meursault with my (at times) severe emotional detachment and moral indifference. I was Willy Loman with my ability to use extreme optimism to mask my insecurities. And I was Billy Pilgrim in that I too have often felt quite "unstuck in time."

Growing up, books opened my eyes to many of life's harshest realities, but in a very fragile and nonthreatening kind of way. *The Giving Tree* taught me about impermanence, *Are You My Mother?* taught me to hang on to my mother tightly, and *Tikki Tikki Tembo* forced me to see that "Erma" really wasn't that horrible a name. However, while it's quite obvious that these "grown-up" books have harsh lessons within them as well, I struggle to want to open my eyes to them. The theme of the vast majority of my readings in high school has ultimately been tragedy and heartache. *Equus, Hamlet,* and *Paradise Lost* were all about tormented souls and that tricky wheel of fortune, and books like *The Color Purple, Hiroshima,* and *Black Boy* dealt with harsh issues like slavery and war. I walked away from these books feeling selfish for the things that I had, and worried about the similarities I had with the characters or their situations. I didn't want to be like the people in the stories, although I knew inside that I was just like them. I have never been thrilled to hear that I had similar characteristics to that of someone full of despair and pain. I know I'm not alone when I say this, but these issues are all too real and far too depressing for me to actually want to hear about, let alone read about. They are important issues, and pieces in our history, but I can't honestly say that I want to know about them. I don't like to feel sad, and I certainly don't enjoy re-evaluating my entire life upon the finishing of a novel.

All those years of being taught how to read and interpret what is being read did absolutely nothing to prepare me for the kind of reading I'd be doing here at college. All of my literary self-doubt returned upon my arrival at CU. I was never really taught how to read factual texts, including textbooks, and rarely did so in high school. Simply put, I'd rather be reading fairy tales. Unfortunately life isn't a fairy tale, and I'm a business major, so I'm stuck reading about domestic spending and worker productivity. I hate reading about current events (it's horrible I know) and thus, it takes me approximately three hours to read about fourteen pages of nonfiction with any chance of retention. Those three hours are added to the previous weeks' three hours and are kept in a section of my brain marked: "Reasons why reading totally sucks." Unfortunately, that section of my brain has significantly outweighed all others for the past six months, almost diminishing all hope for the revival of my reading career.

So, as is fairly obvious, I am torn between my love of books and my dislike of reading. It's quite annoying to be so on the fence about something that so many people list as a hobby. Sometimes I'll see my roommate reading on her bed, and I yearn to ask her what the secret to success with reading is. Perhaps I'm chasing something that is never going to be for me. It sounds ridiculous, my longing for a used book collection, but I could never fully explain why I need this in my life. More than any reason I could ever come up with, I need this desire fulfilled to hold on to my mother for a little bit longer. I would give anything to feel the same sadness I felt when Jack the dog in *Little House on the Prairie* went missing. I'm saddened when I think about how simple life used to be. So simple that the idea of four grandparents sleeping in the same bed—from *Charlie and the Chocolate Factory* of course—had me rolling on the floor in laughter, instead of contemplating how disturbing that notion could be. I hate that I can never get lost in a story again. I'll always question the validity of the tale and I'll forget to enjoy it. I hate that life's complexities have influenced me so greatly, and I've been sucked into a hole of eternal realism. I hate that I let them.

I tried reading *East of Eden* as a part of Oprah's book club, but I quit after the second chapter. Another failed attempt. Unfortunately I no longer have any excuses. I'm not in Mr. Epstein's class anymore, so he can't really be blamed. I've forgotten what most of those literary terms mean anyway. My mom stopped reading to me years ago, so I can't really fault her any longer. She stopped for a good reason—I wasn't a baby anymore, nor am I now. I've just got to grow up and face the music: Reading just doesn't take me away, as I don't feel safe in a make-believe world anymore. The make-believe world of today has become all

> Life in all of its pain and glory has forever taken me away from a place where salvation could be found in a book.

too realistic. Life in all of its pain and glory has forever taken me away from a place where salvation could be found in a book.

The world is unkind, and I've wasted huge chunks of my life trying to come to terms with that. The desire to read eludes me because of its simplicity. The books have grown more complex, and the plots more real. These past few years, I witnessed myself changing—not only from a child to an adult, but from an optimist to a realist. I've been afraid of my realism, because it has opened my eyes to a whole new world of hurt and cruelty. But, it's taken me until now to see that the world is also filled with forgiveness and love, and I've sheltered myself so intensely that I've failed to notice it. So, I think I'm finally ready to embrace my realistic view of the world. As I look to my bookshelf I notice that my copy of *East of Eden* sits right next to *Charlotte's Web*. My childhood and adulthood paired off, and Steinbeck's big words are slowly overpowering poor Wilbur and essentially, my youth. I've had a death grip on my childhood ever since I realized that it could end before I wanted it to. But maybe, like my mom, these books will wait for me to grow up. Maybe the only way to learn how to read is to learn how to grow up.

Finding Pretty

Russell Fox

Personal Narrative: Sample Essay 3

WRTG 1150

Instructor: Tobin von der Nuell

In this richly descriptive essay, Russell reflects on a question he's asked about his girlfriend. By giving us details that appeal to our senses—sight, smell, sound, and touch—he not only tells us about what drew him to Jenny, but he also shows us pictures of important moments. Russell's use of language allows us to enter into his experience and understand its significance.

It was a glorious afternoon. The grass on the field was short and crisp, and the fragrance from the recent cutting still lingered in the early June breeze. I was coaching Little League baseball, adjusting the fourth graders' bat grips and stances at the plate before they were called to the infield to meet their arriving parents. Ben waited. He was the most gifted athlete on the team; he had hand-eye coordination more acute than most high school players and a fearless desire to improve. I assumed he wanted help hitting the ball farther, and I was preparing to tell him that the only possible way for him to do that would be to wait to get bigger. Instead, he stood in front of me and asked, "Russ, do you have a girlfriend?" All the fourth-grade boys would ask that question, and when I would tell them yes, they would "aw" or smirk, then laugh at my lack of knowledge of how dangerous of a situation I was in. Ben nodded, no giggling or awing, and simply asked another question: "Is she pretty to you?"

I don't know what answer I gave Ben, because I didn't know how to answer him. "Is she pretty to you?" What does that mean? He may have wanted to know what she looked like, and if she was attractive, or if she was nice and kind and gentle; or maybe if I liked her, if I loved her, and how much, and simply didn't know how to ask. The truth is that I still don't know what it is Ben wanted, but his question has been the most profound thing ever asked or said to me.

The first time I saw Jenny, I was a sophomore in high school. She was the little blonde sitting in the front row so close to the board that she could see her reflection in Mr. Myers's glasses. I sat in back talking with all the other boys who didn't do their homework. The back row turned test day into a community effort of shuffling papers and writing so un-identifiably in an effort to make our tests impossible to read. Jenny wasn't like me; she mastered all her work, aced every test, always perched in the front.

It wasn't until two years later that I first met Jenny. She was shoved in the back seat of a beat-up Explorer with me and three of my friends who dragged Jenny along with us after their volleyball game. It was December and we raced through Niwot blaring music with our windows rolled down, freezing our cheeks and yelling whatever lyrics we could make out through the crackle of the speakers. The night cold was pouring into the back seat, and the wind whipped around and tangled the girls' hair in their faces. It may have been the cold, or because she was being pushed, but she spent the ride leaning up against me.

I could have answered Ben's question then. Jenny was 5'10" and skinny. Her hair was blond with even lighter streaks from a summer on the Florida beaches, and her skin was smooth against my arm. That night I could have told Ben, yes, she is gorgeous. She sent lightning through my veins.

Between fall cross-country season and spring track, the early winter afternoons of my senior year consisted of leaning against a car in the parking lot, with friends, talking about girls and college. The snow melted off the lot and always kept our shoes damp and as we stood it flowed across the lot in thin sheets of cold evaporating water. Eventually, when we'd get too cold to stand outside, we would drive to the Phillips on the corner of the only two roads in our town. The clerk, a Chinese-American woman who didn't speak English well, always offered us advice on what number scratch ticket was the lucky card that day. We would blow twenty bucks on number five, or number two, scratching and losing, happy our feet were drying. Sweeping the shimmering scratched dust from all of our cards into a pile, we sat content. We didn't play to win money. We played because under the shimmering surface was something unknown; we played to guess at what we couldn't know, and if right, rewarded to buy more tickets, and then guess some more. We would sit at that dusty table all afternoon, and when our money ran out, we sat sipping our sodas, watching the afternoon grow old.

On the days when we didn't make a trip down to the station and the sun dragged across the sky low and late in the afternoon, I asked Jenny to come and spend those short hours with me.

It was my cats that attracted her. Nine kittens, covered in silk fluff so thick that they looked round. The gray ones were her favorites; there were two, stuck somewhere between speckled and striped. She would tuck four or five kittens in her coat and carry them around talking to them; she said protecting them from the cold of the dusty barn. Jenny and I would sit out in the barn, just talking; most of the time I talked at her, she nodded and listened and pet the kittens. What I said didn't matter; she was sitting there, listening. I would ask her questions, trying to scratch away the shimmer that concealed her; sometimes she'd answer me, sometimes not and just look up and smile with her eyes that burned sharp and bright. Dust, hay, grain, and old wood filled the air that smelled warm, despite the cold of the Colorado winter. Much of the barn was covered in thin dust expelled from the hundreds of bails of hay. The kittens and the wood were all dirty, and you could see little paw prints on the saddles layered in dust. You could see across the cart cover where they would slip and swipe the leather clean. The barn was a safe place for me to go on the frigid afternoons; the chickens and the horses all wandered. Nothing they did was in order, yet it all was natural and all made sense. I felt that same way about Jenny, too. I didn't understand her; she was too rich and colorful to be understood. I was just happy there in the barn with her.

She kissed me one day after coming from the barn. By her car, she simply kissed me and said, "Have a good day Mr. Fox!" in her flirtatious, cute manner. Turning abruptly, leaving a swirl in the gravel driveway, she got in her car and drove off.

In the spring we took salsa classes, and I taught her swing. The speed and swing and jazz camouflage intimacy. Spinning through a crowd of others, dragging swirls across the floor with our feet, she taught me to lead with clarity, and she trusted my every step. The trumpet and saxophone's soulful notes mixed with the swirling air from the fans and the sweat beads on the forehead of the dancers.

The air hops with life that cannot be duplicated with a song or a dance, but only with the exact passion of song, dance, and trust. I loved those nights with Jenny. A time to immerse ourselves in a room full of people, and a time to be close and intimate.

As my infatuation with Jenny formed to love, so did my impression of Ben's question. Jenny was much more than beautiful. The heat of a July night would force us to spend evenings down at the lake by her house. The lake was small, but deep and cool. We would swim out to the floating dock in the middle, her long arms slicing the black water, letting long smooth ripples flow behind her. I would paddle and pant, scratch and claw my way after her, dragging my vertical body through layers of cold water that she seemingly glided over. We would lie on the dock surrounded by the black water and gray trees on the bank; I would pant and she would laugh, and lay her head on my damp shoulder, and listen to my pounding breath. Some nights we would sit on the bank, drink beers, and talk about everything. Her articulate ideas and beliefs would force my own to slowly accept others. Those summer nights, when our words would mix with the buzz of mosquitoes and crickets, she taught me how to be kind, how to laugh.

Waking up in the middle of my summer trip with her, when the outside air was still chilled, seeping up off the river surface, Jenny would squirm in her down bag, bring herself up on her knees in her burnt red cocoon, and peer at me. She'd burst out, "It's too cold! Malo..." then she'd flip around the tiny tent, rolling over me and the bags tucked in the corner. She'd stop to ask if I was too cold as well, and I'd laugh when she'd continue her rolling routine, shaking the tent feverously, calling out, "You're a crazy, too cold, you're a crazy." Jenny's passion for life flowed in her voice. There were times when she'd sit next to me and talk in French with the elegance of a native. When she was done with her idea, she'd sit and look at me, waiting for a response, knowing full well that not a single word had registered with me. Other times she would insert an English word, and highlight it, so within a twenty-second French spat, she would give you two words that didn't mean anything without their French context. Her games made me squirm in anticipation just as she did avoiding the cold.

Whenever I'd turn the spotlight to her, she would dismiss her flawless GPA and refuse to acknowledge that she was one of the top volleyball players in the nation. She'd look at me and say, "Don't be silly, Russell, you're making it all up," while a stack of scholarship offers sat behind her. Yet with all her games and all her play, her elegance and intelligence would command attention that hid in the beauty of her voice. I don't understand her reluctance to take credit for her achievements, but through her reluctance I began to notice my attempts to draw attention to mine.

I have tried to answer Ben's question hundreds of times. Is she pretty to you? The question is powerful because it can't be answered with a sentence or idea. Beauty is held in uncertainty, emotion is muffled in clarity. The un-timed rhythm of the barn animals, the mix of sweat and jazz in the dance hall, the speckled gray of the cat, and the ripples in the summer lake all lack order. But they capture the beauty of our unstable world. This beauty is found in the cracks of life, the time not documented.

> Beauty is held in uncertainty, emotion is muffled in clarity.

Summer beauty is not the child running down the dock and jumping into the lake. Pretty is the thud. . . thud. . . thud. . . of his feet stomping the wooden planks, the gasp of air as he tucks his knees, the moment before he crashes into the shimmering water, exploding the uniform ripples into a passionate dance. Jenny is that space between the cracks of my life.

I wish I could answer Ben again. I would tell him that his question was beautiful, and then I would tell him that I love her, that I love her so very much. He wouldn't understand, not at eight; but later, when he falls in love, confused and content, he might.

Path to Heritage

Lena Kang

Analysis: Sample Essay 1

WRTG 1150

Instructor: Lonni Pearce

> *In this essay, Lena responds to an assignment that asked her to analyze a significant theme or concept in a short text. By using concrete details from the text and relating them to the "bigger picture" of the social context out of which Alice Walker's story was written, Lena articulates her interpretation of what is significant and important in Walker's story.*

Alice Walker's "Everyday Use" focuses on the cultural struggles faced by many African-Americans during a significantly changing time in history—the Civil Rights Movement. Individuals were unsure of how to incorporate their traditional African heritage and family traditions into their daily lives. Such is the basis for Walker's short story; "Everyday Use" explores this difficult concept by means of a simple family whose members are distanced from one another. Mama is the hard-working head of the household who is unsure of how to deal with her daughters; Dee is the haughty older daughter who is unable to identify with her family in many ways; Maggie is the timid younger daughter who is afraid to stand up to her sister, Dee. Throughout the course of the story, Walker identifies the characters with many aspects of the Civil Rights Movement. Walker is able to capture this struggle in her writing with distinct characterization of the three main characters and a dominant theme of heritage.

Walker gives Mama, Maggie, and Dee (Wangero) well-defined personalities in order to illustrate the various attitudes of African-Americans during the Civil Rights period. Mama is described as "a large, big-boned woman with rough, man-working hands" who wants to gain approval from Dee and give acceptance to Maggie (75). She makes a reference to how she sometimes dreams her life is like one on a TV show. She would be "a hundred pounds lighter, [her] skin like an uncooked barley pancake[. . .]" (75). This is because Dee is a superficial person and is always criticizing her family for looking ragged and poor. Walker also allows the reader to see Mama's acceptance of Maggie. In the beginning of the story, Mama describes Maggie as "a lame animal, perhaps a dog run over by some careless person rich enough to own a car, [who] sidles up to someone who is ignorant enough to be kind[. . .]" (75). In the end of the story, however, Mama takes Maggie's defense when Dee tries to steal the quilts and then sits in the company of Maggie until the sun goes down.

Much like the situation in the story, the characterization of Mama is typical to many "colored" people during this difficult time. Like Mama, the "colored" people wanted to be accepted by the whites, but were unsure of what to do in order to gain that acceptance. When Mama is talking about the TV show she dreams of, she mentions how "Johnny Carson has much to do to keep up with [her] quick and witty tongue," but then she says "who ever knew a Johnson with a quick tongue? Who can even imagine me looking a strange white man in the eye?" (75). Mama realizes that although she does want to be on an equal level with the white people, she, as an individual, feels unable to find a way to receive the acceptance she craves. In addition, the tensions caused by the Civil Rights Movement made such communication between the white and black people very difficult due to extreme amounts of racism and hatred.

On the contrary, Maggie plays a very passive role in the story. Maggie is self-conscious due to "the burn scars down her arms and legs" and difficulty in learning (74). She feels inferior to her "accomplished" older sister, Dee, who "has held life always in the palm of one hand" (74). Near the end of "Everyday Use," Dee asks Mama for some family quilts that had been saved for Maggie. When Mama objects, Maggie says, "She can have them, Mama. . . . I can 'member Grandma Dee without the quilts." Even when Dee attempts to take the quilts that mean the world to her, Maggie remains quiet and allows her sister to do as she pleases. This quote also shows the strength that Maggie does have. Even though she is viewed as the lesser of the two sisters, she does not feel the need to hold on to material possessions in order to remember her heritage.

Maggie's character symbolizes another large group of African-Americans during the Civil Rights Movement: those who were too afraid and ashamed to demand equal rights from those they found superior—the white people. Like Maggie, many of the black people had been so oppressed and belittled over the period of their lives that they felt physically and psychologically inferior to the white race. Because of these feelings of complete mediocrity, this particular group found it very difficult to find their place in the Movement. They were too afraid to openly object to their position in society, even though they knew it was wrong and wanted a change.

On the contrary, the character of Dee exemplifies yet another group of African-Americans. Dee is educated, witty, and action-oriented, which proves to be overpowering when compared to the personalities of Mama and Maggie. Such is the case when Dee comes to visit her family. Dee proceeds to take everything that she wants even though she knows that her mother and sister cherish the items, like the butter

> Dee proceeds to take everything that she wants. . .

churn that has been in the family for so many generations that "you could see where thumbs and fingers had sunk into the wood" (80). The butter churn symbolizes the traditions of Dee's family. This particular item has been passed down through so many generations of their family that the indents from their fingers are permanently imprinted into the grooves of the wood.

Dee's character more closely identifies with the particular group of people who were very active in their demands for equal rights. People like Dee were at the forefront of the Civil Rights Movement and were the ones who most loudly voiced their objection to the mistreatment of African-Americans in the United States. This particular group led the way for people who were more like Mama and Maggie because the more timid people weren't willing to jeopardize the few freedoms they had gained for the purpose of complete equality. Without the leadership and sacrifice of people like Dee, the concerns of African-Americans across the country may never have been heard.

Although Walker has many themes in her short story, the theme of heritage is the most obvious. The story in its entirety is a parallel to the process of discovering one's background. Dee most outwardly exhibits her newly discovered African heritage by changing her name to Wangero in order to be free of the name the "people who oppress" (78) gave to her. She then decides that she wants many of the items that signify her family's history and culture—the butter churn and the family quilts. Dee believes that by changing her name and owning those items, she will be better able to identify with her past. In contrast, Mama learns about her heritage in a much more subtle way. It isn't until Dee attempts to acquire the quilts that Mama had been saving for Maggie that she fully understands the great deal of culture she and Maggie have. Mama realizes that "it was Grandma Dee and Big Dee who taught [Maggie] how to quilt herself" (81). Mama recognizes that all along, Maggie has been the one who has helped to hold on to their traditions by learning the family tradition of quilting from her grandmother. Mama, unlike Dee, lives the simple, traditional life her family has always lived rather than modernizing. In this she is holding on to traditions that are a part of her family heritage.

Alice Walker's "Everyday Use" embodies the significance of the Civil Rights Movement and family tradition by using distinct characters and themes. The struggle during the Civil Rights Movement is often difficult to grasp, especially on the level of individuals. Unless a person actually lived during that time, it is almost impossible to understand the conflicts at the time. Walker's short story gives the reader a small taste of these struggles in a family setting. People can more easily relate to family hardships, so Walker connects these simpler issues to the much larger issue of Civil Rights.

Teen Pregnancy in Hollywood: Nine Months of Deception

Amanda Lubeck

Analysis: Sample Essay 2

WRTG 1250

Instructor: Petger Schaberg

Although we know that the stories portrayed in films aren't real, they help shape our ideas about reality. In this essay, Amanda analyzes the film Juno *by looking at ways that it presents an unreal view of teenage pregnancy. By examining scenes and explaining how these scenes might affect teenage girls, Amanda suggests that we should be careful to examine the messages that we take from films.*

In the summer of 2008, rumors began surfacing about a group of young girls attending Gloucester High School in Gloucester, Massachusetts. Going into summer break that year, an astonishing 18 girls were pregnant (Kingsbury). As more and more of these girls were interviewed by newspapers across the country, the adolescents eventually admitted to making a pact with each other to become pregnant at the same time so that they could all raise their children together. School officials and parents alike were shocked to discover that these young women willingly became pregnant, but Amanda Ireland, a Gloucester student who gave birth her freshman year, was not. She explained to *TIME* magazine that before she gave birth, the girls that had created this pact frequently approached her at school to tell her how lucky she was that she was going to have someone that would love her unconditionally (Kingsbury). This statement sent shockwaves throughout the nation. Many found it absurd that girls as young as fourteen would feel the need to have a child, but both Kingsbury from *TIME* and

Allen-Mills from TimesOnline in the United Kingdom suggest that Hollywood is a probable cause. Movies and television shows such as *Juno* glamorize teen pregnancy by portraying the soon-to-be teen mothers with desirable characteristics such as recognition among their peers, resolution of many of their previous emotional problems, and a newfound sense of maturity. Pregnancy in Hollywood can be seen as a coming-of-age event, which turns the characters in these films and shows into role models for young girls all over America.

The 2007 film *Juno* follows 16-year old Juno MacGuff, played by Ellen Page, through her pregnancy. Although Juno is forced to face hardships such as debating the option of abortion, telling her father and step-mother about the "blessed miracle," and eventually giving her baby up for adoption, the majority of the film consists of jokes and comical scenes in order to illustrate Juno as a strong and optimistic individual. Even during one of the most serious scenes, Juno cracks jokes about abortion, causing Juno to appear absolutely assenting about her decision to abort her unborn child. Upon making the appointment, she tells the receptionist that she's "calling to procure a hasty abortion" and asks if she can hold because her hamburger phone is "kind of awkward to talk on" (Reitman). However, when Juno goes to the abortion clinic, she cannot force herself to go through with the procedure because she discovers that her baby "already has a beating heart and fingernails"; the film glamorizes pregnancy by suggesting that the fetus already has an absolute value of life which Juno is responsible for protecting. Many teen girls would see this as a positive aspect of pregnancy and would be proud of Juno for making such a decision. Juno's decision to save the life of her unborn child allows Juno to become something of a hero.

Although Juno does appear very sure of her decision when she is making jokes about abortion, she eventually decides to give her baby up for adoption, causing adoption to seem like an easy solution for pregnant teens. Since roughly 2% of pregnant teens decide to take the path of adoption, however, the fact that the filmmakers fictionalize the simplicity of the decision further implies the film's unconscious support for teen pregnancy. After easily deciding the fate of her unborn child, Juno explains herself by saying that she could "give [her baby] to someone who totally needs it like a woman with a bum ovary or a couple of nice Lesbos" (Reitman). Even while making this tough decision, Juno's hilarity shows her strength while under pressure, which not only causes young girls to begin to subconsciously see her as someone they would like to be one day, but also to believe that giving a baby up for adoption is an easy feat. Juno's humor, although it could be seen as psychological compensation for her emotional turmoil, serves as a tool to show her tenacity which shines even while facing potential havoc. Because Juno's humor is so obvious throughout the film, teens see that Juno is still a strong-willed and likeable individual, all the more so because she is pregnant at such a young age.

Just as Juno's decision to give her baby away is simple, the rest of her pregnancy and the other choices she must make for her child continue to be filled with few complications, which subconsciously shows young girls that pregnancy as a whole is an uncomplicated event. In fact, even the seemingly-impossible task of telling her family that she is pregnant is rather simple. When Juno decides to inform her father and step-mother that she is pregnant, they seem surprised at first but, shockingly, do not react with much anger or disappointment. Furthermore, her step-mother even responds with unrealistic excitement about the situation, calling Juno "a little Viking" due to her insistence to have the child, and offering to schedule her pre-natal appointments for her (Reitman). Juno's parents' approval is nonchalant, and seems to offer the idea that something like this would eventually happen to Juno anyway because all teenagers make mistakes. This acceptance, unfortunately, may give teens the wrong idea about pregnancy. Because Juno's parents react with such approval, teens may transpose this into their own ideas about pregnancy. Young girls most likely see this event and assume that pregnancy is as easy as it appears in the film. It is not shocking that teenagers would wish for the nine months of excitement that Juno experiences.

Not only is Juno's pregnancy relatively simple, but it also seems to resolve many problems in her life, making her existence less complicated and happier. Though many would believe that teen pregnancy would rip apart a family, it actually brings Juno's closer together, which turns this complex situation into a beneficial one. After Juno discovers that Mark, the baby's prospective adoptive father, was planning to leave his wife, Vanessa, Juno asks her dad if it is possible for two people to stay in love forever. Juno's dad responds by telling her that he will always love her, a sentimental family moment which had not yet been seen in the film. The analogy of parental love as synonymous with romantic love is both disturbing and inaccurate, but it does show the filmmaker's subconscious support for teen mothers by depicting parental love as everlasting, even through an event as overwhelming as teen pregnancy. Juno's pregnancy forces her to examine the meaning of relationships, and she discovers that, no matter what, her family will always be there for her. When Juno becomes pregnant, she also realizes that she must face the emotional complications which she feels for the baby's father, Paulie Bleeker. It seems that Juno's insecurities have caused her and Paulie to remain only friends, even though both secretly wish to be together, until she becomes pregnant. Though both Paulie and Juno agree that they should not date while she is pregnant, the pregnancy gives them a reason to discuss their relationship. At the end of the film, Juno tells Paulie, "You're not like everyone else. You don't stare at my stomach all the time, you look at my face. And every time I see you the baby starts kicking super hard. I think it's because my heart starts pounding every time I see you," which begins their fairytale relationship (Reitman). Juno's baby takes her and Paulie from awkward to happily ever after, confirming that pregnancy makes permanent adolescent high school relationships.

Juno's pregnancy not only resolves her own personal issues, but also Vanessa Loring's. When Juno is looking for prospective adoptive parents, she sees Mark and Vanessa Loring's photograph in the penny-saver and states, "They were even perfect in black-and-white" because in their photograph they are both aesthetically beautiful and appear to be very much in love (Reitman). Although Juno believes that she has found her baby a perfect set of parents just by seeing their picture, the complications of adoption soon cause Juno to discover that no one is perfect. After becoming very close with Mark, he discloses to Juno that he is planning to leave Vanessa. Mark eventually does separate from Vanessa, and though it seems like her world is falling around her, she still decides to adopt Juno's baby. Though afraid to be a new mother, Vanessa becomes happier than she ever was while with Mark. At the end of the film, the audience sees Vanessa happily smiling and holding her new baby, and although filmmakers ignore crucial aspects such as the financial responsibilities of being a single mother, Juno's child helped Vanessa discover Mark's inability to love and provided Vanessa with someone whom she could love unconditionally that would also love her. Because Vanessa's problems are solved when she adopts Juno's baby, teens who see this film are likely to believe that babies born to teenagers have the potential to solve many adults' problems, even though this is unrealistic.

While Juno's pregnancy does resolve the problems in both Juno's and Vanessa's life, filmmakers seem to make the attention that Juno receives from being pregnant even more important. During one of the first scenes in the film, Juno walks down the hall and must push past her classmates who seem to treat her as if she were invisible. After she develops a large baby-bump, however, her classmates make an aisle for her to walk through on her way to class. Though this change is most likely negative because some of the individuals in the hall give her dirty looks, it is still a change. Juno went from being completely unknown at her high school to being a sort of celebrity. This, of course, is a desirable change for many teen girls who are struggling to make a name for themselves. While seeing Vanessa at the mall one day, Juno even tells her that "At school everyone's just grabbing my belly all the time...I'm a legend" (Reitman). When most people think of the word "legend," they associate it with some sort of mythical provenance and more importantly, fame. Although many would agree that teen pregnancy does not necessarily amount to a great deal of positive attention, many young girls may not be able to make this distinction, like Juno. To some, attention may be positive no matter how it has been gained because, for many teens, attention is the equivalent to esteem. When Juno becomes pregnant she also seems to earn some admiration from her classmates. While in the lunch line, Juno's best friend Leah remarks, "I wish my fun bags would get bigger," alluding to Juno's increasing cup size (Reitman). Leah, like many teen girls, chooses to focus on the positives of Juno's situation and fails to see the negatives and equates maternity with sexuality, which, once again, causes Juno to become something to be envied by young girls.

When Juno becomes pregnant, she also gains a false sense of maturity. To begin, the initial act is a privilege that is supposed to come with maturity. Juno jumps into sex seemingly on a whim, surprising even Paulie. Juno later tells Paulie that the only reason that she had sex with him was because she was bored, showing her immaturity in a situation that requires immense maturity. However, young girls may see this act as something that automatically allows you to be mature because it is something that adults do. Juno's pseudo-maturity continues as she decides what to do with her child. After Mark leaves Vanessa, Juno must confront the idea of giving her child to a single mother. Though she does struggle with this dilemma, she confidently makes this life-altering decision to give her baby to Vanessa because she feels that she is mature enough to make such a choice for her child. Almost every young girl craves maturity because it causes them to feel older than they actually are. One plausible cause of this desire is that many girls find their teen years to be the most difficult. In the case of the Gloucester girls, school superintendent Christopher Farmer stated that because there are so many broken families in Massachusetts, "Many of [Gloucester's] young people are growing up directionless"

(Kingsbury). Growing up in a dysfunctional home may cause teen girls to yearn to start a new home, and it is likely that they feel that having a child will give them the maturity they need to do so.

Since its release in 2007, Juno has received 38 nominations and an astonishing 49 awards, including an Oscar for Best Writing. Its popularity was certainly the cause of a phenomenal screenplay, talented actors, upbeat underground music, and most importantly, a provocative storyline. Despite all of the reasons for Juno's success, the fact that the film is so well-liked should be disturbing to those who view the movie. The film portrays a young girl who makes a huge mistake. Strangely enough, America fell in love with a pregnant teenager, even though many of those who enjoyed the film would probably scoff at a teen in such a situation in on the street. The popularity of movies and shows such as *Juno, Secret Life of the American Teenager, Knocked Up,* and *16 and Pregnant* are all caused by our intrinsic interest in the dramatic. This interest has been transposed into everyday life as the teen pregnancy rate in America rises. Teens see funny, popular, and seemingly mature teen mothers in Hollywood so often that it is not surprising that many of these young girls view them as role models. Teen pregnancy rates will continue to rise in America until Hollywood ceases the glamorization of pregnancy by depicting it as a coming-of-age event.

Works Cited

Allen-Mills, Tony. "Teen 'Pregnancy Pact' has US Town Reeling in Shame." *TimesOnline.* 22 June 2008. Web. 21 September 2010.

Kingsbury, Kathleen. "Pregnancy Boom at Gloucester High." *Time,* 18 June 2008. Web. 1 October 2010.

Reitman, Jason, dir. *Juno.* Fox Searchlight Pictures, 2007. Film.

Happily Horrified

Kelsey McDonald

Research: Sample Essay 1

WRTG 1150

Instructor: Daniel Brigham

A research essay begins with a good question. In her investigation of why many people enjoy horror films and haunted houses, Kelsey asks a question that not only is personally interesting to her but is also interesting to other people. By drawing on the work of scholars from a variety of fields, Kelsey looks at several explanations for people's enjoyment of the horrific. She then compares the scholarly explanations with her own experience, weaving together the academic and personal as she researches this popular cultural phenomenon.

"You may enter." The knobbly, cracked hand of the hooded speaker sweeps slowly across his body and comes to rest upon the arched doors. For a moment, all are silent; his eyes laugh menacingly at ours. Then, he pushes, and the solid oak doors creak open. I suck in my breath; I can hear my blood pulsating in my ears. The hand pulling mine gently leads me into the black uncertainty. As my eyes gradually adjust, I see that I am following my friends' figures down a long corridor, our shadows drifting silently along the peeling walls. My eyes fall upon the silhouette of a young girl floating in a pool of light at the end of the hallway. We creep forward; one foot, then the next. Suddenly, the pool of light is enveloped by blackness. We stop: a noise behind us. I spin around. The girl is now standing where we had just been a half minute before. Her long, black hair clings to her cheeks as she lifts her head. I start pushing. "Run! Just go!"

I sprint down the hall, through a bathroom smeared with sanguine blood. I shove my way through frigid, hanging corpses, past cackling clowns with knives held high in their clenched fists. Finally, an empty room; I slow. My heavy breath hangs in the air, and a bead of cold sweat trickles down through my hair.

Now where? The lights are dimming, the walls seeming to cave in. Then, the roar of a starting chainsaw. Again my legs, though I can't feel them, are carrying me faster and faster. The roar overpowers my eardrums, then grows softer, more distant.

Finally, I'm back in the cold night air. My hands hit my knees, my chest heaves. My best friend Kati is beside me now. The rest of our group appears, laughing hysterically.

"I didn't know you guys could run so fast," Chris manages between bouts of laughter.

"That was awesome!" I say, and Kati agrees.

We pile into Chris's '93 Pathfinder. As we drive back to Kati's house, the others laugh and compare favorite rooms and characters of the haunted house we just left, but I'm lost in my thoughts. Why is that considered entertainment? What makes people want to put themselves in situations like that? I was so scared in there, but I loved it!

It seems so paradoxical. One of the most fundamental assumptions of natural human behavior is that we avoid the repulsive and seek the pleasurable. As Noel Carroll, professor and author of 15 books and hundreds of articles on philosophical subjects, so eloquently points out, "We do not, for example, attempt to add some pleasure to a boring afternoon by opening the lid of a steamy trash can in order to savor its unwholesome stew of broken bits of meat, moldering fruits and vegetables, and noxious, unrecognizable clumps" (275). So how can it be that, in the case of horror films and haunted houses, not only do we seek the revolting, but we find pleasure in it?

The human species has historically always acknowledged that the world is full of "dark" and "evil" aspects ("Horror Story" 245). Beyond this simple acknowledgement, however, humans have always maintained a fascination for the "other-worldly." The ancient Egyptians are remembered today for their preoccupation with the realm of the spirits and their diligent earthly work that would prepare them for what they believed would follow death; ancestor worship began with the Zhou Dynasty in China in 1500

B.C.; classical mythology depicts characters such as Medusa (who turned onlookers to stone and brandished a scalp of snakes), the Hydra (a many-headed water beast who acted as guardian of the Underworld), and the Cyclops (a one-eyed giant). Many of these tales involved a hero (for example, Orpheus or Heracles), who was driven to journey through the land of the dead in order to accomplish his mission or reach his destination (Wilson).

The modern horror genre, however, began its development in the late eighteenth century. As the Enlightenment Movement continued to find scientific explanations for seemingly every aspect of life, many fought against this "rational, ordered world" with tales of terror, now known as "Gothic" literature. These stories related heinous evils and were often framed against an ominous medieval backdrop. This history may offer insight into another reason the horror genre remains popular today. Science and technology continue to define and shape our world in an increasingly ordered and deliberate fashion. It is possible that many find the impossibilities of the horror genre as an outlet for rebellion against today's scientific, classified, formulized universe. To be sure, however, the legacy of Gothic literature continues to awe and entice hordes of indulgers to the present day, and will inevitably continue to do so, as the human fascination with and curiosity toward evil has not waned ("Horror Story" 245).

Perhaps much of our fascination is a result of the religious framework that seems to inevitably encompass the horror genre. In almost every religion there is an ongoing battle between the epitome of good and the ultimate evil. I believe we are intrigued by these ultimate forms of evil, the work of Satan and demons, unknown magical forces. These films and simulations represent, for most people, their greatest fears. Viewers and participants are often required to confront death, and perhaps even what may follow death, and the greatest forces of evil imaginable to the human mind. Through the atrocities that horror films and even haunted houses offer to us, we must necessarily explore religious themes and essentially our personal beliefs and views on the struggle of good versus evil. And because these situations are only simulations, we are able to leave the situation with the sense that we triumphed over that evil.

Our fascination may also result from the impossibility of what we are offered through horrifying simulations. Senior lecturer in Moral Philosophy at the Scottish University of St. Andrews, Berys Gaut, claims in his "The Paradox of Horror" that because monsters are "physically impossible according to our conceptual scheme, we are [. . .] curious about them, and find them fascinating" (296). Carroll agrees, expressing his belief that because monsters are so unusual to us and to our cultural understanding, we have a natural desire to learn about them (281). Take, for example, the monster in Lovecraft's "The Dunwich Horror":

> Bigger'n a barn. . . all made o' squirmin ropes. . . hull thing sort o' shaped like a hen's egg bigger'n anything, with dozen o' legs like hogsheads that haff shut up when they step. . . nothin' solid abaout it—all like jelly. . . great bulgin' eyes all over it. . . ten or twenty maouths or trunks astickn' aout all along the sides. . . (Carroll 281)

However, Gaut also points out that "not all horror fictions involve monsters," that an extremely prominent and popular subcategory of horror is the depiction of the serial killer (296). In the 2007 thriller *Disturbia,* actor Shia LaBeouf, through his teenage character Kale Brecht, demonstrates the natural human inquisitiveness inspired not by a "monster," but by such a "slasher."

Under house arrest for "popping" his Spanish teacher, and lacking the TV, Internet, and gaming services (which his mother had promptly aborted following his incarceration), Kale is left with nothing better to occupy his time than building Twinkie towers and spying on the unsuspecting residents of his wealthy suburban neighborhood. Kale learns that the suspect in an abducted woman's investigation (a case similar to several homicides in a nearby town) is thought to have been driving a blue 1967 Ford Mustang with a dented front left fender. Kale later observes his neighbor, Robert Turner, pushing just such a car, dented front left fender and all, into Turner's garage. Kale informs his friends, Ronnie and Ashley, of what he had discovered, and they all decide to "stakeout," keeping both binoculars and a video recorder trained on Turner's house. Later that night, the trio spots a frantic woman racing hysterically through Turner's hallways and rooms, while through the curtains, they see Turner's silhouette brandishing a glaring, silver knife. The three lunge forward, leaning as close as possible to the glass of Kale's bedroom window, straining to see what will happen. Their rapid, heavy breathing fogs the window; their large, frightened eyes dart from woman to Turner (Disturbia). All three are visibly petrified, but none can tear their eyes from the sight. Their fascination towards the scene has glued them to the sight of it, despite their fear. As Carroll suggests, "One wants to gaze upon the unusual even when it is simultaneously repelling" (286).

So we see that, through the fascination, we can still feel fear. But through the fear, can we also feel pleasure? Some researchers believe not. These proponents of the "aftermath model" assert that the observer does not, in fact, enjoy the fearful experience (the haunted house or horror film) itself, but rather the relief at the resolution of the experience, when the brain finally relaxes after its tensed, stressful state. As the University of California at Los Angeles assistant research psychologist Raphael Rose stated, "There is a profound sense of relief when the terror ends," and it is for this immense release that so many endure the fear and displeasure of, say, a horror film or haunted house (Pressley).

The flaw, here, is the aftermath model's underlying assumption that positive emotions can only occur after the fearful stimulus has gone; that the human species can only experience one emotion at a time.

I know different. As the dramatic music resonates in my ears, my anticipation heightens. I'm certain something big is about to happen. Actress Julia Stiles, as mother Katherine Thorn in the 2006 film *The Omen,* is staring questioningly at her reflection in the mirror. Then, there it is! The haunting reflection of a red-eyed demon breathing down her neck! I jump about a foot in the air. I pull my eyes away to turn and look at Colleen, sitting next to me on the couch. My jaw hangs agape in shock and fright, yet my lips are turned up at the corners in an excited smile; I'm terrified, and I'm having a great time!

This cannot be, according to the aftermath model, but is in direct concordance with the theory of "co-activation." Andrade and Cohen believe that individuals are in fact capable of experiencing positive feelings in addition to fear, and all at the same time. These researchers analyzed the responses of 75 students from the University of California at Berkeley to a frightening stimulus. Each student first observed two minutes of a documentary (to standardize emotional levels), followed by four and a half minutes of a horror movie. The participants were asked to report their levels of happy and fearful emotions, and if and when they experienced these emotions simultaneously, at intervals throughout the film. From the study, Andrade and Cohen concluded that not only did participants feel both fear and pleasure at the same time, but that the more fear they felt, the more pleasure they experienced as well (291).

As I myself agree with Andrade and Cohen's theory, because I know that I do in fact enjoy the scary movie or haunted house as

I experience it, I grew curious as to what my fellow University of Colorado at Boulder students would have to say on the subject. And so, I decided to conduct a study of my own. I polled 20 CU–Boulder students who claimed to enjoy horror films and/or haunted houses. Each student was asked when he or she found their experiences most pleasurable: during the experience or after the stimulus had gone. Nine of the ten males questioned responded that they enjoyed the experience most while it was occurring, and nine of ten females responded in the same way. Thus, it seems that the aftermath model is inaccurate and that co-activation offers the better explanation.

But it seems to me that "co-activation" of emotions is not so well-defined as one might think. As Gaut suggests, "There is no pattern of physiological changes or set of sensations peculiar to each emotion, and an emotion may be associated with different sensations…" (302). For example, the physiological manifestations of our responses to fear are extremely similar to that of love at first sight: sweating; muscle tension; rapid, pounding heartbeat; difficulty breathing. Stanley Schachter, author of "The Interaction of Cognitive and Physiological Determinants of Emotional State," proposes that excitation is not specific to pleasurable or displeasurable emotions, and that the excitation from either of these causes is the same. Therefore, when they are experienced in sequence, they add to each other. For example, if one experiences excitation from a pleasurable experience, say a funny line or scene in a horror film, the following murder attempt on the hero's life will serve to intensify the emotion the viewer had experienced in the scene before.

Can this suggestion, termed the "excitation transfer theory" by Dolf Zillman, be explained scientifically? In fact it can, by the brain's dispersion of catecholamines. These neurotransmitters are released to signal your body to respond to a stimulus, whether fearful or pleasurable. The effects of these catecholamines, however, diminish relatively slowly, and so, excitation by a previous stimulus or emotion is intensified by subsequent or simultaneously occurring emotions (Zillman). This makes it possible to "find both negative emotional responses and their objects pleasant," due to their intensification of pleasurable stimuli (Gaut 302).

I know this to be true. I always find a horror film that contains at least some comic relief to be more enjoyable. The tension is briefly broken and I am excited by a positive emotion. When the next scene cuts to a portrayal of the murderer, I am already enjoying the movie, excited and intrigued, with attention fully focused. This next scene, therefore, seems even more enjoyable than it would have been had the previous scene been excluded.

Gaut takes the excitation transfer theory one step further: He proposes that negative emotions may not be experienced at all; that while the objects (or experiences) that cause the emotions may be negative, the emotions themselves are not necessarily so. Simply because what we are witnessing may be unpleasant does not require that what we are feeling is also unpleasant (300).

These emotions can be interpreted as enjoyable, because the individual understands that what he or she is experiencing is merely a simulation. "Because we know that the monsters are only fictional, the fear and disgust they arouse in us are muted in comparison with what they would be if we were to meet such monsters in real life, which allows the pleasures of curiosity more easily to outweigh the displeasures of fear and disgust" (296). This is commonly referred to as the "control thesis": When the individual feels in control of his situation, in the case of horror films and haunted houses, he realizes that nothing will really happen to him.

Andrade and Cohen refer to this psychological security, and its resulting detachment from depicted events, as the "protective frame." In order to analyze the degree to which enjoyment was affected by the protective frame, Andrade and Cohen recruited 83 University of California at Berkeley students, and again asked them to watch four and a half minutes of a horror film, while reporting their levels of enjoyment at intervals throughout the clip. The procedure was then repeated with the same students, but this second time, the researchers installed within their subjects a stronger protective frame: During the horror clip, Andrade and Cohen placed pictures of the actors in their every-day clothes next to the screen, reminding the viewers that the characters were fictional (293). The results showed that enjoyment levels increased from the standardization experiment, in which no pictures of the actors were placed next to the screen. From this, we see that when people feel sufficiently disengaged and detached from the events, they can feel pleasure along with their fear (294).

It seems to me, however, that this psychological security has individually defined boundaries. I have often heard fellow horror film patrons complain that they did not enjoy a particular movie because they did not experience sufficient fear. For these individuals, the stimulus they experienced was unable to adequately overcome the erected barrier of their protective frame, and they were therefore prevented from enjoying the arousal that is triggered in response to fear. Yet, the situation also loses its pleasure if a simulation becomes too real and evokes too much fear.

"No way, guys! No way! I can't go in there!" Our line was at a standstill. The high black walls of the haunted house had been shrinking over the past several feet, and we now found ourselves staring down the only exit: one tiny door, about three feet high. Kati was on the floor, almost in tears; she would not, could not, convince herself that if she tried to crawl through that door, she would come out all right on the other side. For Kati, what she was being asked to do was just too frightening, too real. The experience had more than surpassed her psychological barrier, and the pleasures of curiosity or fascination, or any pleasure for that matter, were not enough to allow her to enjoy the fictional experience.

When, however, an experience strikes the perfect balance (is fearful enough to trigger emotional responses yet remains just unrealistic enough that psychological security is maintained), not only can an individual enjoy the curiosity and fascination, along with the emotional responses that are triggered by such an experience, but also a sort of mental stimulation.

The screen comes into focus. Two men lay, beaten and bruised, in an abandoned, rusted bathroom. One is chained to a pipe, while the other is similarly bound to a bathtub. Clues have been left for the men that lead them to a saw. Once the tool is discovered, however, the two quickly learn that the blade is too dull to sever the wrought-iron. It soon becomes apparent to the audience that the capturer has intentionally left the fate of each man in his own hands: Will he choose to amputate his own foot above the chain that binds him, and escape; or will he keep his appendage, but die, chained in the cement room *(Saw)?*

"Oh my gosh!" I turn to Emily. "I don't know if I could do it! What would you do?" She thinks for a while. "I'd do it," she finally replies.

Through simulations such as haunted houses and horror films, we are given the opportunity to place ourselves in a particular situation which, if real, would test every ounce of our strength, both mental and physical. But because the situation is only a representation of the actual event, we are able to question, debate, and discover how we ourselves would react. "We can have the experience without dealing with the repercussions," said a friend of mine, Tim McNerney, when discussing possible explanations for people's enjoyment of horror films. Graham Masterton, author of more than 60 horror and thriller novels, wrote that people enjoy horror because the genre

> depicts ordinary people dealing with extraordinary threats. They like to imagine, What would I do if a dark shadow with glowing red eyes appeared in my bedroom at night? What would I do if I heard a sinister scratching inside the walls of my house? What would I do if my husband's head turned around 360 degrees? (Hoffner and Cantor 43)

They have the opportunity to imagine how they themselves would react, how their decisions would differ from the characters', and how the outcome might therefore change. Perhaps this allows an individual to somehow feel superior to the characters by believing that his "better" decision would have allowed the monster to be defeated, the victim to be rescued, or for the story to have an all-around more satisfactory conclusion.

I have discovered, however, that while all of these theories and studies accurately describe why many people put themselves in haunting or horrifying situations, there is one particular explanation that remains the most common and most universal. I asked 20 University of Colorado at Boulder students whether they enjoyed the adrenaline rush they experienced when watching a horror film or visiting a haunted house. All 20 students (10 male and 10 female) responded that yes, they did enjoy this rush and that this was the number-one reason why they chose to engage in such frightening experiences.

So obviously, most people have heard of, and probably experienced, an adrenaline rush. But what exactly occurs in such a response? And what makes it enjoyable?

The answers lie in our bodies' natural "fight-or-flight" response, of which epinephrine, commonly known as adrenaline, is the main ingredient. This hormone is released from the adrenal medulla, located just above our kidneys, and enters into our bloodstream. Epinephrine causes our heart rates to increase, along with our respiratory rates, our arterioles (which carry and direct blood-flow) to dilate, our muscles to tense, and "our attention to focus for quick and effective responses to threats" (Choi). The sudden increase in epinephrine levels also signals the brain to produce endorphins. These hormones, released from the pituitary gland into the bloodstream, and from the hypothalamus into the spinal cord and brain, are the body's natural painkillers. Binding to opiate receptors in the brain, they contribute to an individual's sense of well-being and happiness, and elicit feelings of euphoria. In a sense, endorphins are the body's natural drug and are responsible for a natural "high," contributing significantly to the enjoyment of the rush.

Sylvia Kriebig and a team of researchers conducted a study to determine the effects of adrenaline on emotions caused by fear. Kriebig and her team used electrodes to measure the respiratory and heart rates, and the electrodermal reactions of their subjects, in response to a "fear-inducing film." The team also videotaped the facial expressions of the subjects as the film was watched and recorded their verbal responses following the film. The subjects reported their levels of emotional intensity using a ten-point scale. This was the standardization trial. For a second viewing of the film, each subject received a supplementary injection of epinephrine. Based on all collected data, both the physiological and verbal responses, the team determined that the increased levels of epinephrine led the subjects to experience "higher intensity of emotions," both fearful and pleasurable (801). Higher intensity of both fear and pleasure means higher levels of endorphins, and so, greater enjoyment.

When the danger, or simulation of such, subsides, however, no adrenaline (or no epinephrine) is released, and begins the body's return to homeostasis (its normal functioning state). Though no research has been conducted on this point, it seems to me that, from a developmental standpoint, when this occurs, the restoration must mean that the individual has "won" his battle, overcome the obstacle, defeated the danger, which in itself is accompanied by an overwhelming sense of excitement, triumph, and pleasure.

In reality, no one theory can account for the human enjoyment of horror. In fact, our pleasure is derived from aspects of all the theories and models explored above. Each individual's enjoyment may depend on a unique combination of these explanations, and in varying proportions. Throughout this investigation process, I have come to see each of these aspects of enjoyment in my personal pursuance of horrifying experiences. I believe the fascination and curiosity are the most heavily weighted, which, due to my psychological security, I am able to solicit and relish, without fear of consequence. Yet, for others, it's all about the adrenaline; still others: the triumph.

Well, I'd better go. We're back at Kati's house, and the others have just started the movie. I'd hate to miss the beginning of *Silence of the Lambs!*

Works Cited

Andrade, Eduardo, and Joel Cohen. "On the Consumption of Negative Feelings." *Journal of Consumer Research* 34(2007): 283-300. Print.

Carroll, Noel. "Why Horror?" Neil and Ridley 275-293.

Choi, Charles. "Why We Love to be Scared." *Live Science.*30 Oct. 2006. Web. 1 Nov. 1007.

Disturbia. Dir. D.J. Caruso Perf. Shia LaBeouf, David Morse, and Carrie-Ann Moss. Dreamworks, 2007. Film.

Gaut, Berys."The Paradox of Horror." Neil and Ridley 295-306.

Hoffner, Cynthia, and J. Cantor. "Factors Affecting Children's Enjoyment of a Frightening Film Sequence." *Communication Monographs.* 58 (1991): 41-62. Print.

"Horror Story." *Compton's Encyclopedia.* 2nd ed. 1994. Print.

Kreibig, Sylvia. "Cardiovascular, Electrodermal, and Respiratory Response Patterns to Fear- and Sadness-Inducing Films." *Psychophysiology.* 44.5, 2007: 787-806. Print.

Neil, Alex, and Aaron Ridley, eds. *Arguing About Art.* 2nd ed. New York: Routledge, 2002.

The Omen. Dir. John Moore. Perf. Liev Schreiber, and Julia Stiles. 20th Century Fox, 2006. DVD.

Pressley, Gretchen. "A Fascination with Fear." *The Columbia Missourian.* 30 Oct. 2007. Web. 1 Nov. 2007.

Saw. Dir. James Wan. Perf. Cary Elwes, Leigh Whannell, and Danny Glover. Lions Gate, 2005. DVD.

Wilson, Karina. "The Roots of the Genre." *Horror Film History.* 2005. Web. 6 Nov. 2007.

Zilman, Dolf. "Arousal Processes and Media Effects." *Encyclopedia of Communication and Information.* MacMillan Reference USA. n.d. Web. 1 Nov. 2007.

Makeover Feminism

Olivia Kahlo

Research: Sample Essay 2

WRTG 1150

Instructor: Nona Olivia

The increase in cosmetic surgery is currently a subject of much debate. Olivia's essay goes beyond summarizing this trend to help us understand the ongoing and contradictory developments within feminism. By relating Makeover Feminism to significant questions about various feminist groups' changing perceptions of what it means to be liberated, Olivia gives the topic of cosmetic surgery a much-needed "facelift."

Most viewers of commercial television or consumers of popular magazines have seen striking images of women whose appearance has been dramatically altered. Many of these "made-over" women changed their body image through diet and exercise regimes, skillfully applied makeup, or elective cosmetic surgery. Possessed of higher education, prestigious careers, and families, these successful women often report that they felt some aspect of their appearance prevented them from reaching their goals. Responding to criticism from feminists, they defend the choice to enhance their appearance as a tactical effort to win power in normative society. Drawing on popular media interpretations of third-wave feminism, women compelled to politicize a personal decision to "improve" their image have wrapped this act in ideological jargon.

"Makeover Feminism" is a cheeky new slogan meant to express the idea that conformity to cultural norms of physical beauty achieved through artificial and sometimes extreme means asserts female power. These women deny submission to patriarchal fantasies of the feminine ideal, claiming agency in the choice to alter their faces and/or bodies. Significant numbers of females submit to costly, dangerous, deforming, and potentially lethal procedures in an effort to claim power through beauty. This trend is visible in the annals of medical journal statistics that demonstrate an increase in the number of elective surgeries undergone by women in the last ten years (see Figure 1).

Year	Total Annual Procedures
1992	1,515,222.00
1996	1,937,877.00
2000	13,585,134.00
2001	13,254,795.00
2002	12,824,683.00
Total	43,117,711.00

Figure 1

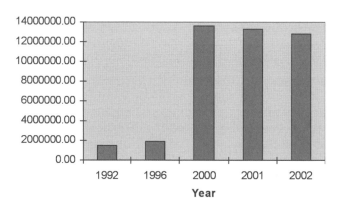

National Plastic Surgery Statistics

Figure 2

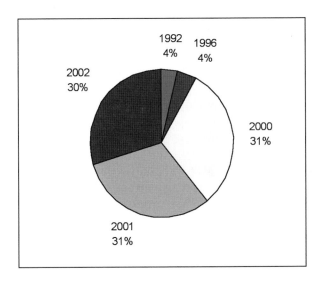

Figure 3
(Data courtesy of American Society of Plastic Surgeons)

These statistics (figures 2 and 3) indicate an overall increase in elective cosmetic procedures over the past decade. Further inquiry into this data source revealed the following: Women comprise 85% of cosmetic patients included in this database. Women 19–34 undergo a greater number of breast augmentation and Otoplasty (ear) surgeries, but women 35–50 account for 45% of female surgery patients (based on average numerical data from the American Society of Plastic Surgeons website from 1992–2002). The number one elective nonsurgical procedure is Botox injection, at an average cost of $400.00–450.00 per treatment, used to paralyze muscle and superficial fascia in order to prevent wrinkling from facial expression. The number one surgical procedure is cosmetic rhinoplasty, more commonly known as a "nose job," at an average fee of $3,500.00.

This data supports popular knowledge that cosmetics and cosmetic surgery is a multi-billion dollar industry, growing rich off the anxiety of Americans, especially women, who fear and dread aging, weight gain, or nonconformity to normative standards of appearance.

Research has shown that attractive people are hired and promoted more frequently, and also earn more income. Attractive women are perceived as friendlier and more competent than their non-attractive peers (Franzoi 374). Women, valued culturally for their sexual and reproductive role in the lives of men, uniquely suffer this association of virtue with beauty. Feminism traditionally attempts to deconstruct these cultural attributions by questioning the enshrinement of idealized feminine imagery in art, literature, theology, and law (for instance, iconic images of the Blessed Virgin Mary, or popular images perfect mothers such as Donna Reed or June Cleaver). Feminists argue that women must be taken seriously as human beings who contribute to the community and the larger culture. Women should not be valued solely as objects of male sexual gratification, or the surrogate means through which he may own his progeny. If women conform to the pressure to be beautiful, thin, and glamorous just so they can have equal opportunities, they capitulate to an oppressive patriarchal paradigm. Supporters of Makeover Feminism argue that positioning beauty and feminine sex appeal within dominant power structures—coupled with the skills, credentials, and authority to support those positions—undermines stereotypes of sexually attractive women as stupid and/or incapable. Although women obtain cultural power through beauty, and have every right to do so, it is nonetheless a contradiction in terms to call such tactics feminist. Makeover Feminism fails to construct political meaning or power for women, either psycho-socially or semantically.

The core ideologies of feminism are stood on their heads by apologists for the multi-billion dollar cosmetic industry, at the expense of a rich and valid feminist intellectual canon. I do not believe that women who choose cosmetic procedures make themselves enemies of feminism. The personal ethics of choosing to alter one's appearance is not at issue, but whether adaptation to an oppressive system in an attempt to gain power can be considered subversive. Beauty serves the individual in negotiating subtle (or not so subtle) dynamics of attraction and preference in the social competition for resources. However, this fails as a collective tool for political and socioeconomic revision of women's status. Women who gain power through cosmetically or surgically enhanced beauty do not create a stable base of power for all women. Further, by referring to their alterations as feminist actions, Makeover Feminists move the discourse of female meaning and power back into the realm of woman-as-object. This clearly violates the intention and agenda of traditional, socially-engaged feminism.

The construction of self-as-other has been the locus of feminist critique since at least the late 1700s when a Frenchwoman named

Olympe de Gouges wrote and distributed a pamphlet entitled *Le Droits de la Femme (The Rights of Woman)*. For her efforts, Olympe de Gouge was assassinated by guillotine (Donovan 1). In 1792 Mary Wollstonecraft published *A Vindication of the Rights of Women*, a response to Enlightenment-era discourse on the inalienable rights of men. Wollstonecraft recognized that women were confined to a position of objectification: "Strength of body and mind are sacrificed to libertine notions of beauty, to the desire of establishing themselves—the only way women can in the world—by marriage" (qtd. in Donovan 8). Although Wollstonecraft introduces the tension between woman's experience of herself as subject vs. object, the main thrust of her work centers on garnering civil rights for women. This original emphasis in feminism shaped first-wave feminist theory. Feminism's second wave penetrates social and political layers to explore psychological, religious, and philosophical understanding of misogyny. In 1949, Simone de Beauvoir wrote, "The situation of woman is that she—a free and autonomous being like all human creatures—nevertheless finds herself in a world where men compel her to assume the status of the Other" (qtd. in Donovan 117). It is not necessary to situate this argument within existentialism to understand the self-alienation implied by de Beauvoir's statement. A woman inhabiting an identity of Otherness lives from a displaced center; her actions and choices reflect the desires and preferences of the subject through whom she exists as other. Feminism, simply understood, seeks to redress this disassociation by establishing woman as subject.

A Feminist discourse on embodiment now includes arguments for and against cyborgs as representations of feminine consciousness, arguments for self-mutilation as gender performatives, Bordeau's defense of eating disorders as statement, and the ongoing discourse of appearance treated in this paper.

The term Makeover Feminism may serve heuristically to summon concepts of individuality, choice, and embodiment. A woman undergoing surgeries, diets, hair coloring, and wardrobe transformations may be acting autonomously to recreate her image. However, the normative beauty standards against which she measures her image are probably not her own. It is always the patriarchal eye she is seeking to please, and through which she hopes to establish power. One doesn't hear, for instance, of a woman going under the knife to acquire a second chin in order to appear older, wiser, matriarchal, and therefore powerful. Claiming agency in her self-presentation, a woman conforming to normative standards of thinness and youthful appearance reinforces gendered subjugation to such standards. The truth behind the bravura of choice and agency in these women's arguments may be a bit more constrained. In fact, women who have been valued for their appearance and submissiveness all their lives may find it difficult to establish power through other means. One experiences great anxiety when moving from a familiar territory of power into new terrain. For women accustomed to the male gaze of approval, letting go of favored status as a pretty woman summons childhood fears of abandonment, and adult dread of the emptiness of death. For, if a self exists only as other, that self ceases to be if no longer "beheld."

Although feminist discourse on embodiment has become increasingly bizarre[1], its original meaning centered on the immanent spiritual value of particularly female flesh. Feminists rewrote the female body as source of origin, nurturance, comfort, and the rooted center from which one lives a life of conscious negotiation with the world. Makeover Feminists position the self as object and locate a woman's power in the act of being chosen. This brings us full circle in the argument for women's status as fully human beings that exist in, of, and for themselves primarily—as do men—not merely as relational creatures.

I would like to discuss briefly some theories and misunderstandings of third-wave feminism. In the 1980s, authors such as Camille Paglia and Naomi Wolf emerged into the mainstream with new critiques of feminism that were accepted popularly as third-wave theory. In fact, these writers offered poor interpretations of second-wave feminist theory, reducing a complex evolution of feminist query to a single point—what they referred to as "victim feminism." Popular media, historically hostile to feminism, embraced these dissident voices, granting their arguments an authority not recognized in feminist academia. More respectably, the late 1970s and 1980s did bring some important criticism of feminism as a movement overly concerned with the issues facing white, educated, middle- and upper-class women. To quote feminist scholar Amanda Lotz, "During the 1970's and 1980's many women recognized that existing feminist theory was not sufficiently complex to understand or explain how oppression can be experienced differently within the broad category described as 'women'" (Lotz 4). The theories of women of color feminists and third-world feminists predate

---

1   Feminist discourse on embodiment now includes arguments for and against cyborgs as representations of feminist consciousness, arguments for self-mutilation as gender performatives, Bordeau's defense of eating disorders as statement, and the ongoing discourse of appearance treated in this paper.

and better define academic third-wave feminism (Lotz 4) than do antagonists such as Paglia.

Regardless, popular theories of third-wave feminism persist and include such new culture "power imagery" as Madonna, Buffy the Vampire Slayer, Kim Possible, the Spice Girls, Power Rangers, Britney Spears, Lara Croft, and Courtney Love[2]. Although these "power images" construct positive role models for girls and women, they reinforce normative feminine aesthetic standards. A woman's attainment of peak artistic, athletic, or intellectual mastery is seldom celebrated or rewarded in popular media unless paired with a pleasing face and body. Although each of these female icons performs skillfully and exhibits physical prowess rivaling any man, her intimidation factor is held in check by acquiescence to social norms of feminine hygiene and appearance. A beautiful, slender woman who "kicks ass" may find media approval, but an unshaven woman lawyer who makes partner before her male colleagues is a "granola dyke." The real message to women, I believe, is that powerful women are embraced only if they are thin, sexy, young, and beautiful.

Certainly, media figures exist who embody female agency and cultural power without conforming to ideals of feminine beauty. Former Secretary of State Madeline Albright, former Attorney General Janet Reno, and primatologist Jane Goodall inhabit public space as autonomous women seated in their own authority. Although these women have won cultural power, they are frequently criticized or humorously belittled for their appearance. In spite of this, I am not convinced that these women would have carved a deeper niche into the patriarchal belt by appearing younger, thinner or more buxom, or more obviously concerned with their sexual image. In fact, many beautiful, intelligent, capable women suggest that female attractiveness can be a hindrance as well as an asset. Some attractive women experience prejudice from teachers, colleagues, and employers who believe that a pretty woman cannot be bright. Other beautiful, successful women have endured accusations of having "slept their way" to positions of power. This no-win situation for women is what anthropologist Gregory Bateson termed a double bind (qtd. in Laing 113). The problem then shifts from media manipulation of imagery to the psychosexual arena of gender politics, and this is where feminists must situate their struggle.

---

2   Interestingly, I stumbled across the phrase "makeover feminism" in an on-line article analyzing Courtney Love's physical transformation.

Makeover Feminists will argue that they situate the problem appropriately by asserting their right to be beautiful, sexual, self-determining in their aesthetic choices, and use these tools to wrest power from the brokers. I agree that women must reclaim their sexual nature, and even see the possible realm of embodied power as "other" if played with consciously. However, a social movement for liberation must include all expressions of a true self: instincts, drives, needs, and desires for things basic to survival, for relationship, and for transcendence. One cannot live a fully authentic life as object/other without recourse to varied states of empowered being. It is impossible to build a free society if the psyche is split and enslaved to shadow projections.

As previously asserted, feminism is basically a shift from woman as eternal Other—always defined from outside—to woman as Self. Makeover Feminism, despite its sincere discourse within the tradition, cannot accomplish the goal of female liberation.

Works Cited

American Society of Plastic Surgeons. n.d. Web. October 2003.
Donovan, Josephine. *Feminist Theory: The Intellectual Traditions of American Feminism.* New York: Continuum, 1992. Print.

Franzoi, Stephen L. *Social Psychology.* 3rd ed. New York: McGraw-Hill, 2003. Print.

Laing, R.D. *The Politics of Experience.* New York: Ballantine, 1973. Print.

Lotz, Amanda D. "Communicating Third-Wave Feminism and New Social Movements: Challenges for the Next Century of Feminist Endeavor." *Women and Language* 26.1 (2003): 2-9. Print.

The Use of Technology in Barack Obama's 2008 Presidential Campaign

Holly Williamson

Research: Sample Essay 3

WRTG 1150

Instructor: David Rothman

> *To assert the power of media in our culture has become a cliché. But to actually examine how it influences specific events, such as the recent presidential election, takes careful research and analysis. Holly's essay demonstrates a well-researched examination of specific ways that Obama's use of various media contributed to his victory.*

Barack Obama successfully utilized media technology and innovative strategies to broadcast his message of change in the 2008 presidential election. Through the use of new media technology, specifically the Internet, social networking sites, and mobile marketing, he was able to directly connect with people and help volunteers self-organize, creating an enormous grassroots movement from the bottom up. Targeted advertising helped him to identify and appeal to specific groups, enabling him to win key counties in Republican stronghold states. These technologies also helped to raise an unprecedented amount of money by giving him access to millions of supporters who could each donate in small increments. These innovative techniques were utilized more successfully than ever because of his unique approach of using them to enhance his clear and concise message and as a result, empowered and inspired a diverse audience.

Historically, Democrats have been faster to catch on to new media. Barack Obama is not the first Presidential candidate to capitalize on new technology. His techniques are reminiscent of many historic figures. In the 1930s, Franklin Roosevelt used the radio to communicate his message to a broad audience, while John Kennedy took advantage of television technology by appearing in the first televised debate in 1960 (Baumann 35).

The newest use of technology in politics involves the Internet, which was first used to aid in campaign efforts in 1996 (Pollard 576). The most noteworthy attempt to take advantage of this new technology was made in 2004 by Howard Dean, Governor of Vermont. His efforts demonstrated the potential power the Internet had to influence the campaign process. Dean used online programs and databases such as Meetup Inc. and VoteBuilder to organize meetings and gather detailed information about voters in order to help democratic candidates customize their campaigning (Ives 12; Talbot 25). He raised over $3 million through the use of his website, marking the importance of the Internet in fundraising efforts (Case 15). Although a more primitive version, his efforts laid the direct foundation for Obama's innovative use of the Internet.

Since then, Ron Paul has used social-networking tools to break previous records by raising $6 million in one day, and Mike Huckabee has used online networking to organize 12,000 campaign volunteers (Pearson 1). All of these trends show a movement towards the use of social networking in politics, but Obama was the first person to fully capitalize on it. Although supported by the groundwork these people laid, his success primarily came from his synthesis of the tools available and their full integration into the message he was broadcasting.

Obama's campaign was centered on creating change. The previous administration had left the country in a disastrous state of division, frustration, and uncertainty. In a chaotic mess of economic crisis, overseas wars, and poor international reputation, Americans yearned for something different. Obama's message provided the country with just what it wanted: change. He replaced negative feelings towards dysfunctional policies with hope and confidence that he could create a new era in American politics (Street X). By inspiring optimism and mending racial, political, cultural, and spiritual divisions, Obama unified a diverse group of supporters towards a common cause for change.

The components of his message appealed to people's emotions and passions, while addressing the changes Americans so desperately wanted to see. Obama's objectives capitalized on improving the mistakes and failures of the previous administration. His platform revolved around solving issues related to the weak economy, becoming more peace-oriented by ending overseas wars, and restoring America's international reputation and relationships that had been damaged by the Iraq war. He also provided forward-thinking ideas on issues including the improvement of the nation's health care and education systems, as well as reducing our dependence on fossil fuels by focusing on new energy sources (Barack).

Obama had a clear, strong message backed with innovative technology to enhance the message and inspire his voter base. His strong rhetorical skills and vocabulary of change resemble Kennedy's while his ability to create human connections is similar to Bill Clinton's (Creamer 1). Obama's innovative approach and progressive ideas gave voters confidence that the campaign would mimic new and different patterns in American politics he would create if elected into office. In comparison to Obama, Republican opponent John McCain had a weak platform coming into the campaign. He also invested far less in Internet tools because of the assumption that the traditional Republican base was less tech-savvy, so it would be difficult to appeal to them through the use of new technologies (Schifferes 1). It was Obama's innovative utilization of new media technology that exploited these differences in platform, position, and public relation to fully take advantage of them.

Although the use of Internet tools has been increasing in recent campaigns, Obama's campaign has been the most successful and effective at embracing these new strategies because of its media plan's utilization of technologies to broadcast and enhance Obama's message. The campaign provided a consistent and clear message by putting emphasis on simple yet effective communications and making such clarity fundamental to all areas of technological tool use. Obama's simple message of change was the most important component of the campaign[1].

Political consulting firm, GMMB, was responsible for managing the campaign's media plan and bold advertising (O'Leary 2). In creating Obama's primary website, GMMB utilized branding strategies to increase effectiveness. The website's smart design and functionality made its web pages clean and easy to navigate, while the aesthetics

---

1   Obama distinctly stuck to spreading the message of change, even when opportunities to veer off topic were presented. During the economic crisis he stuck to his campaign, carefully choosing which battles to fight. McCain took the opposite approach, attempting to take advantage of any opportunity for publicity. His defeat was due in part to his mismanagement of the financial crisis and his focus on negatively attacking Obama. These ideas come from "Five Lessons for Managers From Obama's Campaign" by Liz Ryan. *(Business Week.* 12 Nov. 2008.) and "Barack Obama and the audacity of marketing" by Matthew Creamer *(Advertising Age.* 10 Nov. 2008: 1+. *Academic Search Premier.* EBSCO.).

of the site enhanced the brand by affirming expectations of what a future president should be: an organized, effective, forward looking leader (Jones 55). GMMB further enhanced Obama's brand by using on-the-ground marketing strategies including audience segmentation, database management, and the cultivation of online communities (Creamer 1).

GMMB's primary goal was to "expand the electorate with broader messages while hyper targeting specific audiences" (O'Leary 2). By re-imagining Obama's potential audience, new voter tactics were amplified to significantly increase new voter loyalty and registration. The campaigns' abundant networks and hyper targeting allowed Obama to further expand the electorate. Additionally, Obama focused on directly connecting with individuals to create a personalized feel and encourage greater participation.

Obama utilized the Internet by developing customized websites, targeted social network profiles, and e-mail databases to create a more immediate way of communicating. These methods were more successful because they created direct and personal connections. Forty-six percent of Americans used the Internet or email to get information about the 2008 campaign, surpassing the number of people who used newspapers or watched the news on TV (Dunham 1). By using the Internet, Obama was able to keep voters better informed while encouraging user choice, which empowered individuals by allowing them to decide how they would like to be reached. The use of these technologies further strengthened the communication of his underlying message.

An email database of over ten million email addresses sent out more than one billion personalized emails from the candidate (Dunham 1). Seven thousand different messages were sent throughout the course of the campaign to target explicit audiences (Vargas1). Fifty percent of these emails were state-specific while others were targeted to specific donation levels (Melber 8). Invite Barack, an email response system, managed non-media requests for Obama to attend local events, while the Obama Answer Center allowed visitors to browse frequently asked questions (Ives 12). These methods allowed the campaign to monitor trends in location requests and create more targeted ads by evaluating popular keywords and their regional correlation. These devices also encouraged two-way communication between the people and the candidate.

Obama made the single largest mobile-marketing event to date when he sent out over 2.9 million texts to announce his running mate, Joe Biden (Steel 1). Text messaging is direct, personal, and received almost instantaneously but had never been successfully used before. As part of his mobile-marketing campaign, he also developed the iPhone application Obama Mobile to empower users to contact their friends (Melber 8). The application allowed Obama to tap into personal networks and generate many additional new voters and supporters. Obama Mobile also used area codes to sort contacts by key battleground states in order to help the user focus their efforts on those contacts with potentially decisive votes.

The innovative use of new technologies enhanced communication by increasing its speed and distance, as well as the amount and quality of information. It encouraged horizontal communication and user-generated messages, while enhancing personalized messages (Abroms 420). These tools gave supporters easy access to tangible action, making it simple for people to act on their beliefs.

Obama also placed great emphasis on social networking sites to enhance voter participation by creating communities that helped supporters self-organize. He set up his social networking sites earlier than McCain and created customized individual profiles on the sites to better target specific groups of people (Abroms 416). Over fifteen online community sites were maintained. The community of supporters on Facebook was over 6.2 million, 3.2 million of which were college-aged fans of the "Students for Barack Obama" page (Hall 8a). Obama used another Facebook page titled "The Election 2008" to assist and engage voters (Vargas 1). It provided over 800 numbers to call for voting problems and displayed an "I voted" button that supporters could broadcast on their page to let their friends know they voted. Over 5.4 million users clicked on it (Vargas).

Twitter, a micro-blogging site, sent out quick status updates on Obama to 24 times more people than McCain (Pearson 1). LinkedIn invited professionals to discuss the future of American business, while Central desktop was used to recruit and train volunteers. Other sites including MyBatanga, MySpace, Digg, Eventful, BlackPlanet, Faithbase, Eons, Glee, MiGente, AsianAve, and DNC Partybuilder helped Obama further connect to specific audiences (Vargas). Supporters created over 8,000 additional unofficial Obama campaign websites to help in the effort (Abroms 419).

The phenomenon of blogging online was another component of web tool use. Blogging has changed the way citizens participate in political discussions because blogs give citizens a stronger feeling of contribution to the political process, and have the ability to make voters feel more personally connected to the candidate. Blogs also enable people to widely broadcast their opinions and connect with people anywhere to engage in debates. "Obama's online supporters were more engaged in the political debate [than McCain's by a two to one ratio]" (Hall 8a). Over 400,000 blogs alone were posted on Obama's website, recording personal opinions and campaign experiences (Vargas). Blogs also boosted the spread of the campaign's message because they allowed the campaign to publish more self-written reports and test for potential campaign strategies while getting quick results.

Unlike McCain, Obama utilized hyper targeting to appeal to highly specific audiences. Obama's overall campaign was made up of many small, personalized advertising campaigns directed towards particular groups (O'Leary 2). The campaign did not waste resources doing national polling in the general election; instead it focused its messaging on specific voters it needed to persuade (Hagstrom 8). Database technology allowed Obama to build phone bank lists with potential voter profiles to send out more targeted, personalized messages and better equip calling volunteers (Steel 1). Web site programming also helped him to better understand issues important to voters.[2] David Plouffe, campaign manager, used a high level of organization in all technical, logistical, and on-the-ground areas, thereby allowing for such detailed efforts in hyper targeting (Ryan 10; John 97).

Separate media teams also focused on youth, African-American, and Hispanic oriented advertising (Dunham 1). An online Spanish phone-banking tool made calls in Spanish to help target Hispanic voters; Obama won 54% of the Hispanic vote (Stirland 1). The 2008 presidential election also saw the largest turnout of youth voters since Ronald Reagan's election, due in large part to Obama's efforts. His confident personality and flawless rhetoric delivered an appealing message to the younger population by giving younger voters a cause worth working for because he directly related it to their personal needs. Obama created the image of being the hipper, cooler candidate through branding techniques comprised of artwork, stickers, decals, new media technology use, and other things (Bauman 35). He was most effective at energizing this sector because he connected with them through media channels they were

2 Millions of new pieces of information on voters were collected from phone calls and email responses, entered online and stored into databases during the election. This information holds great power for future Democratic endeavors because it will provide all democratic candidates access to enormous amounts of valuable data, key to creating personalized connections in campaigns.

accustomed to interacting with everyday. Most technological use in the campaign was targeted at the crowd under thirty (Hagstrom 8). For this reason, 66% of voters under 30 voted for Obama (Dunham 1).

Hyper targeting allowed Obama to spend more time and energy on directly targeting swing state voters. In Virginia, for example, Obama spent $24 million on TV ads compared to McCain's $7.4 million (Schouten 59). Obama was able to close the gap by winning key counties in Republican strongholds, such as Colorado, Nevada, North Carolina and Virginia (Creamer 1). In the four days prior to the elections, over three million calls were made from the campaign's virtual phone bank, reminding voters to go to the polls (Vargas 1). On the day of the election, voters in battleground states who had signed up for alerts received three text messages encouraging them to get to the polls as well (Vargas). Poll watchers were also deployed to create call lists for Election Day. Runners would gather information regarding who had and had not yet voted and delivered it to campaign headquarters. This information would then be entered into a database to easily allow universal access. Volunteers used this data to organize canvassing efforts and create call groups directed at those who had not yet voted. They were able to evaluate who needed encouragement to get to the polls to vote, increasing the turnout of Obama supporters.

A key component to Obama's campaign was his enormous grassroots movement. He focused on empowering and engaging individuals to create a loyal, passionate, and excited volunteer force on his behalf. Obama realized the potential that large groups had for spreading his message on an immense scale, while the Internet enabled him to attract, organize, and quickly mobilize an unprecedented number of supporters. Barack makes this clear in his statement, "One of my fundamental beliefs [...] is that real change comes from the bottom up. And there's no more powerful tool for grass-roots organization than the Internet" (Pollard 574). By helping volunteers self-organize, a record number of people were able to get involved in a bottom-up, grassroots movement. He managed to make every one of the eight million volunteers count by emphasizing their individual small acts of volunteerism (Ewen 13).

Additionally, all communication was made using a participatory vocabulary. Phrasing like "Yes WE Can" and "Change WE can believe in" encouraged the public to see the campaign in terms of how they were a part of it (Ewen). He motivated his team to work as a team and enjoy the experience in order to keep all of his volunteers focused on clearly spreading the message of change.

The campaign's most noteworthy innovation was the My Barack Obama networking site. All components of the website were aimed at making information visible and action easy. The "Donate Now" button was noticeably placed front and center, while visible boxes to enter zip codes gave users personalized nearby listings of Obama events (Barack). These easy-to-use tools helped supporters self-organize on behalf of Obama's candidacy. Over two million profiles were created, allowing supporters to find events and connect locally. Over 70,000 people raised $30 million on their personal MyBarack Obama fundraising pages. More than 200,000 events were planned and almost 35,000 volunteer groups were created (Vargas). The website also received 43% of all visits made to campaign websites (Pollard 583).

The communication of McCain's message was not as strong as Obama's due in part to his lacking support group. Only 8 % of the total campaign website visits were on his behalf (Pollard). US Republican grassroots director, Jeff Burton, attributes this to the fact that "[Republicans] haven't been connecting with the American people like [they] used to and like [they] should" (Ayers 24).

The Internet enabled Obama to raise an unprecedented 600 million dollars in funding, which gave him the flexibility and capability to put intense focus on the communication of his message (Vargas). These funds allowed him to blast his messages in key states and tailor messages to appeal to a wide spectrum of people. Obama was able to build large numbers of individual connections through the web, giving him access to an enormous number of supporters who could each donate in small increments. "3 million donors made a total of 6.5 million donations online adding up to more than $500 million" (Vargas). Over 90 percent of those donations were in increments of $100 or less (Vargas). Online fundraising is more efficient and enhances the individual's sense of involvement because they can instantly support a candidate's efforts.

Obama only spent $21 million of the $380 million spent on paid media communications in online efforts because the Internet provides a cost-effective way to create publicity (Kay 30). YouTube, an online video sharing website, allowed the campaign to provide a wide range of videos to the public virtually free of charge. Over 14.5 million hours of Obama videos were watched free of broadcasting costs; equivalent TV time would have cost $47 million (Miller 1). With this in mind, the campaign produced and cut all ads so that they could exist on TV and online. Obama had five times as many videos uploaded as McCain (Abroms 416). By exploiting this inexpensive way to publicize, Obama increased his exposure by 52 million video views, five and a half times more than that of McCain's (Pearson 1).

Obama's campaign has set a new standard for leadership and organization in all future campaign efforts. Future endeavors must utilize direct communications to personalize messages and inspire voter participation. Media spending should be targeted directly at the voter in order to hyper target key groups with decisive votes (Kay 30). Obama's efforts have put greater focus on the importance of first-time voters and young adults, as well as the use of new media communications to connect with them (Nantis 21). His campaign has served as a reminder of the potential for a group of people, when motivated, inspired, and mobilized towards a common goal, to have a great impact. It has also highlighted the importance of putting the political process directly into the hands of the people. In future politics, there is an even greater potential for people who have not been involved in politics to realize that there are things in the political process that impact them. It will be crucial for candidates to inspire and motivate these people to volunteer on their behalf and work towards a common goal.

The interactive web tools have changed the way candidates communicate with the electorate, advertise to voters, organize supporters, and raise money. These technologies can become tools to encourage intellectual growth and can help rally audiences around a cause they believe in. These tools have increased the power of self-expression by the public and encouraged greater participation (Abroms 419).[3] Such tools have enormous potential for power because of their ability to access, store, and interpret such large amounts of specific data. This information is essential to successful personalization and communication within campaigns. Whom ever gains full "mastery of cyberspace determines who is the most powerful man or woman in the world" because information is power (Baumann 35).

---

3 Methods used in the campaign have even changed the way the President governs. Incorporating technology has created a new level of communication that reinvents how the President connects with people, allowing for greater participation by American citizens. Such tools inherently demand greater authenticity, which is creating new levels of transparency and accountability on the government's behalf. New tools include MyWhiteHouse.gov and Change.gov. These ideas come from "How Obama's Internet Campaign Changed Politics" by Claire Cain Miller (The New York Times. 7 Nov. 2008. <http://bits. blogs.nytimes.com/2008/11/07/how-obamas-internet-campaign-changed-politics/>.) and "Favored Obama Address Begins with http, not 1600" by Richard Dunham and Dwight Silverman (Chron [Houston] 8 Nov. 2008: n. pag. chron.com. Web.)

Obama's campaign had a straightforward message, directed at the change that Americans were looking for. Both his message and means of communication through media technology were distinctly different than that of McCain's. Obama's campaign was successful because of his innovative integration of technological tools into the publication of his message. By leveraging the synthesis of new tools, Obama was able to develop a grassroots movement and fundraise like no candidate ever has before. His highly effective communication skills enabled him to create direct connections and targeted messages. Obama's campaign has increased the expectations and possibilities for all future political campaigns.

Works Cited

Abroms, Lorien C., and R. Craig Lefebvre. "Obama's Wired Campaign: Lessons for Public Health Communication." *Journal of Health Communication 14.5* (2009): 415-423. Academic Search Premier. EBSCO. Web. 20 Sept. 2009.

Ayers, Nick. "Movers & Shakers." *Politics* (Campaigns & Elections) 30.10 (2009): 24-25. Academic Search Premier. EBSCO. Web. 29 Nov. 2009.

Barack Obama Home Page." *Organizing for America.* N.p., n.d. Web. 14 Dec. 2009.

Baumann, Michael. "Campaign '08: The Power of the Post." *Information Today.* 25.9 (2008): 35. Academic Search Premier. EBSCO. Web. 29 Nov. 2009.

Boehlert, Eric. *Bloggers on the Bus: How the Internet Changed Politics and the Press.* New York City: Free Press, 2009. Print.

Case, Tony. "Top Media & Marketing INNOVATIONS 2008." *Brandweek.* 49.44 (2008): 15-20. Academic Search Premier. EBSCO. Web. 29 Nov. 2009.

Creamer, Matthew. "Barack Obama and audacity of marketing." *Advertising Age.* 10 Nov. 2008: 1+. Academic Search Premier. EBSCO. Web. 14 Dec. 2009.

Crotty, William J.. *Winning the Presidency 2008.* Boulder: Paradigm Publishers, 2009. Print

Denton, Robert E. Jr. *The 2008 Presidential Campaign: A Communication Perspective (Communication, Media, and Politics)*. Lanham: Rowman & Littlefield Publishers, Inc., 2009. Print.

Dunham, Richard, and Dwight Silverman. "Favored Obama Address Begins with http, not 1600." *Chron [Houston] 8* Nov. 2008: n. pag. chron.com. Web. 15 Nov. 2009.

Ewen, Sam. "Can Obama Teach You? Yes, He Can." *Brandweek.* 08 Dec. 2008: 013. Academic Search Premier. EBSCO. Web. 29 Nov. 2009.

Fredreka, Schouten. "Campaign cash haul obliterates records." *USA Today* n.d.: Academic Search Premier. EBSCO. Web. 29 Nov. 2009.

Hagstrom, Jerry. "Obama's Polling And Media Teams Went All In." *National Journal* (2008): 8. Academic Search Premier. EBSCO. Web. 27 Nov. 2009.

Ives, Bill "How Barack Obama Is Using the Web to Further Engage Voters." *EContent 31.5* (2008): 12-13. Academic Search Premier. EBSCO. Web. 14 Dec. 2009.

John F Kennedy School of Governement. *Campaign for President: The Managers Look at 2008.* Lexington, Massachusetts: Rowman & Littlefield Publishers, 2009. Print.

Johnson, Denis. *Campaigning for President 2008: Strategy and Tactics, New Voices and New Techniques.* New York: Routledge, 2009. Print.

Jones, Alwin A. D. "The Politics of Web Strategy." *Black Enterprise* 39.4 (2008): 54-55. Academic Search Premier. EBSCO. Web. 29 Nov. 2009.

Kay, Tim. "Making the Case for TV Buys in the Internet Age." *Politics* (Campaigns & Elections) 281 (2009): 30-33 Academic Search Premier. EBSCO. Web. 29 Nov. 2009.

Melber, Ari. "Obama's iSuccess." *Nation* 287.13 (2008): 8. Academic Search Premier. EBSCO. Web. 20 Nov. 2009.

Miller, Claire Cain. "How Obama's Internet Campaign Changed Politics." *The New York Times.* 7 Nov. 2008. 25 Oct. 2009. Web.

Mimi, Hall. "Internet engaged people in '08 election, survey shows." *USA Today* n.d.: Academic Search Premier. EBSCO. Web. 29 Nov. 2009.

Nantais, David E. "A Digital Defense." *America* 201.9 (2009): 21. Academic Search Premier. EBSCO. Web. 28 Nov. 2009.

Norman, James. "What We Can Learn from the World's First Viral President." *Habitat Australia* 37.1 (2009): 19. Academic Search Premier. EBSCO. Web. 10 Nov. 2009.

O'Leary, Noreen. "Media Plan of the Year: GMMB." *Media Week.* 15 June 2009: 2. Print.

Pearson, Chris. "Use of Technology in the 2008 Obama-McCain Contest." *Social Capital Blog.* N.p., 19 Aug. 2008. Web. 29 Nov. 2009.

Pollard, Timothy D, James W Cheesbro, and David Paul Studinski. "The Role of the Internet in Presidential Campaigns." *Communication Studies* 60.5 (2009): 574-588. Print.

Price, Joann F.. *Barack Obama: The Voice of an American Leader.* New York: Greenwood Press, 2008. Print.

Ryan, Liz. "Five Lessons for Managers From Obama's Campaign." *Business Week.* 12 Nov. 2008. Web. 22 Sep. 2009.

Schifferes, Steve. "Internet key to Obama victories." *BBC.* 12 June 2008. 25 Oct. 2009. Web.

Steel, Emily. "Obama's Digital Campaign Allies Seek to Cash In." *Wall Street Journal* [New York]. 31 Dec. 2008, Eastern Edition ed., sec. B4: n. pag. Web. 22 Sept. 2009.

Stirland, Sarah Lai. "The Tech of Obamamania: Online Phone Banks, Mass Texting and Blogs." *Wired.* 14 Feb. 2008. Web. 25 Oct. 2009.

Street, Paul. *Barack Obama and the Future of American Politics.* Boulder: Paradigm Publishers, 2008. Print.

Talbot, David. "Personalized Campaigning." *Technology Review* 112.2 (2009): 80-82. Academic Search Premier. EBSCO. Web. 29 Nov. 2009.

Vargas, Jose Antonio. "Obama Raised Half a Billion Online." Washington Post. 20 Nov. 2008, sec. *Politics:* n. pag. 44 The Obama Presidency. Web. 25 Oct. 2009.

America's Obsession with Celebrities and Celebrity News: When Is It Too Much?

Marcy Franklin

Argument: Sample Essay 1

WRTG 1250

Instructor: Christine MacDonald

> *The latest Britney report, the celebrity baby update—is this news? In this essay, Marcy argues that mainstream news media need to rethink their mission. While she acknowledges that celebrity news has some value (a strategy that demonstrates her understanding of the opposition), she counters that the bulk of celebrity news should be contained to specialized media outlets, rather than overrunning mainstream news media.*

One typical morning, I flipped the channel to CNN to catch up on my current events. I saw uninterrupted coverage with serious anchors and reporters giving the grave news that someone had died. My first instinct told me that it was someone who carried a lot of importance in society; perhaps it was a politician, a humanitarian, or a celebrity. Sure enough, in due time I learned that it was Anna Nicole Smith. She was just a girl who was famous for being famous, a Playboy bunny who frequently graced the cover of tabloids for her less-than-flattering antics. I then checked my local newspapers' websites and saw more disturbing news: Britney Spears had shaved her head. And from there it was a downhill slide. I had to learn more about how Anna died, why Britney shaved her head, why an acclaimed NASA astronaut wore diapers to drive 900 miles to harass her competition for another astronaut's heart. . .

But why did I even care? Why was it so important for me to know who Anna's baby's father was, when I certainly wasn't a fan of hers before her death? It didn't seem all that important to me, and yet I couldn't stop reading these stories.

It is a question that must be asked in our celebrity culture: Why do we care? What possesses us to keep up on our celebrity news? It comes as no surprise that our society is obsessed, mesmerized with fame. We want to be near it, we want to have it as our own. Jake Halpern, the author of *Fame Junkies: The Hidden Truths Behind America's Addiction,* noted a survey given to 635 middle school students in Rochester, New York. One question asked was with whom they would most like to have dinner. The clear winner, with 17.4 percent, was awarded to Jennifer Lopez. Jesus Christ came in second with 16.8 percent, and Paris Hilton and 50 Cent tied for third with 15.8 percent. Additionally, when students were asked to rank which job they would most like to have in the future, the clear winner was the job of a celebrity personal assistant, sweeping the contest with 43.4 percent (Halpern xvi). The children of our nation, according to these results, are more interested in fame and celebrities rather than the scholars and leaders of our time. What is even more disturbing is that children are not even aspiring to necessarily be famous—they want to assist celebrities. They are more willing to be a servant to fame rather than do something noteworthy with their own lives.

Appalling as the results may be, who are we to blame? The finger points in the direction of the media. During the Anna Nicole Smith saga, the mainstream media outlets neglected to inform the public that Al Qaeda had been building operatives in Pakistan that were steadily growing (Herbert, para. 7). Rather, the public was inundated with the news from the Anna Nicole melodrama. And the entertainment business is multiplying daily, while the news industry is on the decline. The talent competition *American Idol* brings in more viewers than the nightly news on NBC, ABC, and CBS combined (Halpern xv). Is our obsession with fame blinding us to the important events and issues of our time, or do we simply ignore them? More importantly, is the media emphasizing celebrity news over hard news, and why?

As a journalism major, I have been faithfully taught that the purpose of journalism is to inform citizens so that we can be a free and self-governing society. It seems so simple and clear-cut to us in theory, but it is harder to act on those purposes. When I see the overwhelming amount of celebrity coverage in the media, it makes me question whether the media is fulfilling its journalistic purpose. It is the role, the responsibility, of the media to give us the information that citizens need to be self-governing. It is essential that the media give us the news that helps our democracy to be self-governing; it is clear that celebrity news is hindering our society's ability to be independent and free.

Many will argue that there is nothing inherently wrong with celebrity news, especially in the form of tabloid journalism. Henrik Ornebring, of the University of Leicester in the UK, and Anna Maria Jonnson, of the Goteburg University and Sodertom University College of Sweden, argue that tabloid journalism is not simply another synonym for "bad" journalism. The authors stress that the mainstream media creates a need for an alternative media to present different issues. The problem, these professors argue, is that these alternative media outlets, especially tabloids, are labeled as deterrents to serving the public interest. The authors write,

> Lay (and sometimes academic) criticism of journalism continues to be based around simple binary oppositions, where emotional is bad and rational-intellectual is good, sensation is contrasted with contextualisation and tabloid journalism is charged with meeting complexity with dumbing down. But emotionalism, sensation and simplification are not necessarily opposed to serving the public good. (Ornebring and Jonsson 284)

As the authors mention later, tabloid journalism throughout history has attracted a new public by discussing issues that have been ignored in the mainstream media, therefore better serving the public interest (Ornebring and Jonsson 287). Celebrity news has a similar effect on the public; celebrity gossip media outlets like the E! Channel or *People* magazine bring in audiences looking for celebrity gossip that is not found in mainstream media.

Furthermore, some argue that interest in celebrities, or as psychology professionals define it, "celebrity worship," is not necessarily a bad thing. According to a psychological study, low levels of celebrity worship correlate with high levels of extraversion in people. Psychology researchers John Maltby, Liza Day, Lynn E. McCutcheon, Raphael Gillett, James Houran, and Diane D. Ashe write, "Celebrity worshippers who do so for entertainment-social reasons are extraverted, seek information and support, and are able to display emotions" (423). These characteristics defend the purpose behind celebrity news. Bonnie Fuller, the chief editorial director for American Media Inc., the tabloid conglomerate that publishes the *Star,* the *National Enquirer,* and the *Globe,* said,

> What's going on is that we all have fewer people in common. When you're in high school, or at a small college, you know everybody's business and you can follow their romantic goings-on and discuss them with your friends. But when you grow up and you're out in the work world, you don't have that. So celebrities give us a whole world of people in common—people to gossip about at work over the water cooler or at a dinner party. (Halpern 147)

Celebrity news then serves to bring people together socially and give people an escape from mainstream media. Fuller's argument then seems to justify the validity of celebrity news. However, it should be noted that Fuller's career depends on the validity of celebrity news.

This is not a paper criticizing people's desire to learn about celebrities. However, I believe that the argument that celebrity news is valid within the mainstream media contains loopholes too big to ignore. I will concede that celebrity news is not a bad thing when it is contained to alternative media outlets like the E! channel or *People* magazine. These media outlets are no different than any other specialized media—for example, a sports channel or a sports magazine. This is because they cater to the audience's interests, and indeed, there is a very large audience that is interested in celebrities. But when celebrity news crowds out other news on mainstream media outlets, then it becomes a problem. It has changed what news agencies are pursuing as news. Sue Cross, a vice president of the Associated Press, reported that the news wire service now gets requests from as far away as Indonesia and Germany to report on celebrity stories (Merina, para. 32). Additionally, a study done by Thomas Patterson of Harvard University found that, from 1987 to 2001, "soft" news stories, which includes celebrity news, have increased from 35 percent of stories to 50 percent of stories (Valencia, para. 6). Celebrity news is taking up valuable space, time, and resources that could be dedicated to pursuing stories that make a difference in society.

The Anna Nicole saga may be the most recent prime example. The amount of airtime, page space, and resources dedicated to following the drama was overwhelming in comparison to the coverage of other news stories. Nick Madigan of the Baltimore Sun reported in his editorial that according to the Project for Excellence in Journalism, the Smith story was the number-one story on cable television for a week, and that it took up half the news airtime in the first two days after her death (Madigan, para. 21). In addition, the major mainstream media outlets spent more time dedicated to Smith's story than a developing story about the haphazard conditions and substandard care for wounded soldiers at the Walter Reed Army Medical Center. One website that tracks media coverage, TheLeftCoaster.com, tracked the number of references to the Smith story and the Walter Reed story on news networks. On March 2, Fox News had 10 references to the Walter Reed story, compared to an astounding 121 references to Anna Nicole Smith. The other mainstream media outlets did not fare much better than Fox News; MSNBC had 84 references to Walter Reed compared to 96 to Anna Nicole. CNN, which appeared to be more serious in its news-gathering, had 53 mentions of Walter Reed compared to 40 references to Anna Nicole (Madigan, para. 22). These reports are dismal and shocking. Perhaps it is no wonder that we as Americans are claimed to be uninformed about important issues of our time. When the media should be providing news about an issue that affects numerous people, citizens are instead learning more about a Playboy bunny whose fame was inherent only after death.

This is not to say that Anna Nicole's death has no worth as a breaking news story. But a mention on mainstream media outlets would certainly have sufficed; there are numerous celebrity news outlets to cover her death. Continuing with the arguments of Ornebring and Jonsson, if the mainstream media have created alternative media outlets, then celebrity news should be kept to those outlets. If people wish to learn about their favorite celebrities, then by all means, they have an abundant number of outlets to choose from. Celebrity news has no place in the mainstream media; there are more than plenty of alternative media outlets to cover celebrities.

However, many argue that celebrity news is needed for the news industry to survive. Another argument in favor of celebrity journalism in mainstream media is that the media industry needs celebrity news to boost its ratings or circulation numbers. Undoubtedly, mediums such as newspapers are losing readers rapidly. But while circulation numbers and ratings are decreasing, the "infotainment" industry is booming. *People, Us Weekly, InStyle* and Entertainment Weekly magazines saw an increase of 18.7 percent in circulation; news magazines like *Time, Newsweek, The New Yorker* and *The Atlantic* saw an increase of 2 percent (Halpern xv). As a result, mainstream media outlets are hopping on the tabloid bandwagon. Jay T. Harris, a former editor of a big city tabloid and the Wallis Annenberg Chair in the Annenberg School of Communication at USC, acknowledged the advantages sensational celebrity news has for journalists. In his opinion, it is undeniable that celebrity coverage sells. In an article for the conference "Reporting on Celebrities: The Ethics of News Coverage," he wrote,

> I guess journalists could argue that celebrity coverage is smart business. Further, I will stipulate that, by extension, competitive pressures provide a plausible justification for celebrity coverage —if I don't do it my competitor will and that will be to my disadvantage. (Harris, para. 6)

If the media believe that celebrity news can rescue them from dismal numbers, then they will certainly keep giving their audiences more sensational news. There is, however, a problem with this rationale. Because celebrity news is able to raise circulation and ratings numbers, this leads to the belief that people must want more coverage of celebrities rather than real news stories.

Although the media seem to believe that their audiences want more celebrity news, it is not necessarily true. The world's largest news agency, the Associated Press, decided in February of 2007 to suspend temporarily its coverage of the famous heiress, Paris Hilton. Editors wanted to see the results if they didn't publish any stories about Hilton (Madigan, para. 3). At about the same time, on February 9, 2007, Brian Williams, the anchor of NBC's Nightly News, posted on his web log, the Daily Nightly, "Viewer warning: There will be no mention of Britney Spears' baldness or rehab in tonight's broadcast, nor will there be any mention of Anna Nicole's 'body possession' hearing" (Deggans, para. 2). He said later,

> I wrote it on a whim...I realized I was watching three cable news networks doing some combination (of stories) on a bald singer leaving rehab for a second time and a dead former Playmate whose body is being argued over. I've got a world to cover...(and) if I thought for a moment that Nightly News was somehow depriving a yearning nation of these twin tragedies, I would rethink that decision. (Deggans, para. 4)

Now, was there uproar over Williams's decision to not give time to Britney and Paris? Were news agencies clamoring for more Paris stories from the Associated Press? Not quite. The Associated Press, to its surprise, found that no one requested any Paris stories during its suspension, athough, in all fairness, the agency did note that nothing out of the ordinary happened to Hilton: "No [media outlet] felt a newsworthy event had been ignored" (Madigan, para. 6). Rem Reider, an editor for the *American Journalism Review,* agreed that the AP's experiment exposed something about the American public. He was quoted as saying, "I don't think the world would be diminished if there were a Paris Hilton blackout—with all respect to Paris Hilton" (Madigan, para. 1). Brian Williams found support for his decision from his viewers. Comments on his blog were actually in support of his decision. Wrote Matthew Cowan Mechanicsburg of Pennsylvania, "Your judgment is excellent. I was so glad to see some news last night. I was afraid I'd see nothing but Anna Nicole" (Williams 2007). Williams even responded to those who opposed his decision to not give Smith any coverage. He said that if people disagreed with his editorial decision, they could get that news from a number of other news sources. He wrote on his blog,

> It's not as if there aren't other news outlets for those viewers dissatisfied with our treatment of the story and the end of a tragic life. People watch our broadcast presumably because they trust our reporting and our people, and because they agree with our editorial take on the day more often than not. The great thing about this era of media choice is that all those who find our broadcast lacking in any way are free to go to any number of Web sites where they can find video showing a cat flushing a toilet, or the explosive properties of Diet Coke and Mentos when mixed together. (Williams, para. 2)

However, Williams did receive some criticism for not covering Smith. Wrote Eric Deggans in an editorial in the *St. Petersburg Times,* a respected journalist like Williams could have provided an insightful look into Smith's story rather than the mindless coverage on every cable channel (Deggans, para. 7). But Williams recognized that people do not want as much celebrity news as the media believe.

In fact, the study by Patterson found that audiences actually preferred issue stories rather than soft news stories, celebrity news included. The study, which looked at over 5,000 stories from the LexisNexis database of two television networks, three prominent newspapers, and 26 local dailies, found that the foundation of news audiences are those who read hard news stories (Valencia, para. 12). People look to the mainstream media outlets to get the news, not to be informed of the latest celebrity happenings.

Furthermore, some argue that using the "infotainment" strategy actually hurts rather than helps news organizations in the end.

Media scholars Bill Kovach and Tom Rosenstiel argue that when news turns into entertainment, news organizations must compete with media other than their own, a competition that they cannot win (154). "Infotainment" also creates audiences that are not reliable in terms of ratings and circulation numbers. Kovach and Rosenstiel write,

> The strategy of infotainment, though it may attract an audience in the short run and may be cheap to produce, will build a shallow audience because it is built on form, not substance. Such an audience will switch to the next "most exciting" thing because it was built on the spongy ground of excitement in the first place. (155)

The media's argument that validates celebrity news's worth in the mainstream media is therefore faulty. Celebrity news doesn't just hurt the audiences, but it hurts news organizations as well. In a time when the news industry is struggling to survive, news organizations should be wary of the dangers that celebrity news has.

Therefore, celebrity news is a viable threat to both our media and our democracy. According to Kovach and Rosenstiel, the primary purpose of journalism is "to provide citizens with the information they need to be free and self-governing" (17). The media have a responsibility to citizens to inform the public, or democracy suffers. Jay T. Harris, a former editor of a big-city tabloid and the Wallis Annenberg Chair in the Annenberg School of Communication at USC, sees the possible damage that celebrity news has for the future of our society. He said,

> We [journalists] are the essential plumbing—we carry useful information, including information on changing values, priorities, and shared challenges. But we also carry (or maybe spread is the better word here) that which weakens, that which corrodes, that which debases. (Harris, para. 9)

Additionally, actor Ed Asner, at the "Reporting on Celebrities: The Ethics of News Coverage" conference, called out celebrity news for contributing to the "moral decay" of the country (Merina, para. 39). It's ironic that such harsh criticism of the journalism field comes from an actor, who is one of the many players in the crisis of celebrity news.

So then, what are the consequences of celebrity news? Why is it so damaging to our democracy? We can look to the theory of agenda-setting to explain the possible effects of too much celebrity news. According to the book *Questioning the Media: A Critical Introduction,* the news media have the power to define what is news and what is not. Therefore, whatever the news media give the most prominence to, we consider to be important. The definition reads, "News media power is based not so much on how the media interpret events to us as it is on the sheer fact that they can set our agenda of things to think about in the first place" (Downing et al., 478). To follow this theory, if mainstream media are emphasizing celebrity news over important news stories, then we are more likely to think about celebrities rather than the issues that are pertinent to our democracy. The consequences of this are huge. Suppose that all we cared about is Anna Nicole's baby or Britney's meltdown rather than the issues that make a difference in our lives. How can a democracy possibly survive on paparazzi photographs and celebrity hook-ups without the information it needs to be self-governing? It cannot. Famed journalist Edward R. Murrow put it wisely in 1958, to the Radio-Television News Directors Association Convention, "For surely we shall pay for using this most powerful instrument of communication [television] to insulate the citizenry from the hard and demanding realities which must be faced if we are to survive. I mean the word survive literally" (para. 5). Journalists cannot insulate citizens with celebrity gossip, for it will be detrimental to society.

In all of my research, I found that no one in the journalism field was eager to take sides on the issue. Although many were quick to gripe about the huge amount of celebrity news that appears in mainstream media, they also recognize that without it, news media would not survive. Although many see celebrity news as demeaning to their work, they also realize that many people want it. So then, what are mainstream media to do? Do they run by profits and market demands or by what they believe to be right? Do they give citizens more celebrity news or the news that they see as important? Who, then, decides what news is important and what news audiences need? These are questions with no easy answers, but it distresses me greatly to see that my work in the future, the field and career that I am committed to, may be diminished to following trails of the latest celebrity gossip. I certainly didn't become interested in the field of journalism because I wanted to follow rumors of Britney Spears's antics. I became passionate about journalism because I believed that the stories that I would write would make a difference in my democracy, in my society. Do stories about Britney Spears indeed help the citizens and make a difference? For entertainment purposes, maybe, but I would have to argue they do not inherently help citizens. But I will continue to believe, with perhaps a bit of blind optimism, that the purpose of journalism is not to simply give audiences fluff, information that they do not need. I will believe that the purpose of journalism still is, and always will be, to provide the citizens with information that our democracy needs to function. Therefore, I urge the entire mainstream media to retrace its steps back to the roots and principles of journalism. I challenge the industry to think outside the market demands, the world of ratings and circulation numbers, and to once again consider the audience and what it needs. As Kovach and Rosenstiel worded it so eloquently, journalism's first loyalty is to the citizens, and its first obligation is to provide those citizens with the information they need (13). Celebrity news in the mainstream media is hindering our news industry from fulfilling its journalistic duties, and in turn hurting the citizens of our democracy.

Works Cited

Deggans, Eric. "Anna Nicole and Britney? Yes, they are news." *St. Petersburg Times.* 27 Feb. 2007. Web. 14 Mar. 2007.

Downing, John, Ali Mohammadi, and Annabelle Sreberny-Mohammadi. *Questioning the Media: a Critical Introduction.* 2nd ed. Thousand Oaks, CA: Sage Publications, 1995. Print.

Halpern, Jake. *Fame Junkies: the Hidden Truths Behind America's Favorite Addiction.* New York: Houghton Mifflin, 2007. Print.

Harris, Jay T. "Why Do We Care About Celebrities?". *Poynter Online.* 21 Jan. 2004. Web. 21 Mar. 2007.

Herbert, Bob. "From Anna to Britney to Zawahri." *The New York Times.* 22 Feb. 2007. Web. 26 Feb. 2007.

Kovach, Bill and Tom Rosenstiel. *The Elements of Journalism.* New York: Three Rivers P, 2001. Print.

Madigan, Nick. "Media Say 'Enough Already.'" *The Baltimore Sun.* 11 Mar. 2007. Web. 14 Mar. 2007.

Maltby, John, et al. "Personality and Coping: a Context for Examining Celebrity Worship and Mental Health." *British Journal of Psychology* 95 (2004): 411-428. Thomson Gale. Web. 23 Feb. 2007.

Merina, Victor. "Celebrities in Journalism: the Ethics of News Cover age." *Poynter Online.* 22 Jan. 2004. Web. 23 Feb. 2007.

Murrow, Edward R. "Keynote Speeches." *Radio-Television News Directors Association.* n.d. Web. 18 Apr. 2007.

Ornebring, Henrik and Anna Maria Jonsson. "Tabloid Journalism and the Public Sphere: A Historical Perspective on Tabloid Journalism." *Journalism Studies* 5 (2004): 283-295. Academic Search Premier. Web. 23 Feb. 2007.

Valencia, Monica. "The Wet Stuff, the White Stuff, and the Pooch: Sensationalism and Gossip in News." *Poynter Online.* 21 Aug. 2001. Web. 14 Feb. 2007.

Williams, Brian. "About Last Night..." MSNBC. 9 Feb. 2007. Web. 21 Mar. 2007.

Harry Potter and Christianity: Treacherous Duo or Surprising Partners?

Kelsey Lindsey

Argument: Sample Essay 2

WRTG 1250

Instructor: Christine Macdonald

When people interpret the meaning and influence of a text differently, it can lead to contentious debates. The meaning of the Harry Potter *books has been one of those debates. Kelsey uses her own experience to launch her argument for looking at* Harry Potter *as consistent with some of the core tenets of Christianity. Drawing on a variety of sources—scholarly, religious, and popular—Kelsey addresses Christian parents and argues that they should take a closer look at Harry Potter before banning their children from reading about the boy wizard.*

Introduction

I remember the first time I felt unwelcome in church. I was thirteen years old, starting a new Bible study for middle school girls. In an effort to get to know each other, all the girls in my group shared the usual little tidbits of information: our name, grade, school, favorite color and (game changer!) our favorite book. It was my turn and, trying to control the shake in my voice I would always get from public speaking, I shared what I knew. Name: Kelsey Lindsey. Grade: Eighth. School: Moore Middle. Favorite Color: Yellow. And, last but not least, Favorite Book: *Harry Potter.* I looked up after I shared these vital pieces of information, only to find pursed lips and raised eyebrows greeting me. Obviously I said something wrong.

Panicking, I reviewed the past monologue in my head, searching for the devious slip that caused such a ripple of shock in the circle. After five seconds of very awkward brain racking, I narrowed the culprit down to two suspects: either the group disagreed with my fondness of *Harry Potter,* or all ten girls had a strange dislike towards the color yellow. As I was drawing to my conclusion, the small blonde girl next to me leaned over and validated my hypothesis. In a hushed whisper that seemed to reverberate around the circle, Sarah exclaimed, "You like *Harry Potter?* But isn't that like, all about witches and stuff?"

Since the first book's release in 1999, the *Harry Potter* series written by Scottish author J.K Rowling has been disturbing the calm waters of Christianity, mainly because of the central practice of magic found throughout the seven books. The series tell a tale of a bespectacled orphan Harry Potter who, at the age of eleven, radically discovers that he is no ordinary boy, but a wizard. Whisked away from his dreary life with his only living relatives, the Dursleys, Harry is enrolled in the famous Hogwarts School of Witchcraft and Wizardry, where he meets his best friends Ron and Hermione. With them, Harry progresses through school and life's challenges, always with the ominous threat of his parents' murderer, Lord Voldemort, gaining power and rising again. While the inclusion of sorcery is troubling to some Christians, the humungous popularity of the books is the main catalyst for the religious uprising against young Harry and his friends. With more than 350 million copies worldwide (Hoover Par 3), *Harry Potter* has been published in more than fifty-four languages (Nexon and Neumann 3), making it internationally known and loved. This success is unsettling to Christians, mainly Christian parents, who think that the popularity of the book will provoke the curiosity of their kids, luring them into reading the magical series.

But what is the driving force behind this alarm? As a Christian myself, I strive to understand the fear that is involved in the banning of any source of literature, much less a wonderful series that opens many doors in children's learning and the development of the imagination. Through an examination of the Bible, I do believe that I found the reason behind the action of condemning *Harry Potter,* but through the same source, I have also found evidence to support the reading of these novels. The main goal of this paper is not to recruit you as Christian parents into the large fandom of *Harry Potter*, but to help you explore the many different lessons found within the series. All I ask for is an open mind, and maybe a little faith that these books could be used for good rather than bad, perhaps even as a teaching tool to help your children understand the word of God.

Witchcraft, the Bible and Today's Modern Interpretation: What's in a Word?

Let us first look at one of the most fundamental and inadvertently overlooked discussion points in this argument: that is the use and negative connotation found within the word "witch." Throughout history and popular literature, witches have been associated with evil, wrong doing, and ill intentions. There are the witches of Macbeth, countless evil witches of Disney fame, and of course, the infamous Salem Witch Trials of 1692. While all of these popular and well known influences have subconsciously implanted negative stereotypes within many people's minds, the latter may be the most important, as the blind hysteria found in these trials may be connected to Christians' banning of *Harry Potter.* From June to September 1692, the town of Salem, Massachusetts condemned thirteen women and six men to hanging on the charges of witchcraft and fraternizing with the Devil, imprisoned hundreds of others, which created a town-wide hysteria ("The Dead" par. 1 and Linder par. 1). It is important to notice that the majority found guilty in these trials were women, thus diminishing the negative effects of the male equivalent to the witch in today's society. Wizards are looked at as wise and powerful, in the example of Merlin or Gandalf in The Lord of the Rings series. Because of this acceptance of magic in the word of "wizard" and not "witch," it may be safe to say that some of the fear towards Harry Potter is subconsciously provoked from the inclusion of the words "witch" and "witchcraft" found within the novels. As this may be, I will cease to use these marked words in this paper, as fighting the negative connotations associated with both would be pointless, as they have already been imbedded within all of our minds from early childhood on through many sources. The tragedy at Salem is a prime example of how this underlying discrimination towards the word "witch" has been causing problems many years before Harry Potter.

Biblical Evidence

There are a plethora of Biblical quotes condemning sorcery, many of them used as evidence in the case against *Harry Potter.* Notice the inclusion of the word "witchcraft" within all three of these quotes, as it may as well strengthen the impact these phrases have on readers. Deuteronomy 18:10 says, "Let no one be found among you who sacrifices his son or daughter in the fire, who practices divination or sorcery, interprets omens, [and] engages in witchcraft," and found in 2 Chronicles 33:6: "He...practiced sorcery, divination and witchcraft, and consulted mediums and spiritists. He did much evil in the eyes of the LORD, provoking him to anger." With Galatians 5:20 linking witchcraft with sins such as jealousy, anger and discord, the Bible clearly states that he who deals with magic is not welcome within the Christian community.

Modern Magic and Harry Potter

What may not be so clear is the exact definition as to what is truly witchcraft, and what does the practice of magic look like. There is no description found within the Bible, but many present day "witches," or Wiccans, offer up an explanation as to what their religion of Wicca is. On the website The Pagan Federation, Wicca (the religious name for the study of witchcraft) is defined as a nature-based religion and craft, the purpose of which is to put the practitioner at peace with the "cosmos" through the craft of psychic healing ("What is Wicca?" par 2). The main goal of the followers of this religion is to achieve a "deep communion with the powers of Nature and of the human psyche, leading to a spiritual transformation of the self" (par 1). Because this practice of magic is far from similar to the waving of wands and brewing of potions in *Harry Potter*, it is surprising to me that Christians find fault with the books, as they have no direct correlation to the modern Wicca religion.

But find fault they do, and in the argument against *Harry Potter*, the greatest ally might be found in the form of Laura Mallory, an anti-Harry Potter mother who first found conflict with the series when she discovered that they were being read in her children's classrooms. From then on, she has been one of the most active crusaders in the fight to ban *Harry Potter* from the classroom, on the main basis that the book cleverly disguises and promotes the use of witchcraft to young children. In an interview with The Loganville Tribune posted on her website His Voice Today, Mallory provides several examples of children trying to learn the practice of witchcraft as her main evidence against the book belonging in classrooms. She states that the presence of the magical series promotes the practice of the Wicca religion, and that this solicitation of religion is fertile ground for the removal of the books (Swanepoel par. 19 and 22). Mallory correlates the banning of the *Harry Potter* books with the same law that bans the Bible from the classroom, in the effort to separate church from state.

While Mallory, as a Christian parent, might be easy for you to identify with, I feel the need to bring up a vital downfall in her argument: she has never read a *Harry Potter* book. This unfortunate action causes me to pause, because I do believe that if she had taken the time to read the books, the countless number of hours and resources wasted on her case to remove the series from classrooms would have been saved for better use. In the books, magic is not performed for spiritual acts or evil rituals, instead it is used as we might use technology: accomplishing everyday tasks and generally making life easier for ourselves. As we use the dishwasher to accomplish our chores, spells are used to free the characters of *Harry Potter* from the time spent in washing dishes. In the series, there is no mention of praying or practicing to any sort of deity as Wiccans do, only instead useful spells produced in achieving a simpler life. Even though I cannot relate to you as a Christian parent, I can relate to you as a Christian, and I hope that you might take my word over Mallory's on the sole purpose that I have actually read the books, and have found that there is no harm in them.

And while I agree with the above Biblical quotes, and also Mallory when claiming that practicing of magic in the Wicca religion is ungodly, I believe that there is a difference between the spiritual acts they perform and the harmless reading of magic being practiced in a fictional reality. The Bible does not condemn the notion of magic, or even the thought of it; instead it warns against the practical use of sorcery and divination. In the argument that Harry will lead children to sorcery, the key evidence that I have against this claim lies within the bookshelves of many Christians, maybe even your own. In mysteries, thrillers, and romance novels, there are many central themes of adultery, deception, and even murder; and while these three genres are read by Christians such as my parents and myself, I do not see any uncontrollable urges to kill and cheat rising within any one of us. As none of these genres see any opposition equal to that against *Harry Potter,* I believe that the Christian community does recognize the distinction between fictional sins performed between the pages of books and that of acting them out in real life. These differences are pivotal in the argument over *Harry Potter's* morality, as is the knowledge of the contrast between reading and doing.

The Other Dirty Harry?

So while I hope that you understand the fact that it is not a sin to indulge in these tales of magic, some other Christian scholars look past the spells and point out the disturbing behavior that the protagonist Harry exhibits throughout the series. Catholic Ian Rutherford states that because Harry and his friends "lie, cheat, [and] break rules and laws" in the wizarding world (37), children reading the series will think that it is acceptable to mimic his actions in everyday life. This rule-breaking is evident, and in his book, The Wisdom of Harry Potter, Edmund M. Kern highlights the exact events that may lead Rutherford to conclude that the boy wizard may be a bad influence on the young susceptible minds of readers. In the third book, *Harry Potter and the Prisoner of Azkaban,* Harry "sneaks off school grounds, wanders about after [school] hours, and lies fairly often to everyone from Stan on the Knight Bus to Lupin in the classroom" (71). In learning that Harry even goes as far as attacking a teacher, your intentions might be in the right place when you ban your children from reading the *Harry Potter* books.

Though this argument is reasonable, the validation of it seems to disappear like (dare I say it?) magic when it is understood that the key evidence in this justification is found when only looking at these delinquencies with no outside knowledge as to why they are being done. Sure, your children will see Harry and his friends acting out against authority, but along with these unruly rebellions they will also discover the reasons behind them. Harry sneaks off school grounds after hours to save an innocent animal from wrongful death. In being dishonest and attacking his teacher, Harry does so for what might be the noblest of reasons: to save the soul of a man who has done no wrong. While the teacher being attacked is about to wrongly condemn this innocent man to the horrific fate of living without a soul for purely selfish and vengeful reasons, Harry's actions to stop him can be atoned. When reading about these dishonorable actions in context, I believe that your children will understand that the breaking of rules was necessary in Harry's selfless missions to help the innocent. For younger children who might blur the lines between good intentions and bad deeds, I recommend you read the books with them, explaining Harry and his friends' actions and the good behind them. With this clarification, it is safe to say that children should be able to recognize that while Harry Potter may break the rules, it is for just and noble causes, and that makes all the difference.

Stepping Stones to the Understanding of Brotherhood and Love

The last argument I have may be in fact the most controversial, but I believe it is the most important. I have thought for quite some time now that the *Harry Potter* series can be used as a tool to help teach children the fundamental values of the Christian religion, most importantly: the values of brotherhood and love. In this statement, I am supported by ordained minister John Killinger, who in his book,

God, the Devil, and Harry Potter, defends the series, stating that they are "a modern interpretation of the gospel" (14). Because the *Harry Potter* series is so popular, I believe that examples from one of their favorite books would help children understand some vital lessons and morals taught in the Bible, furthering their knowledge of this wonderful story.

Brotherhood

The value of brotherhood is important in both Harry Potter and the Christian religion. As all of us Christians are looked at as brothers and sisters in Christ, the love we have for each other is a major defining characteristic of both ourselves and our religion. John 13:35 states; "By this all people will know that you are my disciples, if you love one another." We Christians are simply asked to love our sisters and brothers of Christ, supporting and encouraging them as Jesus himself would do. In explaining this love to children, they might be confused as to why so much emphasis is placed upon the gift of being able to love one another, and that is where the novels of Harry Potter would help. In providing examples from the friendship of Harry, Ron and Hermione, children may come to understand what true, unselfish brotherly love looks like. In all seven books, this famous threesome have truly been there for each other by helping in times of need, giving advice on relationships, and even pointing out where one is in the wrong. The love that they show through these actions is important, as it is one of the only things that the evil contained within the novels is deterred by. This is shown in the fifth book, *Harry Potter and the Order of the Phoenix*, when Voldemort is successfully defeated in trying to possess Harry, all because he lacks the understanding of the true power of love. In the attempt to occupy Harry's body, Voldemort is thwarted because he can not bear to be in contained within a vessel that holds so much love for others within. This extraction of evil is neatly summed up by wise Professor Dumbledore when he says "it was your heart that saved you" (Rowling 844). Harry's love for his friends sets him apart from the evil Voldemort, and ultimately saved him from being overtaken by the wickedness trying to overcome him. This example should help children understand that the love that they have for other Christians may be in fact one of the most powerful things in the world, distinguishing them from others and providing strength in a time of weakness.

Love

Christ's love is the founding force for the Christian religion, centered around a sacrifice so great and awesome it has inspired numerous works of literature, art, and praise. The Bible is full of passages describing the incomparable love God has for all of us, from Romans 5:8, "But God demonstrates his own love for us in this: While we were still sinners, Christ died for us," to 1 John 3:16, "This is how we know what love is: Jesus Christ laid down his life for us." Both of these texts center around the key fact that Jesus died on the cross for our sins, displaying the undying love God has for us: a love that I believe can be found in the *Harry Potter* novels. Throughout the books, it is revealed that Harry's mother gave her life to try to spare her son from the evil Lord Voldemort, and this love possessed the power to save him from the "Killing Curse" and destroy the power of Voldemort. This "great love" is unknown to even the wisest in the novels, unseen but relied upon to vanquish immorality in the wizarding world. This plot sounds eerily familiar to the story of Christ, from the selfless sacrifice to the destruction of evil and protection of the innocent. With this new age representation of Jesus' sacrifice, you can help your children understand the love of God, and perhaps spark some curiosity that propels them to seek out more information about their Creator.

Conclusion

In the banning of the *Harry Potter* novels, I believe that you as Christian parents are missing out on a huge teaching opportunity: an opportunity to use a well loved and popular book to excite children about reading, learning, and God. The blind prejudice against the presence of magic found in the novels must be dropped, and I suggest one simple act to help in this process: read the books. In them, if you are able to read further than the casting of spells and brewing of potions, you will find an inspiring protagonist, many allusions to Christ, and if nothing else, a wonderfully well-written story. Sharing these novels with your children will spark numerous conversations, ignite their imagination, and perhaps even act as a catalyst into their discovery of God.

Works Cited

"The Dead." *Famous American Trials: Salem Witchcraft Trials of 1692.* Web. 27 Nov. 2009.Web.

Hoover, Bob. "Harry Potter a classic? Successful? No doubt. But classic? Time will tell." *Post-Gazette.com.* Pittsburgh Post Gazette, 14 July 2007. Web. 29 Oct. 2009.

Kern, Edmund M. *The Wisdom of Harry Potter.* Amherst, NY: Prometheus Books, 2003. Print.

Killinger, John. *God, the Devil, and Harry Potter: A Christian Minister's Defense of the Beloved Novels.* New York: Thomas Dunne Books, 2002. Print.

Linder, Douglas O. "The Witchcraft Trials in Salem: A Commentary." *Famous American Trials: Salem Witchcraft Trials of 1692.* Web. 27 Nov. 2009.

New International Version. Grand Rapids: Biblica. *Biblegateway. com.* The Zondervan Corporation L.L.C. Web. 27 Nov. 2009.

Nexon, Daniel Ha, and Iver B. Neumann. *Harry Potter and International Relations.* Lanham, Md.: Rowman and Littlefield, 2006. Print.

Rowling, J.K. *Harry Potter and The Order of The Phoenix.* New York: Scholastic, Inc., 2003. Print.

Rutherford, Ian. "Harry Potter: Situation ethics candy-coated for kids." *New Oxford Review 69.4* (2002): 36-39. Academic Search Premier, Norlin Library, University of Colorado. Web. 28 Sept. 2009.

Swanepoel, Sharon. "Harry's Harshest Critic Speaks Out." *The Loganville Tribune.* 29 June 2007. Rpt. in His Voice Today Web. 19 Jan. 2010.

"What Is Wicca?" The Pagan Federation. *The Pagan Federation.* Web. 27 Nov. 2009.

Corporate Political Power and Market Failures

Nate Neligh

Argument: Sample Essay 3

WRTG 1250

Instructor: Bruce Bassoff

A successful argument presents clearly articulated reasons and credible evidence that support the central claim. However, an effective argument must also pay attention to and acknowledge opposing views. In his argument, Nate presents his views on the necessity of campaign reform for the restoration of our democracy. But he also addresses the counterarguments, explaining and refuting opposing ideas in order to persuade his readers to support campaign reform in order to restore the balance of power.

Markets rely on self interest, but only when self interest is restrained by the laws of society. Once self interest escapes the bounds of the law, trade is replaced by theft, and markets are no longer beneficial to society. In most situations, the law prevents theft and other harmful self interested behavior. Unfortunately, there is no law for those who make the law. When an entity gains enough political power to manipulate the law of the land, it is no longer subject to the laws of supply and demand either, because it can enact a variety of helpful legislation. The company could push through subsidies and have the taxpayer pay a portion of its production costs. It could receive contracts that provide an enormous flow of taxpayer money with little or no accountability. The corporation could even demand deregulation that would allow it to do business without regard to the social impacts of doing business, or "externalities"

171

(Mankiw 11). The political power that some corporations wield allows them to escape socially beneficial influences of the law and the free market.

Unfortunately, such companies are becoming more common. Current campaign finance laws allow corporations to make large donations in support of political candidates. In addition, companies can muster the resources required to lobby politicians on their behalf. Because consumers are often divided in their opinions, their resources are spread out, and they can't lobby effectively. Citizens are simply too disorganized to wield major influence over high level politicians to counteract the pull of corporations. Also, most people are not politically savvy enough to know what is going on with any particular piece of legislation, much less object to it. Both campaign finance and the ignorance of the electorate aid major corporations. Not all companies, however, benefit from political connections. The vast majority of businesses are small enough that they can't afford to lobby Congress or fund a senator's reelection bid, so the overall effect is that the big companies get bigger and everyone else pays. No one could say that such an outcome benefits society.

One example of government acting a little too friendly towards business should still be fairly fresh in most people's minds. The Bush administration was intimately tied with the private security industry, and their connections are evident from these examples. Donald Rumsfeld began his stint as Secretary of Defense with an enormous amount of stock in Gilead Sciences, which owns the patent to Tamiflu (Klein, 394). During Donald Rumsfeld's tenure, the pentagon acquired a stockpile of Tamiflu for $58 million (Klein 395). The corporate connection permeated the even highest levels of government. Dick Cheney had 189,000 shares of stock in Halliburton, although he gave the profits from these shares to charity (Klein 395). During the Iraq war, Halliburton's stock increased in value by 300% mainly from profits on no-bid government contracts from the government, however, so Cheney is probably making quite a bit of money now that he is out of office(Klein 396). Because they are no longer under scrutiny after retirement, they often profit from questionable dealings in their later years. Because they can deal directly with their friends in government, well connected firms no longer have to deal with inconveniences like competition.

Not only were the contracts in Iraq without bid, but they also lacked accountability. According to Naomi Klein, one company was found to have given the US government funded Central Provisional

Authority "false and fraudulent inflated invoices," but it escaped completely unscathed, because the administration had given US companies blanket legal protection in Iraqi courts, and the Central Provisional Authority was found not to be part of the US government (453). Since the CPA was not part of the US government, the case was not in the jurisdiction of US court, and that meant that US corporations in Iraq could not be sued in any legal system (Klein 453). In essence, these companies were given free license to steal from the American government. Once companies are so well connected, they can get full legal protection; the free market has turned into an expensive robbery.

The connections between the Bush administration and corporations are not anomalous. A similar relationship has persisted between the government and big agribusiness for many years and through many administrations. Again, this relationship allows major corporations to escape the free market. Nowhere is the problem more evident than in the corn market. Because agriculture is a cyclical business, many farmers have difficulty staying solvent through years of low yield or low prices, but during The New Deal a solution was enacted: the government would create a corn pawn shop. Farmers could use excess corn as collateral to take out loans from the government in years of surplus, and in years of famine the corn could be reclaimed and sold (Pollan 46). This solution was good for the farmers, because it prevented sudden price collapses, and it was good for consumers, who got cheaper food when they needed it most. The only people for whom the system was bad were the big food processors who wanted a price collapse. Unfortunately, it was their opinion that ended up mattering. In the 1970's, secretary of agriculture Earl Butz dismantled the corn pawning system, and replaced it with a system under which farmers received direct payments from the government to make up price shortfall for every bushel they produced (Pollan 52). The systems may seem similar, but there is one key difference: under the new system, farmers didn't have to pay the government back. This change gave farmers every incentive to produce as much as possible. In fact, farmers are encouraged to sacrifice sustainable production for present yields, because the target price against which the price shortfalls are assessed is lowered every few years (Pollan 54). Farmers are guaranteed a certain price for their corn, so they have no incentive to consider market demand when they decide how much to produce. This incentive structure has led to massive over production and price collapse.

Some people might point out that if farmers stopped driving up production, congress would stop lowering the target price, but the subsidies have trapped the farmers in what is called a "Nash Equilibrium" (Mankiw 368). In a Nash Equilibrium, each person or organization makes a unilateral decision that is in their best interest, but the net result causes everyone to be worse off. If the farmers all acted together to stop increasing production, they would all be better off in the long run, but there are too many farmers to collaborate, and there is too much incentive to cheat on any supply restricting agreement. If a farmer decides to sell his corn for less than the agreed upon price, he will be able to sell a much greater volume, because everyone will want his cheap corn. The additional profits would be too tempting for farmers to be able to make a supply controlling agreement work.

One might expect consumers to be happy about the low price of corn, but consumers are actually paying for it with their tax dollars. By subsidizing corn production, the law is essentially forcing consumers to use some of their money to buy corn. If consumers do not buy corn, they are losing out, because they have already paid for corn with their taxes. If consumers buy a small amount of corn, they do not benefit much from the law, because they have already paid for the corn with their taxes again. The subsidy does nothing but punish those who don't buy corn, because consumers rarely buy enough corn for the savings to be substantial. It will probably come as no shock that the ones who benefit most from corn subsidies are the ones who helped write the legislation: large, grain devouring food processors like Cargill and Archer Daniels Midland (Pollan 52). The enormous volumes of corn they deal with allow them to take full advantage of corn subsidies. These companies can take four cents worth of corn, break that corn into its basic components, and send those components down the line to General Mills, where it becomes four dollars worth of cereal (Pollan 93). Those profit margins are rarely seen outside movie theater food. How do these companies maintain these enormous profit margins? The biggest input for cereal production is corn, and the corn is being paid for by taxes.

Corn is not, however, the only area of agriculture where big business has a lot of power. Major food companies have managed to push through all kinds of favorable labeling legislation. Although consumers like to think that "organic" means chemical free, locally produced, and absolutely green, corporate pressure has caused the FDA to adopt a very relaxed standard for organic food. According to Michael Pollan, when the organic movement was young in 1990, the FDA applied a set of rules which prohibited all "synthetic food additives" and "manufacturing agents" (155). Big agribusiness, however, could not stand idly by while the organic market grew and made money. Heinz, ConAgra, and Archer Daniels Midland began producing their own organic brands in the 1990's (Pollan 154). Once the corporate pressure was on, the FDA quickly caved, and new rules were implemented allowing organic food to include diverse synthetic additives (Pollan 156). These new rules outraged from the organic movement, but they remain in place to this day (Pollan 154).

Even the USDA beef grading system is a product of lobbying by big factory farms. The USDA policy is to give higher grades to beef with intramuscular fat or "marbling" (Pollan 75). Although this system has become so ingrained into American society that people rarely question it, highly marbled corn fed beef is actually much worse for the consumer than traditional grass fed beef. Corn fed beef may fatten up faster, but it is much higher in saturated fat and lower in omega 3 fatty acids (Pollan 75). Cows grazed on grass tend to be a little leaner, but they are more flavorful and healthier. Unfortunately, grazing cows requires a lot of land. It is much more economical for large operations to cram all their cows together and feed them on the cheapest source of calories available, corn (Pollan 75). Feed lots and corn present many problems to bovine health that can in turn damage human health. Cows are not designed to eat corn, so eating corn raises the Ph of their stomachs to approximately the same Ph as the human stomach. This acidity allows the cows to contract parasites that are transmissible to humans (Pollan 78). The close proximity of the cows also allows quick spreading of disease. The cows need antibiotics to combat the illnesses, and the antibiotics end up in the meat that people eat. When bacteria in the cow and person are exposed to these low levels of antibiotics, they can develop resistance (Pollan 78). Why does the USDA beef grading system reward the production of unhealthy, inferior beef? Because big agribusiness wants the system to be that way.

Big business does have plenty of supporters, however, and people would not support big business if there were no good reasons to do so. Regarding the issue of corporate influence on the government, business supporters would contend that such influence is neither prevalent nor undesirable. Big business as a group loses a lot of lobbying power to internal struggle. For example, the insurance industry is currently battling major employers over government funded health insurance. Wal-Mart, one of the nation's largest employers, is lobbying heavily for a public insurance option, because employer provided insurance is very expensive when a company employs as many people as Wal-Mart does (Reason Foundation).

The insurance industry, on the other hand, is not happy about the idea of government competition, so it is lobbying against the public option. Unfortunately, in most cases, corporations tend to be much less divided than consumers are. For example, environmental protection may have a few defenders from the tourism industry, but such pro environment lobbying is generally targeted at small areas. On the other side, the entire manufacturing and energy industries would prefer looser environmental regulation. In the modern political climate where 55% is considered a landslide, consumers are rarely able to unite on one side of an issue, so it seems unlikely that consumer lobbying will be able to counteract corporate lobbying.

Big business supporters might also argue that corporate influence on the government can be good. Thomas Friedman presents a theory called The Golden Arches Theory of Conflict Prevention in *Lexus and the Olive Tree.* This theory states that no two countries that have McDonald's have ever gone to war. This theory does have a few exceptions such as the most recent war between Russia and Georgia, but the basis of the theory remains sound. When two countries are part of the global market, they are subject to anti-war pressures, because war is bad for business, or at least it was until recently. Naomi Klein mentions that economists often use an indicator called the "guns to caviar index," which measures the number of fighter jets sold versus the number of luxury jets sold (536). Until recently, whenever sales of one went up, the other went down; war hurt profits (Klein 536). In recent years, however, sales of both types of jets have gone up in tandem thanks largely to the booming homeland security and disaster recovery industries (Klein 536). War profiteering is now big business, and the golden arches may now be egging combatants on.

The last major argument against the thesis is this: corporations are just as accountable to consumers as the government is, so corporate influence over the government is just an extension of consumer influence. This argument is actually valid for most corporations. Commerce is a kind of democracy where consumers vote with their money. At first this 'vote with your money' system may seem to favor the rich, but keep in mind that the largest corporations in the world appeal primarily to the middle class. It is unlikely that Microsoft and Wal-Mart would have achieved the success that they have by just appealing to the most wealthy consumers. If consumers truly don't approve of how a business is run, they will take their money elsewhere and that business will fail. Recently the CEO of Whole Foods made statements condemning government interference in the healthcare system, and almost immediately consumers began a boycott of the chain (Grove). Upwards of 22,000 people officially joined the boycott on Facebook alone, and it is likely that many more participate in the boycott unofficially (Grove). Very few companies would be willing to intentionally alienate 22,000 of their customers. The CEO of Whole Foods will probably be more careful in the future. Corporate influence on the government can be a good thing if companies are listening to their consumers. For example, corporate pressure may have helped end apartheid, and why were corporations unhappy with apartheid? Corporations saw that consumers were boycotting goods made under the apartheid government (Waddock 1). If accountability is a concern, one can take heart in the fact that organizations like Transparency International publicize corruption in business as well as government (Waddock 2). Of course, not many people read reports by Transparency International, but more popular news sources sometimes run pieces on corporate corruption as well. Investigative journalists do reports on companies and government alike. Corporations are held accountable in much the same way government is.

The problem arises when corporations are one step removed from consumers or already have monopoly power. Corporations like the previously mentioned Giliead Sciences and Halliburton make most of their money through government contracts. Consumers will never be able boycott these companies because these companies don't have to deal with the free market. In this case, corporate influence on the government allows the corporations to escape not only the socially optimizing hand of the free market but also the moral judgments of consumers. Monsanto, on the other hand, escapes consumer influence because it monopolizes high yield genetically modified crops. Because Monsanto has patents over many vital genetic modifications, modern farmers can't afford to boycott the company. Farmers have nowhere else to go for these genetically modified crops and no way to compete without them. In theory, the government is supposed to move to break up monopolies like Monsanto, but big agribusiness lobbies too effectively for that to ever happen. Once corporations have enough political power to free themselves from the free market, even mass consumer actions will not be able to correct the problem.

There is, however, a solution that is simple in concept and difficult in application. The solution is just campaign finance reform. If corporate donations were banned or donation caps per corporate entity were substantially lowered, legislators would have much less incentive to pander to corporate interests. Direct campaign contributions are well regulated, but "soft money" support is unregulated and can be very substantial. Thanks to a 1978 Federal Election Commission ruling, ads and donations that fund ads are not regulated as long as they don't explicitly say which side of an issue they want people to vote for ("What is the difference between soft money and hard money campaign donations?"). For example, an ad could accuse one candidate of having affairs and embezzling funds, and it could even say that the other candidate spends all her spare time building low income housing, but if it didn't specifically tell the audience to vote for one candidate over the other, it would not be regulated. Eliminating corporate control over the government would require a total overhaul of the regulatory system. Perhaps any ad that specifically mentions a candidate's name, piece of legislation, or political party would be regulated. Ads with visual representations of any of those election choices would have to be regulated as well. Corporations will probably find some way around this regulation as well, but they will have a much harder time than they do under the current system.

The problem is, of course, that all the legislators currently in power got there by using the current system to its full advantage. It is highly unlikely that they would be willing to give up their advantage without a major public movement in favor of reform, and in the modern corporation friendly political climate, such a movement is unlikely. So how do the American people get these changes enacted? How can they break corporate hegemony on government policy and reverse market failures? They must demand campaign finance reform. As long as many issues eclipse campaign finance reform in the public view, legislators will push it onto the back burner, because the current system works in their favor. The American people might even have to elect legislators who are new to politics and don't have as many big business allies. Incumbency is the enemy of reform. Overall, Americans will have to exercise their democratic rights to an extent seldom seen in the last hundred years.

Works Cited

Friedman, Thomas L. *Lexus and the Olive Tree*. New York: Randomhouse, 2000. Print.

Klein, Naomi. *The Shock Doctrine: the Rise of Disaster Capitalism.*
    New York, N.Y.: Picador, 2007. Print.

Mankiw, N. Gregory. *Principals of Microeconomics.* 5th ed. Mason,
    OH.: Cengage Learning, 2009. Print.

Pollan, Michael. *The Omnivore's Dilemma: a Natural History of
    Four Meals.* New York, N.Y.: Penguin Books, 2007. Print.

Reason Foundation. "Wal-Mart Supports Government Health
    Care." *Opposing Viewpoints,* 30 June 2009. Web. 4 Nov 2009.
    Web.

"What is the difference between soft money and hard money
    campaign donations?" HowStuffWorks.com. 26 October
    2000. Web. 17 November 2009. Web.

"That's So . . ."

Madeline Miller

Argument: Sample Essay 4

WRTG 1150

Instructor: Michelle Albert

> *Why do particular words have such power? How can language be misused in ways that are discriminatory? In this short, informal argument, Madeline urges her readers to be more mindful and careful when they use words like "retarded" or "gay." As you'll notice, her essay includes hyperlinks—this essay was intended to be read online, so the references to other sources are formatted as hyperlinks rather than traditional print citations. You can find the URLs for each link in the footnotes.*

I was eating lunch with my friend Jess the other day, talking about a very confusing and difficult test we had just taken and she commented, "That test was retarded." She obviously was insinuating the test was stupid, not characterizing it as having a disability. Something really struck me about that comment. My friend is an intelligent and compassionate person; I was confused why she would be misusing the word *retarded*. As a college student I hear words such as *gay* and *retarded* used as derogatory terms every day of my life. You would think our vocabulary would have changed by now. Adults, especially in the media, have become more aware of their speech due to fear of potential lawsuits or losing their job. However, many young adults, especially college students, have not learned the negative implications that come from abusing words such as *retarded* and *gay*. It is absolutely necessary that our generation stop this misuse of language. If we don't change our word choices, our generation will continue spreading discrimination and further alienate people.

Recently campaigns such as "The R-Word: Spread the Word to End the Word"[1] have raised awareness about how painful it is for the word *retarded* to be used to describe something that is seen as stupid, defective, or bad. People who are mentally retarded and their friends and family are tired of this word being used so incorrectly and insensitively. The phrase itself *mental retardation* is not an insult, but when used to describe something or someone in a negative or joking way it becomes offensive. When people use *retarded* in this negative way they are unconsciously associating stupidity and defectiveness with people who are mentally retarded. Most people who casually use this word will argue that is not their intention, but ultimately this careless language leads to stereotypes and prejudices against people with disabilities. When a person is too lazy to pick a better word rather than *retarded* to use, that person is creating stereotypes and harming people's lives.

Now let's talk about the word *gay*. The word *gay* is abused in the same way as the word *retarded*. For example, a boy in my dorm says *gay* in just about every sentence he can. Upon hearing how high his rent was: "That's gay"; when disagreeing with a friend: "Dude, quit being gay." I'm confused again. How can his rent be homosexual? Why is he calling his heterosexual friend a homosexual? This boy graduated top of his class, but I'm curious why he can't seem to understand the definition of *gay*. The sad fact is he, like many others, is aware of what the word means, but he persistently uses it as a term to refer to something he doesn't like. When used correctly and in context *gay* is not bad. But when *gay* is used to describe something or someone we don't like or something strange it becomes an offensive term. It is the same with the word *retarded*. So many young people use this word as a derogatory term, and believe it's harmless. But using words in this negative way keeps discrimination alive. When *gay* is used as an insult, it implies that to be gay is something bad and stigmatized. This is incredibly offensive to homosexual individuals and implies some sort of inferiority about a person's sexual orientation.

There are many college students who do understand the effects of abusing these words and continue to use them anyway. While we cannot force such people to change their language, I would argue that many people do not realize the effects and prejudices they create. Because so many teenagers are not in positions to lose jobs

[1] "R Word." http://www.r-word.org. Web. 12 March 2013.

or suffer serious consequences because of this bad habit, they feel no incentive to quit using these words incorrectly. But pretty soon we will be the working adult population and we need to drop the bad habits. It may not be that people are trying to be hurtful; they might just be too lazy to *use a different word*! It's not rocket science or something life altering. There are some simple steps to stop using gay inappropriately.[2]

Some may argue that being politically correct is overrated. Sure, there are cases of political correctness being taken to extremes. People who choose not to misuse *retarded* and *gay* are not extreme cases of political correctness. They just are respectful and conscientious people. Those who abuse these words often contest that using them is not a big deal; they don't mean anything hurtful. Well, why don't you abuse *retarded* in front of someone with a developmental disability, or comment that something is *gay* in front of someone homosexual? You never know who around you has a best friend with Down's Syndrome or a brother who is gay. Often those who fight for political correctness are criticized as being rigid, strict, or boring. I'd say those who continue to abuse the words are rigid thinkers and boring. It's still happening, but it has become so stale and unattractive to throw around these words.

My eleven-year-old little brother has autism. The word *autistic* is not as commonly thrown around in a negative or insensitive way, but, unfortunately, I have heard it used as negative slur before. My hope for him is that by the time he goes to college, students will have found better words for expressing their feelings. I believe that it is entirely possible to restore these words to their original meaning and speak with sensitivity and dignity.

In high school I found myself abusing *retarded* and *gay* occasionally. I heard people doing it constantly, so I didn't think anything of it. But soon after I started using them, I felt like I was being mean and saying something wrong. I went to a very diverse high school and there were and many of my friends who were homosexual or had disabilities. Every time I misused one of those words, I realized I was taking a stab at those people, possibly making them feel inferior.

It wasn't a difficult change. If I heard myself saying something was *retarded* I quickly choked it down and expressed to those around me that I was trying to not abuse that word. Soon those phrases were just erased out of my vocabulary and people around me

---

[2] "How to Stop Using the Word Gay Inappropriately." http://www.wikihow.com/Stop-Using-the-Word-%22Gay%22-Inappropriately. Web. 10 March 2013.

began to cease carelessly using them as well. I started becoming so irritated when I heard people using these words as slurs, I just gently asked them to stop, and they did! If you are still using these words carelessly, it's time to stop. You are hurting real people and keeping discrimination and hateful speech alive. Don't be lazy—pick another word! If you don't abuse these words, you'll be a part of the solution. Call people out on their poor language choices and explain why it's important to you!

Reagan's "Bear" Parable

Megan Cruise

Persuasion and Rhetorical Analysis: Sample Essay 1

WRTG 1150

Instructor: Darin Graber

How do texts function persuasively? This is the central question we ask when we analyze rhetoric at work. In this essay, Megan demonstrates how the language and images in this particular political ad functioned to influence voters during the 1984 presidential election. Megan writes about specific appeals and strategies used in the ad to sway voters to view Reagan as the best candidate for president. Through rhetorical analysis, as Megan's essay shows us, we can gain a better understanding of the multiple ways a text influences its audience.

In 1984, Republican presidential candidate Ronald Reagan ran for reelection against Democrat Walter Mondale. Most of Reagan's campaign advertisements were focused on a serene message of America's progress during Reagan's first term as president. This is characterized by the well known advertisement "Morning Again in America." Yet as election day drew nearer, Reagan boldly moved toward a new approach aimed at the issues of foreign affairs. Reagan's most effective political commercial proved to be "Bear," which was a metaphorical reference to the Cold War and the arms buildup. In this 30-second clip:

> an enormous grizzly bear is shown prowling the forest, mean, angry, hungry, as the voice of a narrator is heard: "There is a bear in the woods. For some people, the

> bear is easy to see. Others don't see it at all. Some people say the bear is tame. Others say it is vicious and dangerous. Since no one can really be sure who's right, isn't it smart to be as strong as the bear—if there is a bear?" (Schram, "Reagan Aides" 1)

The bear, commonly used to represent the Soviet Union, grabbed the attention of viewers. In fact, it combined the appeals of logos and ethos to solidify Reagan's message of peace through strength. This advertisement redefined the way that voters looked at the arms buildup and the Cold War in general. It resulted in Reagan's reelection and another four years as President of the United States.

The "Bear" commercial acted as an agent to justify the arms race without increasing Cold War fear. It had a clear and logical message even though "the ad never mentioned the Soviet Union, never mentioned Democratic presidential nominee Walter F. Mondale, never betrayed the fact that it was a political ad until the very end." Typically, when a political advertisement begins by stating which candidate it is about, people of opposing beliefs will immediately turn their attention away from the commercial. By disguising the commercial as something other than political, people of all types of ideologies watched the parable without personal beliefs to distract them. The ending reveals a patriotic-looking picture of Reagan before the flag with his campaign slogan, "Peace Through Strength." Viewers "watched the bear foraging with the sort of interest they would devote to, say, a scene from 'The Wild Kingdom.' Then they would talk with each other about what they had seen." Through this commercial, individuals are given the task of discovering the meaning behind the bear. This keeps their attention focused on the advertisement, even though they may be Mondale supporters. Rather than trying to scare people with the topic of the Cold War, the

> bear proved to be a soft, easy way for them to talk about a tough problem [. . .]Their problem was that people had fear responses to ads about nuclear war and defense and international strength. Their problem was—how do you defend a hard-edged policy in a way that is widely accepted? (Schram, "Reagan Aides" 1)

Unlike Lyndon B. Johnson's controversial "Daisy" advertisement, Reagan wanted to reassure viewers about nuclear war rather than incite fear. Although fear is easily associated with the Cold War, a combination of the soothing narrator's voice and the serene natural environment keeps viewers alert yet at ease. Even the dialogue is causal and more conversational due to the use of contractions. Reagan effectively reassured people of his qualifications to handle the arms race while managing to ease the common concern of a nuclear war outbreak.

A key component of Reagan's "Bear" commercial and all of Reagan's advertisements during the 1984 election was the ethos incorporated in the writing and narration. Hal Riney, writer and narrator of "Bear" and other 1984 Reagan advertisements, was recognized for his "ability to cloak a strong message inside of a softer approach [. . .] Most political advertising hits viewers over the head, while his work makes just as strong a point but in a less confrontational and more soothing manner" (Raine 3). Unlike other powerful and to-the-point commercials, nothing was controversial about this advertisement, and yet it still influenced the way people viewed "Reagan's extraordinary military buildup" (Raine 1). Most importantly, weeks later viewers remembered seeing the commercial. "Bear" was "memorable in part because it was not what people expected political advertising to be—nasty and combative. 'It was attractive, it was beautifully executed'". The neutral and cool color palate is the opposite of loud accusations normally portrayed in a political advertisement. This contributed to peoples' trust in Reagan because he comes across as capable of handling the USSR while remaining rational and collected. Another bonus to Riney's narration was that his "approach mirrored Reagan's philosophy of communication" (Raine 3). Reagan was recognized for his clear and authoritative style of speech. Thus, the advertisement came off as trustworthy and truthful because it was what people would expect from Reagan. The tone of personal credibility set by Riney's writing and narration is original and trustworthy.

Reagan and his strategists tried to maximize the effects of the message in the "Bear" advertisement by strategically airing it on television prior to the presidential debate and repeating it numerous times. While all of Reagan's previous advertisements were focused on domestic progress, "Bear" was the first one to focus on foreign matters and was aired "on the eve of the presidential debate on foreign policy" (Schram, "Mondale Ads" 1). In order to win the election, "Each campaign views the final days as a chance to package its message and pound it home on an emotional level that will speed supporters to the polls" (Mayer 1). Strategists have often agreed that the more advertising a political candidate has, the better off the candidate is. The Reagan campaign "expects to have spent $30 million with an additional $7 million coming from the Republican National Committee." This was a strategic move that had the Republicans outspending the Democrats two to one (Mayer 1). National security was considered Reagan's greatest weakness during the 1984 campaign. As a result, his officials tried to change national security from a disadvantage to an advantage in Reagan's qualifications to continue as president. To do so, the campaign needed to continuously repeat its message of peace through strength until voters accepted and believed the message. Reagan officials attempted to get the most out of the "Bear" advertisement by airing it while millions of people were watching and repeating it enough to make it believable.

"Bear" is also effective when considered in context with Reagan's first term of presidency, which is associated with his focus on having military superiority over the USSR. As far as foreign and Cold War relations went, "Reagan's was the most anti-Soviet administration in decades". In fact, during Reagan's first term, he "pushed forward the largest peacetime military buildup since 1940" (Schulzinger 295). This background knowledge helps to prove that Reagan was the candidate most concerned with the potential threat of the Soviet Union. He had four years in office to demonstrate his tough stance against Soviet power. Some critics of Reagan argued that the "military buildup raised the specter of nuclear war" (Schulzinger 296). Reagan tries to disprove this in "Bear" by deeming it necessary to be stronger than the Soviet Union because it is impossible to predict what the USSR may do. Reagan wants to be recognized as the more prepared of the two men to handle the unpredictable aggression of the USSR.

Reagan's risk of airing a political commercial that could be misinterpreted paid off with his reelection. "Bear" was so successful that to this day, political pundits regard this campaign as being one of the most successful in history. Reagan's idea was even paralleled by George Bush in 2004 when he aired the advertisement "Wolves," which referenced September 11th and terrorism (Barnes 1). Yet, present-day political advertising is rarely similar to Riney's tone. Today, vicious attack advertisements and satirical approaches are the norm due to a different political culture. In fact, creativity and originality are almost unheard of when it comes to a twenty-first century campaign commercial.

Works Cited

Barnes, Fred. "Kerry Nation." *The Weekly Standard.* 23 Feb. 2004. Web. 28 Sept. 2008.

Bear. All Politics *CNN Time.* Sept. 1984. Web. 23 Sept. 2008.Mayer, Jane. "Republicans, Democrats Pound Message Home as Final Advertising Duel Begins." *The Wall Street Journal.* ProQuest Historical Newspapers. 1984. Web. 24 Sept. 2008.

Raine, George. "Creating Reagan's Image." *San Francisco Chronicle.* 9 June 2004. Web. 28 Sept. 2008.

Schram, Martin. "Mondale Ads Take Aim at 'Star Wars' Plan." *The Washington Post.* 2 Nov. 1984. Web. 24 Sept. 2008.

---. "Reagan Aides Bullish on 'The Bear' Ads." *The Washington Post.* 2 Nov. 1984. Web. 24 Sept. 2008.

Schulzinger, Robert D. *U.S. Diplomacy Since 1900.* New York: Oxford UP, 2008. Print.

A Rhetorical Analysis of "How Much is Left?" by Michael Moyer

Allison Langley

Persuasion and Rhetorical Analysis: Sample Essay 2

WRTG 1150

Instructor: David Rothman

While we expect political ads and commercials to be persuasive, we don't always consider how "facts" can present an argument, even by themselves. In this essay, Allison Langley succinctly demonstrates how facts—even without a lengthy textual argument—can function to present the writer's viewpoint. As rhetorician Andrea Lunsford has famously written, "Everything's an argument."

Michael Moyer's article "How Much is Left?" is a carefully constructed argument about the future of our planet's resources. Looking specifically at fossil fuels, water, food, minerals, and biodiversity, Moyer presents a timeline of just when and where our resources are expected to run out. He calls his compilation "a graphical accounting of the limits to what one planet can provide."

Because facts and figures can be dense and unwelcoming, the layout of this article is streamlined, eye-catching, and well organized. Moyer uses bold, bright colors and strong visual appeal. By displaying the statistics in this way, Moyer is advertising the information almost as an entertainment article instead of a scientific review, thereby enlarging his audience significantly—and arguing that the data should be relevant to more than just scientists.

This piece is predominantly an argument to inform. Moyer gives a short introduction, but the bulk of the article is quantitative data. Within the five subcategories, Moyer reports the estimated world supply of everything from Indium and Gold to Himalayan Ice and European Rivers. It is an argument about the future – the future of our resources, and the effect of that future on humanity. Moyer uses language mainly as a tool to introduce and explain the statistics he provides. There is no explicit proposal for action, nor is there an argument in the form of a thesis statement. In this case, the appeal to logic is hard evidence, and a lot of it. But what good is evidence without a claim?

Moyer's thesis is never stated, but implied. Since resource depletion affects our generation and our children's generations, there is at least an expectation that we will care about the subject matter. But Moyer wants even more from us. His audience consists of well-educated and curious members of civil society. Certainly, most of them will have heard deliberation about global warming, sources of oil, and so on. But in truth, it is easy to read about these topics without fully realizing their potential impact. What Moyer has done is to lay these issues out on a timeline to give them immediacy and make environmental concerns more tactile. He isn't producing an argument weighed down with political commentary—just the data. His argument, fundamentally, is that we should care about resource depletion, and that we should care about it now.

> What Moyer has done is to lay these issues out on a timeline to give them immediacy and make environmental concerns more tactile.

Moyer's authority as the writer is evident in his sources; although he is not an expert himself, he has done the necessary research. He cites scientific journals as well as lectures and books written by experts. No information or credentials are given about Moyer himself. Therefore, his ethos is demonstrated in a different way: through the creation of trust. From the very beginning – the title – Moyer asks a question which we trust he will answer. In the introductory paragraphs, he notes that "the constraints on our resources and environment…will shape the rest of this century and beyond." In other words, he's answering the question of why the article matters. He presents the information logically and clearly, and appropriately cites his research.

The strategy of Moyer's argument in "How Much is Left?" is to deliver the data with clarity, precision, and accessibility. Moyer doesn't want to overwhelm his audience with facts, so he displays them graphically, in a way which makes them easy to understand.

He uses language to guide the reader through the facts, but there are no unnecessary embellishments or deviations. Using all of these tactics to cement our interest as an audience, Moyer gives us a look into the future, from an era "seemingly without boundaries" to one in which we must face a finite Earth.

Works Cited

Moyers, Michael. "How Much Is Left?" *Scientific American*. September 2010: 74-81.

Speechwriter Assignment: Part 1, The Speech

Patricia Lee Thomas

Persuasion and Rhetorical Analysis: Sample Essay 3

WRTG 1250

Instructor: Petger Schaberg

This student example comprises two pieces. In the first piece, Patricia adopts the persona of a real person in order to compose a speech directed to a real audience. In the second piece, Patricia analyzes the rhetoric she uses in her speech. Taken together, the two show some of the relationships among speaker, message, audience, and context.

Introduction: Flemming Rose, an editor of the *Jyllad-Posten* (a Danish newspaper that printed inflammatory cartoons depicting the Islamic faith) speaks to an audience of American journalists, editors, and other media communications. He seeks to persuade the audience to see that censorship has replaced the freedom of speech, and that something must be done.

I thank you all for being here. I am excited to address the ideas of media and censorship in terms of politics. As an editor, I know that some information must be cut out. Extraneous information, articles that do not necessarily fit our newspaper, *Jyllad-Posten,* and pieces that could lose us funding all fall under that category. However, the self-censorship we impose on our print is imposed only by us; it is not government censorship, and it is not media censorship under government propaganda. Our decision to print the cartoons depicting Muhammad and other aspects of the Islamic faith demonstrates our power, as a media group, to print and say what we feel needs to be seen or heard. The cartoons, especially the one of Muhammad with a bomb for a turban, did indeed create conflict and aggression from the Muslim opposition, but it also gave us an opportunity to discuss the ideas of Islam, violence, and fanaticism with our Danish Muslim communities. More unfortunate than the outraged Muslims were the seemingly uninterested America media. Your response to these cartoons—of not printing them—made me realize that it was not so much the controversial nature of the cartoons that made them unappealing to print, but the oppressing nature and fear of censorship and propaganda throughout the entire media. I am here today to discuss the issues of government propaganda and self-censorship in the media, and to persuade you that change must take place for the sake of freedom.

America has returned to censorship; just as during World War II, when images of the dead were restricted, your president has banned the images of wounded and dead in the media. Ironically, the restrictions in WWII were lifted in order to draw support for the war, whereas your president has imposed these restrictions to keep the public interested in it. Well, the irony has got to stop. Doesn't it enrage you that you cannot print pictures of the flag-draped coffins of all those courageous soldiers who gave their lives for the ideal of freedom? If you didn't realize it before, think about it now: The media have become puppets of propaganda for the government's agenda. President Bush will not allow the images of the coffins to appear in media sources because he needs public approval to stay high; the images of death force the public to reconsider the consequences of war. This censorship, even in the slightest, hinders the pursuit of freedom. By allowing such censorship, the media become accustomed to the infractions committed against free speech, and continue simply because they know no other way.

Apart from propaganda, fear has a profound effect on people and often encourages unconscious self-censorship. In the media, from journalists to editors alike, it is fear; fear of the opposition, fear of losing a job, fear of death, fear of being unpatriotic, that contributes to mass censorship. I attribute the act of not publishing the Danish cartoons to this fear. But you cannot let this pervade your work, and your duty to give perspective and report on a story. Nor should this fear dissuade you from choosing a different article for a layout because it might be less financially successful. No, we must grab fear by the horns and dispose of the beast so that journalism and media communications can again have the freedom of their words and expression.

Your government created a bill called the Patriot Act, mandating cooperation with the government in the name of Patriotism.

Nobody wants to be labeled unpatriotic, and so the media, out of fear of labels, avoid writing or reporting on an issue that might make them seem unpatriotic. In other words, they cooperate to such an extent that civil liberties are taken for granted and ignored. The flag-draped coffins once again exemplify this: The president's ban on these images has not been tested because the media are too afraid of the consequences. Why can't the media show the coffins of all the brave soldiers who died nobly? Isn't it important to report on issues that make people think about their actions? Your fear-imposed censorship transforms you into puppets of the government, making you the government's primary tools of propaganda. Even the name given to this war, "The War on Terror," expresses deep irony; as you report on the "War on Terror," you feed a different kind of terror, the same one that makes you cooperate with the government so easily, so readily. The role of the media in this war is a war in itself; however, the opposition, your freedom of speech, is weak, and the government is winning.

The government has a special relationship with the media, one that is, however, unbalanced; the government has been using the media in ways to benefit its agenda, but it has deeply hurt journalism. Imagine being sent out into the field, embedded with a battalion. You're hot and lonely, and the only people you really talk to are military personnel. You're dehydrated and hungry, but the only way for you to get sustenance is the military. You're tired and scared, and the only way for you to find shelter and receive protection is through the military. What do you think you will report on? The close quarters between the two can often create deep, personal, and of course biased relationships. The use of embedded reporters during this war has also created a union between government and media, two previously sworn enemies. Reporters talk to soldiers freely, whereas in the Vietnam War reporters were something to be wary of. These new relationships influence the footage that makes it to the public, but the press does not always release and show the footage depicting the realness of the war. So what is shown? Censored materials: Government-approved images, and self-censored outside perspectives. Although this helps the government by showing images of the war in Iraq, these images are decided upon in government offices and are not a fair nor reliable account of the entire war.

Journalism has been suffering as the government offers the media an easy substitute for reporting. Media communications reflect an attitude of taking what's given, rather than searching, uncovering, and reporting the issues. This laziness has narrowed media communications, leaving only a government-biased stance, when the media should emphasize outside perspectives and should exercise their privilege of free speech. Outside, non-government-biased perspectives, once reported and printed, reflect the free expression so greatly revered in the US. But outside reporters are scarce, and their articles and perspectives are even more so. Does this lack of perspective make you proud to be a journalist? Does this make you reconsider your freedoms? Does this make you want to make a change?

As savvy journalists and editors, you have a choice about what to write and what to print. The government does not make this decision for you. And if it does, then you should fight it, in the name of your sacred freedom. I urge you to do what I did: Take a chance and print controversial, sometimes offensive material. Print articles that offer an outside perspective on the war. Print images and ideas that are the expression of your free speech. Like the cartoons, this material might bring about some much-needed discussion. Above all, I ask that you consider your civil liberties, your freedom, and make your decisions with that in the back of your mind, always. Don't let your outlet to discuss important issues become corrupt and run-down with government ideas on censorship and propaganda. Stand strong, and support your country's ideology of freedom of expression through speech and press.

Speechwriter Assignment: Part 2, Rhetorical Analysis

Patricia Lee Thomas

Flemming Rose, the editor of the now infamous *Jyllad-Posten* newspaper, in which the Danish cartoons depicting Islam were first printed, speaks to an audience of American journalists and editors. The colloquial diction he uses creates empathy between the audience and the speaker. The structure of the speech centers around two main images of censorship: the ban of the flag-draped coffin images, and the embedded reporters working in the field. I also employ rhetorical devices such as analogies, metaphors, rhetorical questions, repetition, and parallel structure to persuade the audience to move away from a time of censorship, fear, and propaganda, whether government or self-imposed.

The introduction to the speech highlights the speaker's ethos through his use of words, while the ironic analogy to past censorship questions the very basis for why censorship exists. The phrase "as an editor" draws a connection between the audience and the speaker, and establishes, within the first few lines of the speech, an empathetic ethos that holds the audience's attention and elicits respect. The analogy between the "War on Terror" and WWII use of censorship delineates the potential purpose of it. The ironic juxtaposition of lifting censorship to gain support for a war with imposing censorship to gain support for a war makes the latter appear unnecessary and wrong. I use irony to suggest to the audience that their views might also be wrong, through subtle humor.

The visual image of the flag-draped coffins makes an ethical appeal to the press and a pathos-based appeal to American pride. Within the rhetorical question "Doesn't it enrage you that you cannot print pictures of the flag-draped coffins of all those courageous soldiers who gave their lives for the ideal of freedom?" phrases such as "courageous soldiers" and "ideal of freedom" serve as symbols of American pride and freedom. By appealing to the emotions of the audience, I create more empathy between the speaker and audience, increasing the chance of persuasion. The speaker attempts to persuade the audience that the government is one reason for the censorship of images: "The media have become puppets of propaganda for the government's agenda." The metaphor compares the media to puppets, an image that explains that the media have no power, nor do they retain any benefit from serving as the government's tool for propaganda. The government can manipulate the media without any consequences. This metaphor serves as a warning for the audience and might frighten them into persuasion.

Just as the first image uses pathos and ethos, the image of embedded reporters uses logos. The second-person words "you're hot and lonely ... you're dehydrated and hungry. . . you're tired and scared" force the audience to take the place of the embedded reporter and understand what the job entails. The following rhetorical question, "What do you think you will report on?" suggests that the audience can report only with an enormous bias toward the military. The rhetorical question directs the contrived answer but still gives the audience a chance to think and interpret the question for themselves. This encourages persuasion, as the hearers feel as though they have come to a conclusion on their own. The parallel structure creates a fluidity and rhythm in speaking. The use of logos through the rhetorical question adds another element that the audience can grasp and believe.

Apart from the two main images of the speech, the speaker en-courages the thought that fear acts as an overpowering reason for censorship. I use repetition and parallel structure within the syntax to create rhythm, which emphasizes a fluid, charis-matic sound. "In the media. . . it is fear; fear of the opposition, fear of losing a job, fear of death, fear of being unpatriotic, that contributes to mass censorship." The emphasis on the word *fear* suggests that its pervasiveness is the reason for censorship. One must "grab fear by the horns and dispose of the beast so that. . . media communications can again have freedom." This metaphor, comparing fear to a dangerous beast and human power and intelligence to the conquerer of the beast, shows the struggle between fear and human intelligence. The phrase "by the horns" suggests the confidence one needs to face fear, yet juxtaposes this idea with the vulnerability of being head-on to the beast, or fear.

I create a metaphor so that the audience can see, in a more visual manner, the pervasive qualities of fear and the confidence and vulnerability inherently attached to fighting it.

Lastly, the appeal to logos also comes from the statements and refutations of the counterargument. Within the first paragraph of the speech, the speaker presents the counterargument: "The cartoons. . . did indeed create conflict and aggression from the Muslim opposition." By stating the counterargument, the speaker appears confident in his argument, meaning his argument becomes more enticing in its persuasive qualities. The refutation, "but it also gave us an opportunity to discuss the ideas of Islam," demonstrates the superiority of his argument. The logical transition from the counter to the refutation is also found in another counterargument about embedded reporters later in the speech.

Through the use of rhetorical questions, parallel structure, metaphors, and analogies, I develop the speaker's voice as powerful and persuasive. The speech shows the audience the impact of censorship and propaganda with regard to fear and the government. Through these rhetorical devices, the speaker, Flemming Rose, can powerfully persuade the audience to move in the direction of free speech and leave the times of censorship in the past.

Genre Analysis of Letters

Evan Fernandez

Genre Analysis: Sample Essay 1

WRTG 1250

Instructor: Kathryn Pieplow

This short piece provides a good example of genre analysis discussed in chapter five. In it, Evan Fernandez responds to Bruce Ballenger's piece "On the Importance of Writing Badly" by rewriting some of his ideas as a letter to the "grammar police." He then reflects on the generic features of letters, commenting on their suitability for specific audiences.

May 13, 2011

Grammar Police
Grammar Police Building
3434 Ophelia Avenue.
Maui, Hawaii

Dear Grammar Police,

You do not understand how to teach students to write. You are hypocrites who have the effect of discouraging students. You swarm over any mistake, and capitalize on any opportunity to identify and criticize any sentence that isn't perfect. You want students to learn to write successfully, but when you so harshly grade them, it makes them dislike the activity, and plummets their confidence. Not every child is born Shakespeare. Expecting them to learn without giving them the chance and the proper guidance to do so is hypocritical and stupid! I propose that students should begin writing by doing bad and messy writing. This entails simply getting ideas on a page without regard for proper sentence structure, grammar, revision, or quality. This helps students get started and will eventually lead to them understanding more about how to write, and to enjoy the activity at a higher level. A quote I go by is: "What matters in this journey—at least initially—is not what kind of car you're driving, but where you end up."

Sincerely,

Good Writing Teacher (you can also call me Bruce)

Genre Analysis

A letter is a unique genre in that it has a very specific and limited purpose, audience, and format. The Quote Garden puts forth this quote from an unknown author: "What a wonderful thing is the mail, capable of conveying across continents a warm human hand-clasp." An aspect of letters that is very significant is that they have a personal touch that helps to convey their message. This is greatly effective for letters with an important purpose.

The audience for this genre is very specific. This is so because when one writes a letter, they are writing specifically to convey a message to that person or group. For example, a principal of a middle school writes a letter to all the parents of her school addressing how the daily schedule will change once construction of a new portion of the school commences. This information is very important to those students and parents, but anyone outside the school's immediate community could not care less. This demonstrates how the letter only serves a specific audience. The audience could get even more specific. For example, instead of writing a letter to the population of the school's parents, the principal may write a letter just to one parent who has responsibility in the construction. That parent could be the coordinator of the construction. This letter would contain information that would be important to an even more limited audience. An exception to this rule is when letters are used for academic purposes. For example, letters written by important figures in history could augment the knowledge historians have of a time period and aid in their studies. Overall though, the audience for letters is very specific and limited.

The purpose that a letter serves reflects the audience it serves, in that it is very specific. Letters are written when an important and precise piece of information needs to be relayed from one person to another. There are forms of communication such as texting that can be used to relay information, but when information that is more important and detailed needs to be communicated, people resort to writing and mailing letters. This is so that they can describe exactly what they desire to communicate to the exact people/ person they want to. This helps if the information is private and intended only to be read by the desired audience. In today's world, there is less of an exigence for this genre, due to communication forms such as telephone, email, and online chatting, than there was 100 years ago, but it still is important. This is so because it is much more personal of a message when someone composes a letter in their own hand, and sends it to someone personally. This will emphasize the significance of the letter to the reader, and can help the author get what they desire. For example, a person who writes a letter asking their neighbor to stop playing loud music at night will be much more likely to be listened to, than someone who sends an impersonal email. This effect is created by this genre, and helps to illustrate the need for letters in today's society.

The format a letter has is very precise. In the upper right-hand corner, are the address of the author, the date, and the address of the recipient below the date. Then a letter always begins with "Dear Recipient" or some other formal type of greeting. The purpose for the letter is then stated, almost like a thesis statement. The author is explaining why they wrote the letter, and what they desire from the reader. In the ensuing paragraphs, is just additional information elaborating and echoing on the sentiments of the letter's original purpose. At the end of the letter, the author gives a farewell to the reader, by stating the author's name with a farewell phrase. For example, "Sincerely, Bruce." Also, in some cases, letters are signed with the handwritten signature of the author. The format of the genre is very detailed.

In conclusion the letter is a genre that is not left up to creativity. It has a precise audience, purpose, and format. "A piece of handwritten or printed text addressed to a recipient and typically sent by mail," is the definition given to this genre by bing.com. This simple definition reflects how letters are not a device used for creative fun, but are utilized for an exact purpose.

Works Cited

Ballenger, Bruce. "The Importance of Writing Badly." *The Curious Writer*. Upper Saddle River, NJ: Pearson, 2004. 32-34. Print.

A Day to Forget and Remember

Mike Rotolo

Critical Inquiry Sample Portfolio

In some ways, this portfolio might be seen as an example of how the three primary processes involved in critical inquiry—analysis, argument, and inquiry—can work together to explore a topic in depth. This portfolio represents one writer's attempt to make sense of a confusing—indeed, terrifying—event that occurred in his own high school and to use that experience as an occasion to explore larger issues in American education and culture.

All of the samples were written by Mike Rotolo, a student in Paula Wenger's WRTG 1150 class, in response to an assignment sequence that asked students to expand the context for writing about a topic of immediate interest to them. For the first paper, students wrote a personal essay based on their own experience, observation, or perspective. For the next two papers—an annotated bibliography and an academic paper—students identified an issue from their personal essays to explore further through research. The final assignment was a civic essay on another issue drawn from the personal and academic papers or a variation on the issue explored in the academic paper, written for a particular publication with a definable audience. Based on the student's personal perspective, informed and shaped by research, the civic essay presented an argument on the issue to a nonacademic audience. This assignment sequence was designed to take students through the process of using academic sources and skills to deepen personal experience for the purpose of contributing more effectively to work and civic communities beyond the academy.

Personal Narrative

The noises reminded me of a brick of Black Cat firecrackers that I hear exploding every year on the Fourth of July. Even when several teachers ran in and out of my sophomore science class, I thought that some clever seniors were pulling off another prank. I even used the time when my teacher was out of the room to compare test answers with a fellow classmate. It was not until the first pipe bomb exploded and several students fled into our room that I realized that this was more than a senior prank. The noises that I had thought were simple firecrackers were actually the first shots fired during the tragedy at Columbine High School on April 20, 1999.

The students who had fled into our room from the cafeteria on the first floor told us how men dressed in black and armed with shotguns were shooting people outside of the school. I still did not believe the ignorant freshman until a wounded faculty member, Dave Sanders, stumbled through our door and collapsed on the floor. Through the shrieks of my female classmates, I could hear Mr. Sanders screaming in pain. He had been shot through the back of his neck and once through the back and his heart. My science teacher was instructing us to hide behind our desks because no one was sure where the shooters were, or even how many shooters there were. As we hid, our teacher scrambled to turn the television on, looking for any information regarding the chaos that had just begun. The local news told us that up to 150 of our classmates were wounded or dead, and this was 15 minutes after the first shot.

With the fire alarms and passing period bells ringing loudly, I sat behind my flipped desk, while other teachers entered our room and instructed the boys in the class to remove our shirts so that they could be used to stop the blood that spilled from Mr. Sanders's serious wounds. With the shirt barely off my back, I was lifted off my feet by my teacher and given a dry-erase board that read, "1 bleeding to death." I held the sign in the window, fearful that I myself would be a target for one of the shooters, while several local news helicopters flew in to film the message. After being spotted by a crouching police officer, I once again retreated behind my flipped school desk. From the phone inside our room, the police told us that they would have Mr. Sanders and the rest of us out of the classroom in 20 minutes, but the screams coming from our wounded teacher lasted for four and a half hours.

Several of my classmates led us in prayer, but the cries of pain silenced every one of us over and over. Some of the students began to show Mr. Sanders pictures of his daughters, telling him that his three beautiful girls were just one of many reasons why he had to live, and to hold on for the paramedics for one more minute.

I wanted to believe that the paramedics would be there in one minute, but 11:30 a.m. turned to 2:00 p.m., which then turned to 4:15 p.m. With each passing minute, I began to feel more and more frustrated and angry, while previous worries about the destruction that had been taking place in my school began to numb away. When the S.W.A.T. unit finally arrived, the time was 4:21 p.m.—five hours after the first shot had been fired. For five hours, I wondered if any of my friends had been wounded, or worse yet, killed. I thought of all the parents outside of the school who did not know if their child, their baby, had been shot or killed in the school that day.

When the door to our classroom was kicked in, a fear like I have never experienced filled every cell of my body. I wasn't sure if these men in black were the S.W.A.T. team or the killers, but a giant shield that read Denver PD settled all of our hearts. They told us that we would all be fine, and that Mr. Sanders would be taken to a hospital as soon as possible. That moment of security lasted only a second because as we were led from the classroom we heard the weak breath of our wounded teacher scream, "Tell my girls I love them." At the time it did not strike me, but I was later told that those would be Mr. Sanders's last words. We were brought from our classroom and for the first time saw the damage that had been done.

Broken glass, bullet holes, blood-stained carpet, a flooded cafeteria, bullet shells, and even our murdered classmates are what we passed as we were led out of the school at gunpoint by police officers. We were all suspects since the shooters were students. Anyone of us could have pulled the trigger, changed clothes, and fled into a classroom, even me. But the thought of who would do such a thing flopped over and over in my mind.

I felt the tears well up in my eyes when I saw my mom waiting for me at the park next to our school. My helplessness must have been evident from first sight because my mother scooped my 180-pound body up in her arms as if I were a newborn child and held me tighter than she ever has. I wanted to tell her that I wasn't scared, and that I would be fine, but I was worried about Mr. Sanders and all of my friends.

> We sat perplexed, staring into each other's puffy eyes, asking questions that we knew had no answers.

My mother told me that I was the last of my friends to exit the school and that the majority of the 2,400 students who attended

Columbine had escaped within five minutes of the first shot. I also learned that one of my friends, Matthew Kecter, had been murdered that day, along with 11 other students and Mr. Sanders.

I cried with my friends for days. They wouldn't stop hugging me. We sat perplexed, staring into each other's puffy eyes, asking questions that we knew had no answers. Sitting in my basement with all of my friends seemed to be our only escape from chaos, our only safe haven. I remember listening to my friend Jon tell us that we needed to live every day like it was our last, and that our fear and confusion would be diminished as long as we helped one another through our times of need. It was then that I realized how precious life truly is and that each of us needed to live our lives to the fullest, for ourselves and for those whose lives were stolen from them during the tragedy. I miss my friend and I will never forget the events that happened that day in my life.

Violence and Education: An Annotated Bibliography

Mike Rotolo

Research (Annotated Bibliography)

Addington, Lynn Andrea. "The Columbine Effect: The Impact of Violent School Crime on Students' Fear of Victimization." *Dissertation Abstracts International Section A: Humanities and Social Sciences,* Dec. 2002. Print.

> Addington discusses the fear of victimization experienced after Columbine by other students around the nation. This article uses polls to gather responses on the impact of Columbine in the categories of students' fear, protective behavior, and changes in school security. The author also uses the National Crime Victimization Surveys as the basis for much of her study.

> This article makes good use of surveys to find the effects on students who have not witnessed a violent act firsthand, who are still affected by the violence seen elsewhere. This article also gives brief information regarding what actions some schools are taking to prevent such events.

Arman, John. "In the Wake of Tragedy at Columbine High School." *Professional School Counseling* 3.3 (Feb. 2000): 218–20. Print.

> Author John Arman briefly explores the most common causes that are associated with violence among America's youth. He

looks at topics ranging from violence in the media to violent video games and movies. Arman also discusses which of these theories have been the most popular and why.

Arman's article gives me the most popular and least popular reasons that people have come up with as to why students in schools are becoming violent. Although Arman does not go into great detail, he gives a wide range and understanding of the different theories.

Bender, William, Phillip McLaughlin, and Terresa Shubert. "Invisible Kids: Preventing School Violence by Identifying Kids in Trouble." *Intervention in School & Clinic* **37.2 (Nov. 2001): 105–11. Print.**

This article aims to inform the reader of ways to identify adolescents who have the potential for violent outbursts. The authors look closely at the shootings at Columbine High and Heritage High and cover issues spanning from bullying all the way to gun control.

From this article, I was able to find information regarding how the weapons in each of the cases were obtained, as well as many determining factors in why each of the killers acted so violently.

Quinnan, Timothy. "Preparing for the Moment When a Student's Rage Turns to Violence." *Chronicle of Higher Learning* **45.49 (13 Aug. 1999): B7. Print.**

This article discusses the cause of violence among students in schools around the United States. The author uses experiences with students before and after tragedies to explore the cause and effect of such events as Columbine High. This article also looks at possible ways to prepare schools and universities for school shootings or other traumatic incidents.

This article examines many different causes for violence in schools at both a high school and college level. It also briefly touches on effects on students and ways to cope and prevent similar situations.

Soskis, Benjamin. "Bully Pulpit." *The New Republic.* **14 May 2001: 25–27. Print.**

Author Benjamin Soskis focuses on bullying as a factor influencing adolescents to act violently. He explores the differences between the students who bully and the students who are bullied. Soskis also looks at different factors that might make a violent combination if added to being bullied.

"Bully Pulpit" gives me detailed information about what type of children bully and why they do it. This article also looks at how to identify those who are bullied and also how to identify children who seemed troubled by isolation.

Ulschmid, Nancy. "The Psychological Consequences of Community Violence Exposure: What Variables Protect Children in Urban Settings?" *Dissertation Abstracts International Section A: Humanities and Social Sciences,* **Feb. 2002. Print.**

The author studies 121 students, ages 11–15, who have been exposed to violent acts while attending public schools. She analyzes effects ranging from disabilities to stress and anxiety syndromes. This study also looks at the difference in the effect of violent acts on boys and girls.

This article will provide data taken from students who have witnessed a violent act to analyze several effects. This article gives both demographics that had little effect and those that had a greater effect.

Eliminating Violence and Trauma

Mike Rotolo

Argument

As newspaper headlines more frequently involve violence or violent acts and the top story on a local news station is a report about a murder, one may start to wonder why this sort of violence is showing up in classrooms and schools everywhere. There are many beliefs and theories on why violence in schools is becoming more common, but in the wake of such tragedies as Columbine High School in Littleton, Colorado, and Heritage High in Conyers, Georgia, many ideas about causes, as wells as effects, of these acts of violence become seemingly more evident. Regardless of the number of victims or severity of violent acts in schools, the classroom simply has no place for such behavior, and many new methods aim to diminish it. By addressing what causes students to act so violently toward one another, schools will be able to prevent violence before it occurs and eliminate lifelong scars, whether physical or emotional, that come from witnessing a violent act. With this better understanding of our students as both perpetrators and victims of violent acts, parents, teachers, counselors, and principals will possess the knowledge it takes to operate an environment of learning, understanding, and responsibility.

The most common question that can barely be understood through the rivers of tears that stream down the faces of students, teachers, and family members alike when dealing with a traumatic experience is why? Why did they do it? Why our school? Scholars all over the world look for these answers every time violence and schools mix together. Many point the finger at the "darker dimensions of popular culture, such as violent video games and movies, 'gangsta' rap music, and misanthropic World-Wide Web sites and chat rooms" (Quinnan 1). In many cases, the entire American culture, most importantly the media, is being examined and also blamed for many of the violent outbursts that are revealing themselves in our nation's schools.

As entertainment industries make billions of dollars a year selling sex, violence, and action to fan bases reaching nearly every inch of the United States, many are questioning the effect that this may be having on our nation's youth. Even musicians such as Marilyn Manson and other rock stars who stray away from the MTV norm are being accused of making music that provokes violence and anger in young Americans. However, many believe that the violence and anger that are often depicted in music videos, movies, and television shows are not affecting the actual perpetrators of these violent acts seen in schools; instead it is provoking some students to harass and bully their peers who are seen as different. As scholars begin to investigate different causes for America's violent culture, the most common reason offered is that the "bully" is now "the embodiment of a youth culture so cruel that it leads the persecuted to kill" (Soskis 1). In other words, being mocked or mistreated by a peer for whatever reason causes these already emotionally hurt students to snap. Although seventy-five percent of adolescents admit to being bullied and five million elementary and junior high students are bullied each year, many still believe that bullying, despite how common it is, combined with certain personality traits, can be a mixture for an act of violence (Bulach, Fulbright, Williams 1). Still, many wonder why being bullied can push some students to the point of murder and often suicide when more than three quarters of American adolescents experience bullying. The latest acts of violence seen in Colorado and Georgia reveal startling similarities in traits that are found in all of the perpetrators. The first is that each of the white males, T.J. Solomon in Georgia and Dylan Klebold and Eric Harris in Colorado, demonstrated indicators to peers of emotional problems and a low regard for life. Other similarities include alienation from family and friends, warnings given to others in advance by talking about killing someone, average or above-average intelligence, and deliberate actions on the day of the shooting (Bender, McLaughlin Shubert 2). Each of these factors can be combined with the experience of being bullied, or picked on, to generate many scenarios that might be the reason for these violent acts.

> Many believe that if guns were not so accessible in our society, violent and potentially deadly acts would be nonexistent in classrooms and in schools.

The most important of these factors that might create the combination for violence when added to being bullied are emotional factors. T.J. Solomon, the shooter in Georgia, had been under medical treatment for depression, and one of the shooters from Colorado, Eric Harris, was described as a troubled teen who was suffering from obsession and depression. The mixture of bullying and depression creates alienation from not only family and friends but also from the larger school community. This depression and constant battering of self-esteem generates itself into an eventual lowering or declining respect for life. This cycle and disregard for life is especially exemplified in the actions of Klebold and Harris, by the statements of dissatisfaction they made both before and during the shooting, and also by the vast number of victims. By ruthlessly killing whoever they could, Klebold and Harris demonstrated their lack of care and respect for their victims' lives, and by killing randomly they proved their alienation from the entire school community by showing hatred for all. These internal behaviors are often manifested from being picked on by more aggressive students and are evident in prior warnings that went unnoticed: "Prior to the Columbine Shooting, a video made by Harris and Klebold for a video production class showed the boys acting out a scene that involved anger, violence, and revenge". Solomon too showed his true feelings when "following the breakup with his girlfriend he became angry and spoke of suicide and bringing a gun to school." Solomon also told two classmates that he had no reason to live and that he would blow up the classroom, and this just one day prior to the shooting (Bender, McLaughlin, Shubert 2). With underlying emotions of negativity and depression, the only escape from the relentless torment and humiliation caused by being bullied was an act of violence, carried out by hatred and with cruelty.

Despite the popularity of the belief that school bullies pushed the already troubled teens to their breaking point, still others believe in and insist on other causes of school violence. Many believe that if guns were not so accessible in our society, violent and potentially deadly acts would be nonexistent in classrooms and in schools. The Tec-DC9 semiautomatic firearm used by Klebold and Harris at Columbine was purchased by a friend at a gun show and then given to them. Also, Klebold's girlfriend admitted to "buying a Hi-Point semiautomatic carbine and two 1969 Savage shotguns," (Bender, McLaughlin, Shubert 2), all of which were used during the massacre. The weapons used by Harris and Klebold were the first used in a string of school shootings where the guns were actually purchased. Accessibility to guns also helped Solomon execute his plan because he was able to take guns from an unlocked display case in his family's home and the ammunition needed for the weapons from a drawer underneath. In both of these cases, the accessibility of firearms helped the perpetrators unleash their fury in fatal ways. Without this easy access, the teens would have been forced to deal with their depression and anger in other ways, and although they still might have turned to violence, it would have taken place on a much smaller scale. Many believe that the availability of weapons such as guns provoke troubled teens to take the most drastic measures when coping with problems, as opposed to reaching out for help or finding another, more positive emotional outlet. Many point to other causes such as "out of touch parents, unrestricted access on the Internet to information on how to build pipe bombs, the effects of mental illness, over-burdened school counselors, lacking resources for mental health services in schools, racism, and violence in the media" (Arman 3). No matter what the cause, students are still pushed to their breaking point, and violence is usually an inevitable outcome, while the cost of these outbursts is the lives of their victims and traumatic effects experienced by many.

With so many fingers pointing to different causes and putting blame on others, many rarely stop to think about the various levels and types of effects that a violent act such as a school shooting might cause. Although most acts of violence cause trauma to those who were present, tragedies like the school shootings in Colorado and Georgia had effects on students, teachers, parents, entire communities, and even the entire nation. One consequence of violent acts of this size is a feeling and fear of victimization at school among students nationwide (Addington 1). In most parts of the country, victimization felt by students was only moderate and simply increased school security, although very minimally. In towns such as Littleton and Conyers, however, different effects were present because of the magnitude of the tragedy that occurred in their schools, yet even these effects were in different forms and different levels. For example, "Children who directly experience the event face higher risk than do children who witness the event from a distance" (Kirk 1). Already, two different risk levels are set up simply by an adolescent's location or involvement in the actual event. For those who simply witness the act from a distance, a feeling of victimization will again be present, but survivor's guilt also emerges because of relationships with those who were directly involved, either as close witnesses or victims. Although some will experience different levels, most of the students and school personnel who witnessed Columbine "have suffered from survivor guilt, anger, overwhelming grief, and essentially post-traumatic stress syndrome" (Arman 1). Of these symptoms, the most common and the symptom with the greatest risk of disabling the life of a person is post-traumatic stress disorder (PTSD).

Many people with PTSD repeatedly re-experience the ordeal in the form of flashback episodes, memories, nightmares, or frightening thoughts, especially when they are exposed to events or objects reminiscent of the trauma. Common side effects usually result in the witness experiencing emotional numbness and sleep disturbances, depression, anxiety, and irritability or outbursts of anger. Post-traumatic stress disorder can last a minimum of one month; however, each victim will handle his or her disorder differently, so recovery times cannot be accurately estimated.

Other problems experienced by firsthand witnesses include major depression, anxiety, and behavior problems. The side effects that are experienced by those who witnessed the violence can vary because of the gender of the adolescent, but the adolescent response also differs from the level at which adults who witnessed the tragedy are affected. Adolescent girls, for example, reported a wider range of trauma symptoms such as sensation-seeking, atypicality, somatization, social stress, and inadequacy that most boys do not encounter (Ulschmid 1). The differences in effects caused by a violent act are also different than that of adults. Adults or teachers, who are obviously much older, have had a life full of experience and thus are equipped to deal with their emotions on a much more rational level. Although these effects may be on the same level as the students, "adolescents are particularly at risk because of issues surrounding identity formation, self esteem, and developmental differences in coping mechanisms" (Kirk 1). For these reasons, an adult will handle his or her emotions better due to experience, whereas adolescents and young teens are still trying to find themselves and still experiencing new emotions. Although emotions such as survivor guilt, anger, and victimization are usually short-term effects, many witnesses, regardless of gender and age, will experience trauma for a long period of time. Feelings of anxiety, depression, and PTSD will often stay with individuals until they confront the symptoms, which are often prolonged because of denial. Although the long-term effects of witnessing an act of violence such as school shootings are still being studied, it is known that experiencing such an event can be traumatic for long periods of time and can even be life altering. As school violence such as the events in Littleton and Conyers begins to become more common, many people are now focusing their attention on how to prevent these acts from happening by reaching these troubled teens before they act out in desperation.

Initially, the idea of preventing these horrible acts of violence seemed very clear. Identify the children who are in and out of the principal's office because of their bullying, aggressive behavior, or other conduct disorders. These externalizing behaviors that are displayed by these students are immediately noticed by their teachers, and they are identified as potential violent students. However, as school violence seems to be more frequent, evidence is proving that these "aggressive students" are not actually the perpretrators of school violence. Instead, the "students who are easiest to ignore are using violence to offset and counteract their anonymity" (Bender, McLaughlin, Shubert 3). These students have internalized their aggression, as opposed to the more common externalizaton, and it results in an explosion of violence. With these astounding new findings, new ways of identifying teens who are potentially violent are being developed.

After finding that the students responsible for the recent tragedies in many schools were virtually unknown to many school officials prior to the shooting incidents, many schools implemented Warning List and Profiling to identify all students. Although this was an effective way to track children with previous violent outbursts, it was still very difficult to identify those who might potentially act out. Problems with the Warning List method of profiling students arise very frequently because it is "dependent on the teachers' knowledge of the emotional well being of all the students in their class" (Bender, McLaughlin, Shubert 4). This poses huge problems when trying to observe troubling behavior because those students who are internalizing their aggression will not display any violent or anger-driven traits externally. The problems with this method of identifying potentially violent teens were demonstrated by the shootings at Columbine and Heritage High Schools when all three perpretrators were not students recognized as being troubled or showing previous aggressive behavior. In the light of these new findings, other methods of prevention look to peers, not teachers or school officials, to help identify troubled teens before they lash out.

After efforts by teachers to clearly identify troubled teens in their classes failed, many findings suggest that the most effective "set of eyes and ears in the school building are the students" (Bender, McLaughlin, Shubert 5). When looking at the most recent school shootings that have taken place in the United States, researchers note that teachers and principals had no concern about the students' behavior, but other students knew that something was not right. Countless interviews after the shooting at Columbine

High School were filled with students speaking of the Trench Coat Mafia, the violent writings of the perpretrators, and their isolation from other students within the school. However, when officials at Columbine were asked about the information that was given by so many students, they told reporters that they had not previously heard about these things. For reasons such as this, many schools are turning to peer screening as a method to identify teens who are troubled. By using a rating system, teens rate every student in their class on several statements.

Statements such as, "I would like to sit next to this person at lunch" are rated a scale ranging from 1–5, one being strongly agree and five being strongly disagree. After students' scores are tabulated and averaged, teachers can easily identify students who have few friends and therefore may be likely candidates for dissociation from others in the school environment. As this method becomes more popular, analysis shows that not only does this help in identifying those students with few social contacts, but it also allows teachers to implement formal and informal interventions to assist in the developement of socially isolated children (Bender, McLaughlin, Shubert 5). Clearly the Peer Screening method of identifying and preventing possible acts of violence is taking a step in the right direction. However, even this technique might soon present some flaws in the wake of the next act of extreme school violence.

Whether looking for answers to the cause of school violence, analyzing the traumatic effects that it causes in adolescents, or even attempting to prevent it, the extreme violence that has recently popped up it schools in the United States has gathered global attention. Many still blame the aggressive American culture that children are submerged in from birth, while others point the finger at school bullies. Any way you look at it, tragedies like those at Columbine High School and Heritage High School have magnified the problem of troubled adolescents and the ability to deal with pressures of growing up and life at school. By studying the behavior of both perpratrators and victims alike, we can have a better understanding of both how to identify and prevent these acts of violence, and also deal with and help eliminate side effects that might emerge from witnessing an act of extreme violence.

Works Cited

Addington, Lynn Andrea. "The Columbine Effect: The Impact of Violent School Crime on Students' Fear of Victimization." *Dissertation Abstracts International Section A: Humanities and Social Sciences,* Dec. 2002. Print.

Arman, John. "In the Wake of Tragedy at Columbine High School." *Professional School Counseling 3.3* (Feb. 2000): 218-20. Print.

Bender, William, Phillip McLaughlin, and Terresa Shubert. "Invisible Kids: Preventing School Violence by Identifying Kids in Trouble." *Intervention in School and Clinic 37.2* (Nov. 2001): 105-11.

Bulach, Clete, Tenland Fulbright, and Ronnie Williams. "Bullying Behavior: What is the Potential for Violence at Your School?" *Journal of Instructional Psychology 30.2* (June 2003): 156-64. Print.

Quinnan, Timothy. "Preparing for the Moment When a Student's Rage Turns to Violence." *Chronicle of Higher Learning 45-49* (13 Aug. 1999): B7. Print.

Soskis, Benjamin. "Bully Pulpit." *The New Republic.* 14 May 2001: 25-27. Print.

Ulschmid, Nancy. "The Psychological Consequences of Community Violence Exposure: What Variables Protect Children in Urban Settings?" *Dissertation Abstracts International Section A: Humanities and Social Sciences,* Feb. 2002. Print.

Violence at Columbine: Why?

Mike Rotolo

Argument

Note: I am writing this piece for Newsweek's *section called "My Turn." This will give me an opportunity to reach people of all backgrounds, knowledge of the events, and ages. I think that leaving this open to a broad range of audiences is the best way to approach an article that covers a topic that affected the entire country and even world.*

Many different theories have been generated since the school shooting at Columbine High School, in Littleton, Colorado, on April 20, 1999. Some of these theories revolve around violence in the media, bad parenting, and even violent video games. However, the two theories that have sparked the most controversy put the blame on bullying and isolation, or on easy access to guns. Many believe that the combination of bullying and easy access to guns was the determining factor in prompting Dylan Klebold and Eric Harris to such violent rage on their fellow classmates that day. Still, a closer look at what really took place at Columbine High School prior to the shootings seems to reveal a different story than what was portrayed on the news worldwide.

I was a sophomore at Columbine when the tragic shooting that took the lives of 13 students and one faculty member startled the world. At first, many began to put the blame on bullying. For most people the theory that "bullies" had driven these already emotionally unstable teens to snap seemed very rational and probable. Yet, I, along with many other Columbine students and faculty members, was left more confused and dumbfounded than ever. The confusion did not stem from the theories themselves but from the claims made regarding which students, and which types of students, were involved with either end of the bullying.

With an astounding "seventy-five percent of adolescents admitting to being bullied and five million elementary and junior high students being bullied each year," it would be unrealistic to say that bullying did not take place at Columbine High School (Bulach, Fulbright, Williams 1). As a student at Columbine, I witnessed different levels of bullying, and the most severe forms rarely, if ever, involved the students who would later murder their fellow classmates and teacher. The most severe and aggressive bullying was aimed toward athletes by other athletes. Just like in all levels and types of athletics, new team members are often picked on as a rite of passage or as a way to distinguish the freshmen teams from the junior varsity teams, and the junior varsity from the varsity teams. Being a football player, I saw and received bullying from older athletes, not because we were different or because they disliked us and wanted to humiliate us, but instead because it is natural for the older students to seek dominance and power over the younger students. Although one might speculate that these acts of bullying may isolate the athletes who are receiving the bullying, they actually somewhat initiate the athlete into the larger family of athletes who make up all levels of the sport, freshman through varsity. By no means am I condoning or supporting these bullying rituals and vicious cycles that are found in high schools all over the country, but I do question the theory that bullying was the main reason that Dylan Klebold and Eric Harris chose to murder.

Both were members of the Trench Coat Mafia, a group of more than 10 Columbine students who wore black trenchcoats to school daily. Neither Klebold nor Harris was isolated from the entire student population. In fact, a picture and letter at the end of the 1998 and 1999 school yearbook showed the group of friends together and talked about all the fun times they had shared over the past year. At the same time, neither of the students participated in school sports, so neither would have been subjects of the bullying that takes place to initiate younger athletes. What then, if not bullying or isolation, made these two students want to kill? Although there is no definite answer to this very touchy question, I believe that an interest in violence and guns generated from idealizing Adolf Hitler, combined with easy access to guns, not bullying, drove these students to kill.

Both Klebold and Harris demonstrated their interests in violence when a video made "for a video-production class showed the boys acting out a scene that involved anger, violence, and revenge" (Bender, McLaughlin, Shubert 2). In addition, videos recently released by the Jefferson Country Sheriff's Department show the two killers taking target practice at human-shaped targets, thus revealing their fascination with guns and destruction. Although their attraction to guns played a huge role in the violent nature of the two killers, the easy access to these guns helped them turn their violent video-production project into a reality.

Many believe that if guns were not so accessible in our society, violent and potentially deadly acts would be nonexistent in classrooms and schools. The Tec-DC9 semiautomatic firearm used by Klebold and Harris at Columbine was purchased by a friend at a gun show and then given to them. Also, Klebold's girlfriend admitted to "buying a Hi-Point semiautomatic carbine and two 1969 Savage shotguns," all of which were used during the massacre (Bender, McLaughlin, Shubert 2). The weapons used by Harris and Klebold were the first used in a string of school shootings where the guns were actually purchased. Without the weapons, Klebold and Harris would never have had the opportunity to put their violent thoughts and plans into action, thus preventing the tragedy from ever taking place. Although the fascination with guns and violence might still be present, harder access to guns would restrict this fascination from taking over the boys' lives and prevent them from acting upon their violent fantasies.

Since the shooting in April of 1999, a number of theories have been presented about what drove Dylan Klebold and Eric Harris to commit murder at Columbine High School. Of these theories, none have been examined more than bullying and easy access to guns. With so many of the United States' adolescents being bullied each year, some are starting to question why these certain few are pushed to kill and so many are not. This is leading many to believe that other aspects such as easy access to guns, instead of bullying, are provoking students to act upon violent fantasies. As access to firearms becomes easier and easier, so is the ability to put violent plans into action. Instead of looking at who might have caused these killers to act, we should look at what outlets enable these adolescents to act on violent manifestations—in this case, the easy access to guns and firearms.

Reflective Essay

William F. House

Reflection: Sample Essay 1

WRTG 1100

Instructor: Michelle Albert

Reflective writing can be a way of making sense of various thoughts and ideas that have more or less consciously influenced a writer's thinking. Will makes sense of his experience in WRTG 1100 through metaphors that help him relate his own process of writing—and dealing with writer's block—to other experiences, such as taking a run.

For a discussion of reflection and its relationship to writing, see page 11.

What have I learned in my writing class? And what can I say about reflecting on that? What I've learned is that writer's block can be and is one of the most foul and unpleasant things that a person can experience. However, for me, I think it's necessary. Or at least, that's what I've decided I'll let it be. Do I have it right now? No. Have I folded up like a card table at its influence before? You bet I have. I've decided this, though: Write when the tide is in and soak up experience when the tide is out.

When our literary tide is in, the words flow and ideas wash up like smooth, iridescent sea glass. We're buoyed up by this ocean of words and you can't help but write; the sentences are just there. And they come out with little to no prodding. Then, perhaps on a regular basis or maybe at the most inopportune times, the tide will go out. As a writer or student, we begin to panic. We panic or fret because we have a deadline or because our professors are expecting us to fulfill our assignment or because we just feel that we "should" write. We're writers, for the love of Steinbeck! Where are the words?!

I say, take a deep breath and just realize that the tide isn't gone for good; it's just out. And this is the perfect time to explore and soak up experience. This is the time that real writers emerge. They go down and wade out onto the tidal flats and see what lives in the tidal pools. They take in the pungent salt air. They notice the seastars and snails and kelp and mollusks left behind. They listen and feel. They know that their muse is like the moon, always thirsty for the ocean and pulling our words away generally more than she gives them to us (or so it seems at times).

One night a few weeks ago, I went for an evening run. It was getting dark and raining out. And, in fact, it was snowing above us in the mountains. I slipped on my running pants and a warm top and my trusty Sauconys and after a few minutes of stretching, I headed out. I ran to the end of our street and through a tunnel that goes under the road and into the park next door. It was very quiet and I had that excitement that you get at the beginning of a run where you really want to run fast but you know you have to pace yourself. I fell into a pace that was comfortable and ran as the sun slid behind the peaks.

I generally run near Wonderland Lake and then up into the foothills. That night, as I rounded the shoreline, steam was coming off the water as the night air quickly grew cooler than the lake. The trail was nearly deserted as only a few runners passed me. We all smiled at each other like this was the best-kept secret in the whole world. The moon was nowhere to be seen and it grew quiet as I pushed up into some of the trails above the lake.

Soon, I wasn't passing anyone and my feet were growing heavier with mud. I splashed through several puddles to try and get rid of some of the unwanted stowaway dirt. Just as I topped a small hill, I looked over and noticed the warm lights of many homes in the valley as people were having dinner or maybe talking about which ski resort would open first this year. I topped the hill and began going down the other side. The city slid away and there was nothing but night and rain and the sound of breathing and feet hitting the wet soil. My mind felt as quiet as my run. I wasn't thinking about anything in particular, but I was completely lucid and more alert than I'd been all week. And for a moment, I stopped mentally and thought, *This is what we need as writers: simple, but rich experience.* And I thought of all the simple and sometimes profound experiences that we all go through. I thought of sitting with patients at the hospital where I work, listening to their stories and of how they're afraid to die but happy to be alive. I thought of driving home the night before this particular run and how the clouds were lifting from the mountains and the sun was breaking through against the rocks and how I got a lump in my throat just from the sheer beauty of it. I thought of how my dad made up cowboy stories for me at bedtime for as far back as I could remember. I thought of seeing my daughter being born and having her look at me for the first time. I thought of a moment in my life enduring physical pain that was so intense that I thought I would pass out and wished I had. I thought of standing on top of the Eiffel Tower for the first time and seeing the morning sun break over Paris. I thought of sitting at my Uncle Dan's pond as a boy, fishing and getting sunburned. I thought about the first time I started an IV on someone and realized that I knew what being a doctor was like. I thought about the first time I sailed...

...and then, I was running again. I was back down near the lake. I could hear the city noises again. A young girl passed me on the trail and huffed out a quick "hey" as she went by. A man who must have been in his seventies ran by me like I was standing still and made me smile in spite of myself. And I thought, my tide may be out right now, but tomorrow I will write and let all this experience out onto the page.

Writer's block isn't bad. It's just your tide being out. If we view it in that light, a funny thing begins to happen. Before you're even ready perhaps, you'll notice the tide coming back in and pooling into your footsteps, following you back up to higher ground. And even sometimes, the tide comes back in hard and fast and just like the real ocean, it brings an abundance of life back to the shoreline. Our tide of experience can bring new life into our words and into our writing. We just have to allow it.

So, that's what I've learned this semester in my writing class, and this is the best way I know to reflect on it, to simply write it. I think I've known that my strengths are conveying something with a sense of truth and knowing how to drive home fact or elicit an emotional response. My biggest fear and insecurity in writing was simply not knowing how to deal with writer's block. Through the tools I learned in this class and from the encouragement and help of my instructor (and peers), I've learned that I can deal with the issue, though. The class and the lesson have been helpful and important to me in ways that exceed the scope of the class.

All of this reminds me of a favorite line from a Tom Hanks film called *Castaway.* There's a scene where he's describing the incredible hardship of being stranded for years on an isolated island and of the unexpected good fortune he receives. He says, "Tomorrow the sun will rise. Who knows what the tide could bring?" My writing has changed in light of that. It's just like my life; there will be good times and not so good times, but we just keep trying.

The Rules

Caroline Bess

Reflection: Sample Essay 2

WRTG 1250

Instructor: Rolf Norgaard

Rules. Like many accomplished young writers, Caroline Bess was well acquainted with the standard grammatical and stylistic tyrannies, not to mention the individual quirks and obsessions of her teachers. For her final project, Caroline reflects on the role of rules in writing. To what extent do they enable or constrain? And how much "[s]hould we as a society lighten up or buckle down?"

In this essay, Caroline weaves reflection, personal narrative, analysis, inquiry, and argument into her discussion of the rules of language. While this is not a typical reflective essay, Caroline's writing demonstrates how reflecting on the writing process might be connected to a broader inquiry into controversies about language use in our culture.

On the first day of seventh grade, I was sitting down among the faces of the future, waiting expectantly to meet yet another teacher who would have a hand in my intellectual molding, when I saw the sign that would set the tone for my academic career. It said, "Got is Gone." The big red letters on the white tagboard seemed almost as imposing as my teacher's huge, domineering stature as he walked to the front of the classroom to introduce himself. Both the sign and the man had a certain boldness that demanded deference, prohibited skepticism. I did not have to wait long to learn that the sign meant we were not to use any variation of the word *got*. And if we were to use the forbidden word in our writing, our assignment would be penalized one letter grade—that's how serious he was about it.

My teacher had brilliantly boiled down the art of writing to a single rule by which to gauge our progress. In fact, he often didn't even have to read the assignment. He was a certified speed-reader who could scan an entire essay in seconds and, wielding his mighty pen, strike out every *got* he saw obstructing his path. And now, as I reflect back on my early education, most memories grow hazy, but I will always remember watching as he graded my semester project in one minute flat. I grew increasingly dismayed as he eradicated one, two, three variations of *got*. Just like that, I had gotten a "C." And let me tell you, I'll never use that word again.

This early display of grammatical tyranny was the first of many unyielding language rules to come that would reveal an excessively narrow view on the ills of modern American writing. The academic elitism that promotes a constricted focus on nit-picky rules serves as blinders to the degeneration of articulate and expressive writing. The ultimate goal of functional literacy, let alone literary art, falls by the wayside as the path is obstructed by grammatical dogma. What is the point of perfect structure if a phrase has no force? From my seventh-grade take-off point, I was to encounter teachers who would drill into my head ranting oaths about countless grammatical laws, like "never ever, under any circumstances, will the passive voice be used" and "You'll forever abstain from using contractions in your writing." And really, where would I be if it weren't for this word orthodoxy keeping me in line? Surely, I would have been swept away by a swift river of grammatical travesties into a great pool of societal decadence from which this collapse of language spawns. I would have become just another base perpetrator of this "creeping casualness" that so many linguists, teachers, and moralistic grammar police are up in arms about (Eakin).

And what exactly are these conservatives up in arms about? Well, specifically, the "poor grammar, sloppy syntax, misused words, misspelled words, and other infelicities of style" that they see in their colleagues', students', and leaders' writing ("Clues to Concise Writing"). It is they who write enraged letters to the editors for allowing grammatical lapses as if they were moral travesties. William Safire, a self-proclaimed enforcer of proper speech, is one of the squeakiest wheels out there, notorious for his indictments of America's "sloppiness in speech," whether it's caused by "ignorance or apathy" (Safire). And one has to wonder how the moralistic tone entered the song of these "language snobs." Linguistic conservatives fear that the structures, much like grammar, that "provide our security are in danger of collapse" (Williams). Not only do they rail against the language's misuse, but they lament the impending changes of it. They scoff at the annual alterations and additions to *Webster's Standard Dictionary*, such as *gift* and *impact* being amended to be verbs as well as their conventional definitions as nouns.

But the very notion of defending grammar is a little childish and willful. For example, one thousand years ago in Old English, "Happy New Millennium, Everybody" would have been "Bliss on baem cumendum busend leara, Eallum!" (Kurland). No one looks at the status quo of grammar

> "Word Orthodoxy" has no place in our current society. . .

in respect to Old English and thinks, "We're such barbarians—what we've done to our forefathers' language is sacrilege!" People understand that languages, just like people and societies and thoughts, evolve. With a little perspective, it's difficult to imagine the English language had it remained static. It's futile to resist the changes in grammar that are being made today. So the current complaints about the degradation and evolution of the language are pretty myopic, really. Granted, grammatical slippages are jarring to a trained ear, and they can sometimes even be alarming, such as President Bush's comment on the educational testing system in which he says, "You teach a child to read, and he or her will be able to pass a literacy test."

However, one must question how dire poor grammar really is in the face of greater linguistic troubles. Perhaps there's a greater ill that's being overlooked by the likes of the grammar police, and that is a development of "vagueness and sheer incompetence" in the style of modern prose, as the art of style is viewed as superfluous. Perhaps this crusade against grammar trespassers is pulling the wool over our eyes. A more pertinent issue, more significant than a misused *whom* here or an unnecessary preposition there, is how our language has become "ugly and inaccurate because our thoughts are foolish" (Orwell). To this end, a more appropriate, and more alarming, quote from President Bush might be his statement in which he fervently asserted, "I know what I believe. I will continue to articulate what I believe and what I believe—I believe what I believe is right." Articulate? I think not. Neither is it graceful nor moving, as was the style of political leaders past. Perhaps the English language is losing something more important than impeccable subject-verb conjugation.

Our American president's use of dialect nicely highlights the contentiousness between linguistic conservatives and liberals. On the one hand, if our president, one of the most powerful and influential men in the world, can perform his job in the midst of grammatical carnage, then what's the difference? In the grand scheme of things, his slip-ups are not so calamitous. And on the other hand, it is our president, one of the most powerful and influential men in the world, who is consistently breaching grammar laws. Should we as a society lighten up or buckle down? This is the question. And my own experience with teachers buckling down has helped me to come to my own answer.

My teachers' narrow catering to prescriptive grammar hampered the possibility for creative advancement in my writing. In middle school, I abided by the grammar dogma religiously, for my teachers allowed no leeway. High school was not so terribly different; I still took my oaths and listened to various English teachers berate those grammatical urchins who were still writing sentence fragments and run-ons. But this was when we started analyzing rhetorical devices and syntax strategies in masterpieces of literature. We would write perfectly formed essays, with the thesis at the end of the first paragraph, appropriately placed topic sentences, and an all-inclusive conclusion at the end, even as we were writing about unconventional stylistic strategies that have been lauded for centuries. Run-on sentences quickened the pace of one passage to convey a sense of urgency. There was improper capitalization in another to allow for greater flexibility in emphasis. Sentence fragments were a particularly potent way of accentuating a point. Switching tenses mid-piece was not careless writing—it was a deliberate and essential volta in the tone and meaning. So, we students wrote endless essays on these rhetorical devices, but I don't recall ever once being encouraged to write with the same finesse. We were trained to recognize the art that creative writing can generate, but our own expression was shackled by the commitment we had made to convention from our early education. As students, we have been taught in such a way that as we write, we have a constant dialogue of "should" and "shouldn't" that doesn't allow us liberty of expression. I think we've been buckled down too tightly.

So as the intellectual elite are now up in arms about the English language's "abuse and misuse in the news, media, and elsewhere," I find myself wondering what exactly they are aiming to salvage if we as a society are no longer capable of creating art through the language (Society for the Preservation of English). There is a plethora of societal changes that are challenging the creative beauty of writing. We are an increasingly oral-based culture, for one. We get our news through the television and radio versus the newspaper. And when we do write, instead of letters, we communicate via e-mail, in which the writing is condensed as much as possible into clips like "ur," "g2g," "ttyl," and "brb." Letter writing is no longer an art, but a skill in concision. So we, as a society, are no longer reading or writing for news, entertainment, or education. Seems to me that grammar is the least of our worries as far as the fate of the English language is concerned. (Oh dear, thank God for Microsoft Word—had my previous sentence fragment not been underlined with a squiggly green line, I know not what I'd have done. This corporation has dutifully taken upon itself the task of keeping billions of word documents within the checks of pre-ordained grammar laws. But do you know what I'm even more thankful for about Microsoft Word? The *ignore* button.)

In fact, it is even arguable that as the language evolves, and as we deviate from the diction of "privileged classes from the past," we open up a greater freedom and potential for creative expression (Nunberg). So as our standards for grammar and definition evolve along with the times, what will this new voice sound like? Will it really be the voice of slovenliness and foolishness, or will it be the voice of inventiveness and expressiveness? Or perhaps it will merely temper the haughty, condescending tone of our intellectual elite, a point which leads nicely to the counterargument.

On the opposite end of the spectrum from the "language snobs" are the "language slobs." As the linguistic conservatives are trying desperately to prevent any kind of change in the language, these radicals believe that the "rules of language reflect the reality of human speech" and to attempt to control the language is to attempt to control the culture. Rather than make society follow the rails of a preserved language, they believe language should follow the flow of popular culture. Doing otherwise would be detrimental to creative expression. In fact, the present politics of academia have "been on the side of an open-ended diversity" in that grammar is now seen as a "plot to perpetuate the political dominance of white males." The teaching of grammar is suddenly politically incorrect as these radicals view it as preventing students from expressing themselves in their own "idioms and style and punctuation." Of course, strong individual voices would struggle to come out of a shaky verbal foundation in the first place, but "expression without form" is hardly as dire a consequence as "form without [...] energy" (Williams). This is the real issue. The inconsequential changes that are disconcerting some to no end are just that—inconsequential.

"Word Orthodoxy" has no place in our current society (Adams). Such borders sever creative extremities and are not capable of containing something that is so intrinsically tied to our forever-evolving society. Of course proper grammar is an essential tool in the creation of artistic literature. However, this grammatical dogma is more of a limiting tool than a constructive one. If your inner monologue is constantly reciting "I shall not. . ." and "never, ever. . .," it's awfully difficult to hear "what if. . ." or "maybe I could. . ." My seventh-grade teacher would have found three travesties of grammatical justice in this paper. Rather narrow, isn't it?

Works Cited

Adams, Rob. "Comments on 'Orwellian." *Provenance: Unknown.* Ed. Matt Pfeffer. 28 Jan. 2003. Web. 9 Nov. 2003. "Clues to Concise Writing." *Vocabula Review.* Feb. 2001. Web. 9 Nov. 2003.

Eakin, Emily. "Going at the Changes in, Ya Know, English." *New York Times.* 15 Nov. 2003. Web. 15 Nov. 2003.

Kurland, Dan. "Words: Our Evolving Language." *How the Language Really Works: The Fundamentals of Critical Reading and Effective Writing.* Criticalreading.com. 2000. Web. 9 Nov. 2003.

Nunberg, Geoffrey. "The Decline of Grammar." *Atlantic Monthly.* Dec. 1983: 31-44. Print.

Orwell, George. "Politics and the English Language." *George Orwell, 1903-1950: Work: Essays.* May 1945. Web. 6 Nov. 2003.

Safire, William. "Quotations by Author." *Quotationspage.* n.d. Web. 9 Nov. 2003.

Society for the Preservation of English Language and Literature. *Spellorg.* n.d. Web. 9 Nov. 2003.

Williams, David R. "Snobs and Slobs." *Vocabula Review.* Feb. 2001. Web. 9 Nov. 2003.

Appendix A

PWR Course Policies

The following are general course policies that apply to all PWR courses. However, because there may be some variation in the way instructors choose to implement them, it is your responsibility to consult your course syllabus and instructor about particular policies for your class.

Enrollment

Capped at just 19 students, First-Year Writing and Rhetoric is likely to be one of the smallest classes you take at CU. The PWR believes strongly that writing courses should be kept small so that students can work closely with their instructor and also with one another on their writing. PWR instructors are therefore asked not to over-enroll their courses. If you find yourself on a waitlist, you have several options: You can stay on the waitlist in hopes that an enrolled student drops the course during the drop/add period; you can stay on the waitlist in order to be eligible for course reservation the following semester (guidelines for course reservation are online at http://registrar.colorado.edu); or you can look for a section with openings. Staff in the PWR main office can help you decide which is the best option.

Adds/Drops

You must attend your class regularly during the drop/add period. Any student who misses two classes during that period may be administratively dropped in order to make space for students on the waiting list. However, this process is not automatic, so if you decide you don't want to take the class, it is your responsibility to drop it in order to avoid receiving an "F" for the course.

Attendance

In a class as small as this one, your absence will be noticed. Other students depend on your feedback in class discussions and workshops. In short, your presence counts in this course. While any absence may affect your grade, most instructors designate a maximum number of classes you can miss before they officially begin deducting points from your final grade. Thus it is very important that you become familiar with your instructor's particular guidelines and policies for attendance, and that you use your absences wisely, saving some for illness or an emergency late in the semester.

If you must miss a class, you are responsible for finding out what you missed and for keeping up with the assignments. If you know in advance that you will have to miss a class, it's a good idea to let your instructor know ahead of time by e-mail or, better yet, by making an appointment with him or her. (E-mailing your instructor after the fact to ask, "What did I miss?" isn't a good option. Your instructor doesn't have the time to summarize an entire class period or workshop in an e-mail!)

If you need to be absent for a religious observance or for military obligations, you must give your instructor two weeks' notice. In the case of a military obligation, you will need a note from an officer verifying the reason for your absence. You will also need to arrange in advance for any work that needs to be completed.

Faculty Mailboxes

All work should be turned in during class time unless you have made other arrangements with your instructor in advance. In the event that you do need to turn in an assignment outside of regular class time, all PWR instructors have a mailbox in the lobby of the building where their office is located. Please note, however, that mailboxes are only accessible during regular business hours: Monday–Friday, 8 a.m.–5 p.m.

Lateness

Individual instructors' policies on lateness vary; check your course syllabus to find out what the policy is for your class. Generally, walking in late or leaving early displays disregard for the class. If you know that you will be late for a class or will have to leave early, let your instructor know ahead of time. Also, be aware that many instructors count late arrivals or early departures as absences. The same goes for turning work in late. Instructors are not required to accept late work; at the very least, most require that you make arrangements with them in advance.

Appealing a Grade

If you have questions about the grade you receive on a particular assignment or for the course, the first step is to make an appointment with your instructor so that the two of you can discuss your concerns. If, after speaking with your instructor, you believe that the grade you have received is unfair given the assignment or course objectives, you may follow the PWR's process for appealing a grade:

Step one: You may submit a formal, written appeal to the PWR conflict resolution coordinator. (Please see contact information page at the beginning of this book.) All appeals must be made within 45 days of the academic term in which the course was taken.

Step two: If the conflict resolution coordinator deems a review appropriate, he or she will evaluate all relevant course information. It is your responsibility to provide the coordinator with copies of relevant documents (e.g., course policies, syllabus, assignments, clean copies of papers). The coordinator will then have two other PWR instructors independently read and evaluate the paper(s) in question.

The conflict resolution coordinator will speak with you and your instructor about the outcome of the review. The instructor will take the review under advisement in deciding whether or not to change the grade.

Step three: If you are still not satisfied with the outcome of the appeals process, you may then take the matter to the director of the Program for Writing and Rhetoric, who, after reviewing the case, will make his or her recommendation to the instructor. Final authority for any grade rests with the instructor.

English as a Second Language

The PWR dedicates certain sections of its first-year courses for students whose native language is not English; these sections are distinguished by an 800 section number. These sections have the same goals as the standard sections but may address issues of particular concern to nonnative writers of English. If you are a nonnative writer of English, you may prefer to take these classes for a variety of reasons: You may wish to reinforce your understanding of American academic writing; you may want an opportunity to write and read about language differences; or you may feel the need for more formal attention to English grammar and style. If you're unsure whether an 800 section is suitable for you, come by the PWR main office on the lower level of Environmental Design in room 1B60, or call the PWR office at 303-492-8188.

Special Accommodations

If you qualify for accommodations because of a disability, please submit to your instructor a letter from Disability Services in a timely manner so that your needs may be addressed. Disability Services determines accommodations based on documented disabilities (303-492-8671, http://disabilityservices.colorado.edu).

Plagiarism

Plagiarism is the act of passing off another's work as your own. Stealing, buying, or otherwise using someone else's work, in whole or in part, constitutes plagiarism and is against university policy. Such behavior is taken seriously by the Honors Council, to which many such incidents are referred. Consult http://honorcode. colorado.edu to learn more about the CU Honor Code.

Plagiarism does not always take such blatant forms, however. Of equal concern, especially in a course like this one where you will be encouraged to draw on others' ideas in your own writing, are the more subtle forms of plagiarism. For example, you probably know that all words taken directly from a source need to be quoted and cited, and that there are specific conventions for doing this properly. However, you may not know that merely changing a few words in a passage—say, by using the thesaurus function on your word-processing program—does not protect you from the charge of plagiarism. Passages that are similar to their sources in syntax, organization, or wording but are not cited are considered to be plagiarized. In fact, even if you cite the source but do not make it clear to your readers that the phrasing of a passage is not your own, the source is still considered to be plagiarized.

Any time you use another's work—ideas, theories, statistics, graphs, photos, or facts that are not common knowledge—you must acknowledge the author.

Depending on the severity of the offense and on the instructor's particular policy, the consequences for plagiarism vary, from having to rewrite a section of a paper to receiving a failing grade. Therefore, in addition to making sure you understand what constitutes an offense, it is important that you become familiar with your instructor's policy.

In the PWR, we see plagiarism as more than merely a matter of policy or legality. It is also an issue of respect and regard for other readers and writers. Some students are reluctant to cite their sources because they mistakenly believe that in college all their ideas must be original. But the university is a community of thinkers; as such, the writing we produce may be thought of as a conversation with other thinkers. As in any conversation, your "listeners" expect you to build on what has already been said.

We all build on each other's ideas, making our own small contribution to the discussion. At the same time, we all like to see our ideas acknowledged. Acknowledging other people's work can only enhance your reputation as a credible, thoughtful, honest writer. Although the ideas in your paper may come from others, the way you put them together and make sense of them will be uniquely your own.

Appendix B

Campus Resources

The PWR and University Libraries are committed to providing support for writers at all levels, through a range of resources. We encourage you to take advantage of these resources—not just while you are enrolled in a writing course, but throughout your college career.

PWR Resources

PWR Conflict Resolution

We provide a confidential conflict resolution service for students of the Program for Writing and Rhetoric. Students may consult with the conflict resolution coordinator about perceived problems in their PWR courses without their instructor's knowledge. The PWR conflict resolution coordinator will help settle disputes and personality conflicts between students and instructors. The coordinator will also handle student challenges to a grade, plagiarism concerns, and similar problems that may arise in PWR classes. To contact the PWR conflict resolution coordinator, see PWR Contact Information at the beginning of this book.

Writing Center

We are a faculty of professional writing consultants available to help you through the writing process. Better yet, our help is free to CU students! Writing consultants are trained to help individual writers improve their skills. We encourage you to take advantage of this great benefit, not only while you are enrolled in the first-year writing course but throughout your college career.

Our consultants are on hand to help you at any stage of the writing process, from brainstorming and organizing your ideas to finally understanding the mysteries of grammar and style. Please do keep in mind that the Writing Center is not an editing service; our goal is to teach you to become more skillful and aware as a writer by using your own papers as tutorials.

We ask that you bring your draft, outline or notes, and the assignment description with you and that you keep papers to a 10-page maximum per visit. Writing Center consultations last 50 minutes and should be booked in advance.

To book an appointment, please visit our website (http://www.colorado.edu/pwr/writingcenter.html). You'll need to register for a free account to access our appointment calendar. Once registered, you'll have the ability to book up to two appointments per week.

One caution, though: Don't wait until the last minute to seek help; we have a limited number of consultants, and the time slots often fill quickly, especially at midterms and the end of the semester. We advise booking at least a few days in advance.

We are located in Norlin Library close to the revolving doors at the east entrance. Please visit our website for more information about our hours and contact information:

http://www.colorado.edu/pwr/writingcenter.html

Writer's Help

As part of your first-year writing course, you'll be required to purchase access to Writer's Help, an online writing resource that includes information about many writing issues, including:

◆ how to organize an essay

◆ how to cite sources

◆ sample student essays

◆ grammar and punctuation guidelines

To purchase access, buy an access code in the CU bookstore. Your account will give you access for four years, so you'll be able to use Writer's Help not only for your writing class but for your other classes as well.

To access Writer's Help, go to http://writershelp.bedfordstmartins. com/ebooks/helphandbook.php .

For an introduction to Writer's Help and technical support, go to http://pages.mail.bfwpub.com/WritersHelp/Get_Help_Students.

Library Resources

Library PWR Website

The website for the information literacy component of First-Year Writing and Rhetoric is available at http://ucblibraries.colorado. edu/pwr/.

This page includes links to all of the other online resources you'll need for First-Year Writing and Rhetoric, including the reading themes and online tutorials and quizzes (RIOT). If at any point you have a question about how to access these resources, please e-mail pwrhelp@colorado.edu.

Research Tutorials (RIOT)

You can access the PWR Research Tutorials (RIOT) through D2L. Log in to D2L at: https://learn.colorado.edu/ .

Off-Campus Access

You will have no difficulty accessing the library resources such as the reading themes and tutorials from a campus computer. However, if you are using an off-campus computer (your home computer, for example), the system will not recognize that you are a CU student and you will be denied access. To correct this problem, you must establish off-campus access. To find out how, go to http://ucblibraries.colorado.edu/research/offcampusaccess. htm and follow the directions. If at any time you have questions about remote access, please call the ITS Help Line at (303) 735-HELP. A final note, AOL does not work with the library sources; please use Internet Explorer, Netscape, or a similar browser.

ASK US

http://ucblibraries.colorado.edu/askus/index.htm

Do you have questions? Would you like some help with your research? You can ask us for help at any stage of your research.

There are a number of ways to contact us:

Research desk: Stop in the Library and ask questions (Norlin

Library research desk is located on the 2nd floor)
http://ucblibraries.colorado.edu/hours/index.cfm

Chat: Go to the libraries' webpage and ask a question via chat
http://ucblibraries.colorado.edu/askus/index.htm

Consultation: Request to an individual research consultation http://ucblibraries.colorado.edu/reference/researchconsultation.htm

Email: Send questions to pwrhelp@colorado.edu

We would like to help, so don't hesitate to ask us!

Reference Desk

If you cannot make it to the Drop-in Research Center, stop by the Norlin Library Reference Desk, which is staffed by librarians who provide general and specialized research help. Please come to the desk whenever you need assistance with your research. It is open Monday–Thursday, 9 a.m.–5 p.m. and Saturday–Sunday, 1 p.m.–5 p.m.

PWR Contests

PWR Writing Contest

The PWR holds a contest each year for the best writing in its core classes. If you have a piece you would like to submit, see your teacher for the submission guidelines and deadline. You may obtain a contest entry form by going to the PWR homepage (www.colorado.edu/pwr/) and clicking on "Resources." In addition to receiving cash prizes, winning entries will be published in the PWR's online journal, Occasions, and they may also be selected to appear in the next edition of Knowing Words. Several of the essays included in Chapter 6—including "Makeover Feminism," "Cultural Chameleon," and "Learning to Read"—were selected from among past years' submissions. Good Luck!

PWR Cover Art Contest

In addition to the writing contest, PWR holds an annual student cover art contest. The contest is open to all CU undergraduate students—you do not need to be enrolled in a writing course to enter. The contest winner receives a cash prize, and the winning art piece becomes the cover for the next edition of Knowing Words. You may obtain a contest entry form by going to the PWR homepage (www.colorado.edu/pwr/) and clicking on "Resources."

Submission guidelines and deadlines are listed on the form. Good Luck!

Student Affairs Resources

Student Affairs' primary focus is to create a positive learning environment that fosters successful learning and personal development, both inside and outside of the traditional classroom. Student learning and success is enhanced when the academic environment and community support students' full development as individuals—not just as isolated intellects—and when students are seen as important partners in the learning experience.

The first priority of Student Affairs is students' development as successful, intellectually curious learners, and as healthy, competent, active citizen participants in our American democracy. The division provides, in collaboration with other members of the campus community, educational opportunities, resources, and support to help each individual student reach his or her goals. They work to create a learning environment that eliminates barriers standing in the way of student learning, development, and success.

Select websites as resources:
Events, activities, lectures, student group meetings, etc.:
http://inthemix.colorado.edu/

General resources:
http://studentlife.colorado.edu/

Student government:
http://cusg.colorado.edu/

Student Involvement, Activities & Leadership Development Office:
http://www.colorado.edu/atoz/-/s/
u93c726010dbf6ad0d1ff6ec3133c2939.html

Leadership program at CU - Gaining Opportunities through Leadership Development:
http://umc.colorado.edu/quicklinks/gold.html

Academic Advising Resources

The website for the Academic Advising Center is available at: http://advising.colorado.edu/

This website includes resources for exploring your major and the entry point into the advising portal. When you log in to the advising portal, you can schedule an advising appointment and schedule a time to declare (change or add) a major.

Your academic advisor is a good resource and can help you to find and utilize campus resources, round out your academic experience with experiences outside the classroom, and assist you with selecting courses. Advising is generally not required so it's up to you to reach out to your advisor every semester.

You also need to familiarize yourself with your degree audit as this is the tool you will use to track your degree progress, including which requirements remain for you in the Core and your major and a listing of courses that can fulfill those requirements. You can find your degree audit by logging into MyCUInfo.

The busiest time to try to make an appointment with your advisor is when everyone is registering! Plan ahead and schedule your appointments in September and February.

Appendix C

MLA Documentation

When you do research to find supporting evidence for your ideas or arguments, you need to credit your outside sources. Depending on what type of essay you are writing or which type of course you are writing for, you will need to choose a documentation style and continue with that style for the entire essay. Two of the most common styles, especially for freshman and sophomore students, are MLA (Modern Language Association) and APA (American Psychological Association).

If you write in composition, language, linguistics, and literature courses, you will often be asked to use documentation guidelines created by the Modern Language Association (MLA). The *MLA Handbook for Writers of Research Papers*, in its seventh edition, provides a full description of the conventions used by this particular community of writers; updates to the *MLA Handbook* can be found at <www.mla.org>.

MLA guidelines require that you give both an in-text citation and a Works Cited entry for any and all sources you use. Using accurate in-text citations helps guide your reader to the appropriate entry on the Works Cited. For example, the in-text citation given below in parentheses directs the reader to the correct page of the book given in the Works Cited.

> In-text citation➔When a teenager sleeps more than 10 hours per night, it is time to question whether she is having significant problems (Jones 63).

> Entry in Works Cited➔
> Jones, Stephanie. *The Signs of Trouble.* Boston: Dilemma Publishing, 2010. Print.

This chapter provides a general overview of MLA documentation style and an explanation of the most commonly used MLA documentation formats, including a few significant revisions since the previous edition.

Using MLA in-text citations

In-text citations (also called *parenthetical citations*) point readers to where they can find more information about your researched supporting materials. When you use MLA documentation style, you need to indicate the author's last name and the location of the source material (page or paragraph number). Where this in-text information is placed depends on how you want to phrase the sentence that is summarized, paraphrased, or quoted. Be sure that the in-text citation guides the reader clearly to the source in the Works Cited, where complete information about the source is given.

The following are some of the most common examples of parenthetical citations.

1. Author's name in text

When using a parenthetical reference to a single source that is already named in the sentence, use this form: (Page number). Note that the period goes after the parentheses.

➔ Stephanie Jones, author of *The Signs of Trouble*, describes "excessive sleeping, refraining from eating, and lying about simple things" as signs to look for when parents are concerned about their children (63).

2. Author's name in reference

When the author's name is not included in the preceding sentence, use this form for the parenthetical information at the end of the sentence: (Author's Last Name Page number). Note that there is no comma between the name and date in an MLA parenthetical reference, and also note that the period comes at the end of the sentence after the parentheses.

➔ When a teenager sleeps more than 10 hours per night, it is time to question whether she is having significant problems (Jones 63).

3. No author given

When a work has no credited author, use a clipped version of the work's title.

→ In a recent *Time* article, a list of 30 common signs of teenage trouble cites lack of sleep as the most common sign ("Thirty" 3).

4. Two or three authors given

When you use a source that was written by two or three authors, use all the names in the text of the sentence or in the citation.

→ The idea that "complexity is a constant in biology" is not an innovative one (Sole and Goodwin 2).

→ Most signs in English that the authors encountered on the road had "grammar mistakes, misspellings, or just odd pictures" (Smith, Jones, and Best 55).

5. Four or more authors given

MLA documentation style allows a choice when there are four authors or more of an item to be cited. You can either name all the authors or include only the first author's name followed by *et al.* (Latin for "and others").

→ In Hong Kong, most signs are in Chinese and English; however, once you are in mainland China, English is rarely found on signs, except in tourist areas (Li, Smith, Jones, and Franz 49).

→ In Hong Kong, most signs are in Chinese and English; however, once you are in mainland China, English is rarely found on signs, except in tourist areas (Li, et al. 49).

6. Authors with the same last names

If your source material includes items by authors who happen to have the same last name, be sure to use each author's first name or initial in the parentheses.

→ When a teenager sleeps more than 10 hours per night, it is time to question whether she is having significant problems (S. Jones 63).

→ Another sign of trouble can be when you do not see your child for meals (B. Jones 114).

7. Encyclopedia or dictionary unsigned entry

When you use an encyclopedia or dictionary to look up a word or entry, be sure to include the word or entry title in the parenthetical entry.

→ The word *thing* has more definitions than any other entry in the *Oxford English Dictionary* ("thing").

8. Lines of verse (plays, poetry or song lyrics)

For plays, give the act, scene, and line numbers that are located in any edition of the play. Separate the act, scene, and line numbers with periods. For example, the quotation below comes from *Romeo and Juliet*, Act II, Scene 2, lines 43 and 44. The MLA also advises using this method with biblical chapters and verses. Be sure, though, that the sequence goes from largest unit to smallest unit.

→ Juliet grapples with how names can influence feelings as she questions, "What's in a name? That which we call a rose/By any other name would smell as sweet" (2.2.43-44).

Use a slash (/) to signify line breaks when you quote poetry or song lyrics, and put line numbers in the in-text citation instead of page numbers.

→ An early song by Will Smith shows the frustration of children as he sings, "You know parents are the same/No matter time nor place/They don't understand that us kids/Are going to make some mistakes" (1-4).

9. Indirect quotation

When you use a quotation of a quotation—that is, a quotation that quotes from another source—use *qtd. in* to designate the source.

➜ Smith has said, "My parents really didn't understand me" (qtd. in Jones, par. 8).

Using long or block quotations

Long or block quotations have special formatting requirements of their own.

1. Block quote of prose

If you quote a chunk of prose that is longer than four typed lines, you are using what is called a *block quotation*. Follow these MLA guidelines for block quotations:

1. If introducing the block quotation with a sentence, use a colon at the end of the sentence.
2. Begin the quotation on a new line.
3. Do not use quotation marks to enclose the block quote.
4. Indent the quote one inch from the left margin, and extend the right margin to the end of the line.
5. Double space the entire quotation.
6. Put a period at the end of the quotation, and then add the parenthetical citation.

➜ However, Lansky states:

> Despite the statement on <www.signspotting.com> that we don't accept signs with the intention of being funny, people like sending them in. I've opted not to use these as it could encourage people to start making them, sticking them up in their driveway, and snapping a picture. Plus, funny signs are so much more amusing when the humor is accidental. (72)

2. Block quote of poetry, drama, or song lyrics

For songs and poems, be sure to give line numbers rather than page numbers and to use the original line breaks.

→ The Fresh Prince, an early Will Smith character, sings about parents not understanding:

> You know parents are the same
>
> No matter time or place
>
> They don't understand that us kids
>
> Are going to make some mistakes
>
> So to you other kids all across the land
>
> There's no need to argue
>
> Parents just don't understand. (4-7)

Adding or omitting words in a quotation

1. Adding words to a quotation

Use square brackets ([ ]) to point out words or phrases that are not part of the original text.

→ Original quotation: "When we entered the People's Republic of China, we noticed that the signage began dropping English translations."

→ Quotation with added word: She said, "When we entered the People's Republic of China, [Dunkirk and I] noticed that the signage began dropping English translations" (Donelson 141).

You can also add your own comments inside a quotation by using square brackets. For example, you can add the word *sic* to a quotation when you know that there is an error.

→ Original quotation: "When we entered the People's Repulic of China, we noticed that the signage began dropping English translations."

→ Quotation with added comment: She said, "When we entered the People's Repulic [sic] of China, we noticed that the signage began dropping English translations" (Donelson 141).

2. Omitting words in a quotation

Use an ellipsis (. . .) to represent words that you delete from a quotation. The ellipsis begins with a space, then has three periods with spaces between them, and then ends with a space.

> Original quotation➜ "The Great Wall is something that can be seen from space. When we reach a time when advertisements can be seen from space, we have probably gone too far."

> Quotation with words omitted in middle of sentence➜ Frank Donelson, author of *Signs in Space,* remarks, "The Great Wall . . . can be seen from space. When we reach a time when advertisements can be seen from space, we have probably gone too far" (178).

If you omit words at the end of a quotation, and that is also the end of your sentence, use an ellipsis plus a period with no space before the ellipsis or after the period.

> Original quotation➜ "The Great Wall is something that can be seen from space. When we reach a time when advertisements can be seen from space, we have probably gone too far with our advertising and signage."

> Quotation with words omitted at end of sentence➜ Frank Donelson, author of *Signs in Space,* remarks, "The Great Wall is something that can be seen from space. When we reach a time when advertisements can be seen from space, we have probably gone too far. . ." (178).

Citing online sources

In the MLA documentation style, online or electronic sources have their own formatting guidelines since these types of sources rarely give specific page numbers.

The MLA recommends that you include in the text, rather than in an in-text citation, the name(s) of the person (e.g., author, editor, director, performer) that begins the matching Works Cited entry. For instance, the following is the recommended way to begin an in-text citation for an online source:

➜ Roger Ebert says that Shyamalan "plays the audience like a piano" in the film *Signs* (par. 8).

If the author or creator of the Web site uses paragraph or page numbers, use these numbers in the parenthetical citation. If no numbering is used, do not use or add numbers to the paragraphs, pages, or parenthetical citation.

When Web site does not number paragraphs➜ In his review of the film *Signs*, Roger Ebert says that Shyamalan "does what Hitchcock said he wanted to do, and plays the audience like a piano."

When Web site numbers paragraphs➜ In his review of the film *Signs*, Roger Ebert says that Shyamalan "does what Hitchcock said he wanted to do, and plays the audience like a piano" (par. 8).

General formatting guidelines for the MLA Works Cited

If you cite any sources within a paper, be sure to include a Works Cited at the end of the paper. Here are some general formatting guidelines to follow when setting up a Works Cited.

1. Put the Works Cited at the end of your paper as a separate page.
2. Use one-inch margins on all sides.
3. Include any header used for the paper on the Works Cited.
4. Center the title Works Cited at the top of the page, using no underlining, quotation marks, or italics.
5. Place the first line of each entry flush left with the margin. Indent any additional lines of the entry one-half inch (or one tab).
6. Double space the entries in the Works Cited, not adding any extra spaces between entries.
7. Alphabetize the Works Cited. Use the first major word in each entry, not including articles such as *a, an,* or *the,* to determine the alphabetical order. If the cited source does

not have an author, alphabetize by using the first word of the title of the source.

8. Put author's last name first (e.g., Ebert, Roger). Only reverse the first author's name. If more than one author, follow the first author's name with a comma, and add the other author names in the order of first then last names (e.g., Ebert, Roger, and Gene Siskel).

9. Use hyphens when you use more than one source from the same author. Alphabetize the titles, use the author's full name for the first entry, and then use three hyphens to replace the author's name in all entries after the first (see **formats for print sources #3**).

10. Capitalize all words in titles except for articles, conjunctions, and short prepositions. Always capitalize the first word of a subtitle.

11. Use quotation marks for titles of shorter works, including articles, book chapters, episodes on television or radio, poems, and short stories.

12. Italicize the titles of longer works, including album or CD titles, art pieces, books, films, journals, magazines, newspapers, and television shows.

13. Give the edition number for works with more than one edition (e.g., *MLA Handbook for Writers of Research Papers*, 7th edition).

14. Use the word *Print* after print sources and *Web* for Internet or Web sources.

Formats for print sources

1. Books (includes brochures, pamphlets, and graphic novels)

Author's Name. *Title of Book*. Place of publication: Publisher, date of publication. Print.

Lansky, Doug. *Signspotting*. Oakland, CA: Lonely Planet, 2005. Print.

2. Books with two or more authors

A comma is used between the author names, even if there are only two authors.

First Author's Name, and second Author's Name. *Title of Book.* Place of publication: Publisher, date of publication. Print.

> **Maasik, Sonia, and Jack Soloman.** ***Signs of Life in the USA: Readings on Popular Culture forWriters.* 6th edition. Boston: Bedford/St. Martin's, 2008. Print.**

3. Two books by the same author

Use three hyphens and a period in place of the author name(s) in the consecutive entries. Be sure the entries are in alphabetical order.

> **Maasik, Sonia, and Jack Soloman.** ***California Dreams and Realities: Readings for Critical Thinkers and Writers.* 3rd edition. Boston: Bedford/St. Martin's, 2004. Print.**

> **---.** ***Signs of Life in the USA: Readings on Popular Culture for Writers.* 6th edition. Boston: Bedford/St. Martin's, 2008. Print.**

4. Anthology or collection

Editor's Name(s), ed. *Title of Book.* Place of publication: Publisher, date. Print.

> **Smith, Allison D., Trixie G. Smith, and Karen Wright, eds.** ***COMPbiblio: Leaders and Influences in Composition Theory and Practice.* Southlake, TX: Fountainhead Press, 2007. Print.**

5. Work within an anthology

Author's Name. "Title of Work." *Title of Anthology.* Ed. Editor's Name(s). Place of publication: Publisher, date. Pages. Print.

> Tan, Amy. "Mother Tongue." *The Norton Field Guide to Writing*. Ed. Richard Bullock, et al. New York: Norton, 2010. 564-70. Print.

6. Article in a scholarly journal

Author's Name. "Title of the Article." *Journal Title* vol. number (date of publication): pages. Print.

> Holbrook, Teri. "An Ability Traitor at Work: A Treasonous Call to Subvert Writing from Within." *Qualitative Inquiry* 16.3 (2010): 171-83. Print.

7. Article in a scholarly journal that uses only issue numbers

Author's Name. "Title of the Article." *Journal Title* issue number (date of publication): pages. Print.

> Franks, Lola. "The Play in Language." *Child Signs* 73 (2006): 3-17. Print.

8. Article in a newspaper

Author's Name. "Title of Article." *Newspaper Title* Day Month Year: pages. Print.

> Genzlinger, Neil. "Autism is Another Thing that Families Share." *New York Times* 6 Apr. 2010: A4. Print.

Note: when citing English language newspapers, use the name on the masthead but be sure to omit any introductory article (*New York Times*, not *The New York Times*).

9. Article in a magazine

Author's Name. "Title of Article." *Magazine Title* Day Month Year: pages. Print.

Note: only use day if magazine is published on a weekly or bi-weekly basis.

> Musico, Christopher. "Sign 'Em Up!" *CRM Magazine* Nov. 2009: 49. Print.

10. Review

Reviewer's Name. "Title of Review." Rev. of *Title of Work*, by name of author (editor, director, etc.). *Journal or Newspaper Title* Day Month Year: pages. Print.

> **Ebert, Roger. "A Monosyllabic Superhero Who Wouldn't Pass the Turing Test." Rev. of *X-Men Origins: Wolverine*, by Dir. Gavin Hood. *Chicago Sun-Times* 29 Apr. 2009: E4. Print.**

11. Article in a reference book

Author's Name. "Title of Article." *Title of Reference Book.* Ed. Editor's Name. Location: Publisher, date. Pages. Print.

> **Jones, Amber. "Semiotics." *Encyclopedia of Signs.* Ed. Jeffrey Haines and Maria Smith. Boston: Brown, 2003. 199-202. Print.**

12. Religious works

Title of Work. Ed. Editor's Name. Place of publication: Publisher, date. Print.

> **Zondervan NIV Study Bible. Fully rev. ed. Ed. Kenneth L. Barker. Grand Rapids, MI: Zondervan, 2002. Print.**

Formats for online sources

1. Web site

Author's Name (if author given). *Name of Page.* Name of institution or organization associated with the Web site. Date of posting/revision. Web. Date of access.

> **Services Locator. United States Post Office. 2010. Web. 9 Feb. 2010.**

2. Article on a Web site (including blogs and wikis)

Author's Name. "Article Title." *Name of Web site.* Name of
institution or organization associated with the Web site. Date
of posting/revision. Web. Date of access.

Note: If there is no author given, begin the citation with the article title.

**"China's Traditional Dress: Qipao." *China Today.* Oct.
2001. Web. 9 Feb. 2010.**

**Ebert, Roger. "Signs." *rogerebert.com Movie Reviews.
Chicago Sun-Times.* 2 Aug. 2002. Web. 9 Feb.
2010.**

3. Online newspaper or magazine

Author's Name. "Title of Article." *Newspaper Title* Day Month Year:
pages. Web. Date of access.

**Bailey, Holly. "The Sign of the Red Truck." *Newsweek*
2007: 1. Web. 9 Feb. 2010.**

4. Online journal article

Author's Name. "Title of Article." *Title of Journal* Vol. Issue (Year):
pages. Web. Date of access.

**Austen, Veronica. "Writing Spaces: Performances of
the Word." *Kairos* 8.1 (2003): n. pag. Web. 9 Feb.
2010.**

5. Article from an online service, such as General OneFile
or LexisNexis

Author's Name. "Title of the Article." *Journal Title* vol. issue (Date
of publication): pages. Name of database or other relevant
information. Access Provider. Web. Date of access.

**Franks, Elizabeth. "Signing Up for Trouble." *Semiotics
and Signs* 13.4 (2009): 112-7. *InfoTrac
OneFile.* Thomson Gale. Middle Tennessee State
University. Web. 9 Feb. 2010.**

6. Article from an online reference work

Author's (or editor's) Name. "Title of Article." *Title of Reference Work.* Location, Date of publication (Day Month Year). Web. Date of access (Day Month Year).

> **Jones, Amber. "Semiotics."** *Encyclopedia of Signs.* **U of AK, 20 Mar. 2009. Web. 21 Sept. 2010.**

Formats for other commonly used sources

1. Television or radio program

"Title of Episode or Segment." *Title of Program or Series.* Name of network. Call letters and city of the local station (if applicable). Broadcast date. Medium of reception (e.g., Radio, Television). Supplemental information (e.g., Transcript).

> **"Signs and Wonders."** *The X Files.* **FOX. 23 Jan. 2000. Television.**

2. Sound recording

Artist/Band. "Song Title." *Title of Album.* Manufacturer, year of issue. Medium (e.g., Audiocassette, CD, Audiotape, LP, Digital download).

> **Five Man Electrical Band. "Signs."** *Good-byes and Butterflies.* **Lionel Records, 1970. LP.**

> **Tesla. "Signs."** *Five Man Acoustical Jam.* **Geffen, 1990. CD.**

3. Film

Title. Dir. Director's Name. Perf. Actor's Name(s) (if relevant). Distributor, year of release. Medium.

> *Signs.* **Dir. M. Night Shyamalan. Perf. Mel Gibson. Touchstone, 2002. Film.**

You may also include other information about the film, such as the names of the writers, performers, and producers, after the director's name.

> *Signs.* Dir. M. Night Shyamalan. Perf. Mel Gibson. Ex.
> Prod. Kathleen Kennedy. Touchstone, 2002. Film.

If you would like to highlight the specific contribution of one actor, director, or writer, you may begin the entry with that person's name, as you do with an author for a book.

> Phoenix, Joaquin, perf. *Signs.* Dir. M. Night Shyamalan.
> Touchstone, 2002. Film.

4. Advertisement

Name of product, company, or institution.
Advertisement. Publisher date of publication. Medium of publication.

> SunChips. Advertisement. *Newsweek*
> 15 Jan. 2010: 33. Print.

> SunChips. Advertisement. NBC.
> 15 Jan. 2010. Television.

Note the difference in how the citations for print and television advertisements are formatted.

5. Painting, sculpture, or photograph

Artist's Name. *Title.* Creation date (if known). Medium of Composition. Name of institution that houses the work or the individual who owns the work, City.

> da Vinci, Leonardo. *Mona Lisa.* c. 1503-6. Oil on Poplar.
> Louvre, Paris.

6. Interview

Interviewee's Name. Descriptive Title of Interview (e.g., Personal, Telephone, Webcam). Date of interview.

> Elbow, Peter. Personal Interview. 1 Jan. 2009.

7. Lecture, speech, address, or reading

Author's Name. "Title of Speech." Relevant information of where speech was given. Date of presentation. Descriptive label (e.g., Lecture, Speech, Address, Reading).

> **Stephens, Liberty. "The Signs of the Times." MLA Annual Convention. Hilton Downtown, New York. 28 Dec. 2009. Address.**

Sample Works Cited using MLA

Following is an example of how a completed Works Cited would look at the end of your paper.

Your Last name 14

Works Cited

Ebert, Roger. "Signs." *rogerebert.com Movie Reviews.*

    Chicago Sun-Times. 2 Aug. 2002. Web. 9 Feb. 2010.

Five Man Electrical Band. "Signs." *Good-byes and Butterflies.*

    Lionel Records, 1970. LP.

Signs. Dir. M. Night Shyamalan. Perf. Mel Gibson.

    Touchstone, 2002. Film.

Stephens, Liberty. "The Signs of the Times." MLA Annual

    Convention. Hilton Downtown, New York. 28 Dec.

    2009. Address.

Appendix D

APA Documentation

When you do research to find supporting evidence for your ideas or arguments, you need to credit your outside sources. Depending on what type of essay you are writing or which type of course you are writing for, you will need to choose a type of documentation style and continue with that style for the entire essay. Two of the most common styles, especially for freshman and sophomore students, are MLA (Modern Language Association) and APA (American Psychological Association).

If you write an essay in the social sciences, you will usually be asked to use documentation guidelines created by the American Psychological Association. The *Publication Manual of the American Psychological Association*, in its sixth edition, provides a full description of the conventions used by this particular community of writers; updates to the APA manual can be found at <www.apastyle.org>.

This chapter provides a general overview of APA documentation style and an explanation of the most commonly used APA documentation formats.

Using APA in-text citations

In-text citations (also called *parenthetical citations*) point readers to where they can find more information about your researched supporting materials. In APA documentation style, the author's last name (or the title of the work, if no author is listed) and the date of publication must appear in the body text of your paper. The author's name can appear either in the sentence itself or in parentheses following the quotation or paraphrase. The date of publication can appear either in the sentence itself, surrounded by parentheses, or in the parentheses that follow the quotation or paraphrase. The page number(s) always appears in the parentheses following a quotation or close paraphrase.

Your parenthetical citation should give enough information to identify the source that was used for the research material as the same source that is listed in your References list. Where this in-text information is placed depends on how you want to phrase the sentence that is summarized, paraphrased, or quoted. Be sure that the in-text citation guides the reader clearly to the source in the References list, where complete information about the source is given.

The following are some of the most common examples of in-text citations.

1. Author's name and date in reference

When using a parenthetical reference to a single source by a single author, use this form: (Author's Last name, Year of publication). Note that the period is placed after the parenthetical element ends.

→ When a teenager sleeps more than 10 hours per night, it is time to question whether she is having significant problems (Jones, 1999).

2. Author's name and date in text

In APA, you can also give the author's name and date within the sentence, using this form: Author's Full Name (Year of publication)

→ Stephanie Jones (1999) describes the signs to look for and when to be concerned.

3. Using a partial quotation in text

When you cite a specific part of a source, give the page number, using *p.* (for one page) and *pp.* (for two or more pages).

→ Stephanie Jones (1999) describes the signs parents should look for when concerned about their children: "excessive sleeping, refraining from eating, and lying about simple things" (p. 63).

4. No author given

When a work has no credited author, use the first two or three words of the work's title or the name that begins the entry in the References list. The title of an article or chapter should be in quotation marks, and the title of a book or periodical should be in italics. Inside the parenthetical citation, place a comma between the title and year.

➜ In a recent *Time* article, a list of 30 common signs of teenage trouble cites lack of sleep as the most common sign ("Thirty," 2010).

5. Two to five authors given

When you use a source that was written by two to five authors, you must use all the names in the citation. For the in-text citation, when a work has two authors, use both names each time the reference occurs in the text. When a work has three to five authors, give all authors the first time the reference occurs in the text, and then, in subsequent citations, use only the surname of the first author followed by *et al.* (Latin for "and others") and the year for the first citation of the reference in a paragraph.

➜ The idea that "complexity is a constant in biology" is not an innovative one (Sole & Goodwin, 1997, p. 63).

The last two authors' names in a string of three to five authors are separated by a comma and an ampersand (e.g., Jones, Smith, Black, & White).

➜ Most signs in English that the authors encountered on the road had "grammar mistakes, misspellings, or just odd pictures" (Smith, Jones, & Best, 1999, p. 55). The most common mistake was an "incorrect or misplaced apostrophe" (Smith, et al., p. 56).

6. Six or more authors given

When there are six authors or more of an item to be cited, include only the first author's name followed by *et al.* (Latin for "and others"). Use this form for the first reference of this text and all references of this text after that. Note: be sure, though, to list all six or more of the authors in your References list.

→ In Hong Kong, most signs are in Chinese and English; however, once you are in mainland China, English is rarely found on signs, except in tourist areas (Li, et al., 2007).

7. Authors with the same last names

If your source material includes items by authors who happen to have the same last name, be sure to use each author's initials in all text citations.

→ When a teenager sleeps more than 10 hours per night, it is time to question whether she is having significant problems (S. Jones, 1999, p. 63).

→ Another sign of trouble can be when you do not see your child for meals (B. Jones, 2003, p. 114).

8. Encyclopedia or dictionary unsigned entry

When you use an encyclopedia or dictionary to look up a word or entry, be sure to include the word or entry title in the parenthetical entry.

→ The word *thing* has more definitions than any other entry in the *Oxford English Dictionary* ("thing," 2001).

9. Indirect quotation

When you use a quotation of a quotation—that is, a quotation that quotes from another source—use "as cited in" to designate the secondary source.

→ Smith has said, "My parents really didn't understand me" (as cited in Jones, 1990, p. 64).

10. Personal communication

Personal communications—private letters, memos, non-archived emails, interviews—are usually considered unrecoverable information and, as such, are not included in the References list. However, you do include them in parenthetical form in the text, giving the initials and surname of the communicator and providing as exact a date as possible.

→ A. D. Smith (personal communication, February 2, 2010)

→ J. Elbow (personal interview, January 6, 2009)

Using long or block quotations

Long or block quotations have special formatting requirements of their own. If your quotation is prose and longer than 40 words, this is called a *block quotation.* Follow these APA guidelines for block quotations.

1. If introducing the block quotation with a sentence, use a colon at the end of the sentence.

2. Begin the quotation on a new line.

3. Do not use quotation marks to enclose the block quote.

4. Indent the quote five spaces from the left margin, and extend the right margin to the end of the line.

5. Double space the entire quotation.

6. Indent the first line of any additional paragraph.

7. Put a period at the end of the quotation, and then add the parenthetical citation.

→ However, Lansky (1999) states:

> Despite the statement on <www.signspotting.com> that we don't accept signs with the intention of being funny, people like sending them in. I've opted not to use these as it could encourage people to start making them, sticking them up in their driveway, and snapping a picture. Plus, funny signs are so much more amusing when the humor is accidental. (p. 72)

Adding or omitting words in a quotation

1. Adding words in a quotation

Use square brackets ([ ]) to point out words or phrases that are not part of the original text.

→ Original quotation: "When we entered the People's Republic of China, we noticed that the signage began dropping English translations" (Donelson, 2001, p. 141).

→ Quotation with added word: She said, "When we entered the People's Republic of China, [Dunkirk and I] noticed that the signage began dropping English translations" (Donelson, 2001, p. 141).

You can also add your own comments inside a quotation by using square brackets. For example, you can add the word *sic* to a quotation when you know that there is an error.

→ Original quotation: "When we entered the People's Repulic of China, we noticed that the signage began dropping English translations" (Donelson, 2001, p. 141).

→ Quotation with added comment: She said, "When we entered the People's Repulic [sic] of China, we noticed that the signage began dropping English translations" (Donelson, 2001, p. 141).

2. Omitting words in a quotation

Use an ellipsis (. . .) to represent words that you delete from a quotation. The ellipsis begins with a space, then has three periods with spaces between them, and then ends with a space.

Original quotation "The Great Wall . . . is something that can be seen from space. When we reach a time when advertisements can be seen from space, we have probably gone too far" (Jones, 1993, p. 101).

Quotation with words omitted in middle of sentence Frank Jones, author of *Signs in Space,* remarks, "The Great Wall . . . can be seen from space. When we reach a time when advertisements can be seen from space, we have probably gone too far" (1993, p. 101).

If you omit words at the end of a quotation, and that is also the end of your sentence, you should use an ellipsis plus a period with no space before the ellipsis or after the period. Only use an ellipsis if words have been omitted.

Original quotation "The Great Wall is something that can be seen from space. When we reach a time when advertisements can be seen from space, we have probably gone too far with our advertising and signage" (Jones, 1993, p. 45).

Quotation with words omitted at end of sentence Frank Jones, author of *Signs in Space,* remarks, "The Great Wall is something that can be seen from space. When we reach a time when advertisements can be seen from space, we have probably gone too far ..." (1993, p. 45).

Citing online sources

In the APA documentation style, online or electronic sources have their own formatting guidelines since these types of sources rarely give specific page numbers.

The APA recommends that you include in the text, rather than in an in-text citation, the name(s) of the person that begins the matching References list entry. If the author or creator of the Web site uses paragraph or page numbers, use these numbers in the parenthetical citation. If no numbering is used, do not use or add numbers to the paragraphs, pages, or parenthetical citation.

When Web site does not number paragraphs In his review of the film *Signs*, Roger Ebert says that Shyamalan "does what Hitchcock said he wanted to do, and plays the audience like a piano."

When Web site numbers paragraphs In his review of the file *Signs*, Roger Ebert says that Shyamalan "does what Hitchcock said he wanted to do, and plays the audience like a piano" (para. 8).

General formatting guidelines for the APA References list

If you cite any sources within a paper, be sure to include a References list at the end of the paper. Here are some general formatting guidelines to follow when setting up a References list.

1. Put the References list at the end of your paper as a separate page.
2. Use one-inch margins on all sides.

3. Include any header used for the paper on the References page.

4. Center the title **References** at the top of the page, using no underlining, quotation marks, or italics.

5. Place the first line of each entry flush left with the margin. Indent any additional lines of the entry one-half inch (or one tab) to form a hanging indent.

6. Double space the entries in the References list, not adding any extra spaces between entries.

7. Alphabetize the References list. Use the first major word in each entry, not including articles such as *a, an,* or *the,* to determine the alphabetical order. If the cited source does not have an author, alphabetize by using the first word of the title of the source.

8. Put author's last name first and then the initial representing the author's first name and the initial for the author's middle name, if given (e.g., Ebert, R.). If a work has more than one author, invert all the authors' names, follow each with a comma, and then continue listing all the authors, putting a comma and ampersand (,&) before the final name (e.g., Ebert, R., & Siskel, G.).

9. Arrange two or more works by the same authors in the same name order by year of publication.

10. Capitalize only the first word in a title and a subtitle unless the title or subtitle includes a proper noun, which would also be capitalized.

11. Do not use quotation marks for titles of shorter works, including articles, book chapters, episodes on television or radio, poems, and short stories.

12. Italicize the titles of longer works, including album or CD titles, art pieces, books, films, journals, magazines, newspapers, and television shows.

13. Give the edition number for works with more than one edition [e.g., *Publication manual of the American Psychological Association* (6th ed.)].

14. Include the DOI (digital object identifier), a unique alpha-numeric string assigned by a registration agency that helps identify content and provides a link to the source online.

All DOI numbers begin with a *10* and contain a prefix and suffix separated by a slash (for example, 10.11037/0278-6133.27.3.379). The DOI is usually found in the citation detail or on the first page of an electronic journal article near the copyright notice.

CITATION DETAIL WITH DOI

---

stet Detail

Title:
> An Ability Traitor at Work: A Treasonous Call to Subvert *Writing* From Within.

Authors:
> Holbrook, Teri[1] *tholbrook@gsu.edu*

Source:
> Qualitative Inquiry; Mar2010, Vol. 16 Issue 3, p171-183, 13p

Document Type:
> Article

Subject Terms:
> *DISABILITIES
> *QUALITATIVE research
> *MANAGEMENT science
> *SIGN language
> *WRITING

Author-Supplied Keywords:
> assemblage
> disability
> multigenre
> multimodal writing

NAICS/Industry Codes:
> 541930 Translation and Interpretation Services

Abstract:
> In questioning conventional qualitative research methods, St. Pierre asked, "What else might *writing* do except mean?" The author answers, it oppresses. Co-opting the race traitor figurative, she calls on qualitative researchers to become "ability traitors" who interrogate how a valuable coinage of their

---

trade—the written word—is used to rank and categorize individuals with troubling effects. In this article, she commits three betrayals: (a) multigenre **writing** that undermines the authoritative text; (b) assemblage as a method of analysis that deprivileges the written word; and (c) a gesture toward a dis/comfort text intended to take up Lather's example of challenging the "usual ways of making sense." In committing these betrayals, the author articulates her "traitorous agenda" designed to interrogate assumptions about inquiry, power, equity, and **writing** as practice-as-usual. [ABSTRACT FROM AUTHOR]

Copyright of Qualitative Inquiry is the property of Sage Publications Inc. and its content may not be copied or emailed to multiple sites or posted to a listserv without the copyright holder's express written permission. However, users may print, download, or email articles for individual use. This abstract may be abridged. No warranty is given about the accuracy of the copy. Users should refer to the original published version of the material for the full abstract. (Copyright applies to all Abstracts.)

Author Affiliations:
[1]Georgia State University

ISSN:
10778004
DOI:
10.1177/1077800409351973
Accession Number:
47934623
Database:
Academic Search Premier
View Links:
Find Fulltext

Formats for print sources

1. Books (includes brochures, pamphlets, and graphic novels)

Author's Last name, Author's Initial of first name. (Year of publication). *Title of book*. Place of publication: Publisher.

> **Lansky, D. (2005).** *Signspotting.* **Oakland, CA: Lonely Planet.**

2. Books with two or more authors

A comma is used between the author names, even if there are only two authors.

First Author's Last name, First author's Initial of first name, & Second author's Last name, Second author's Initial of first name. (year of publication). *Title of book*. Place of publication: Publisher.

> **Maasik, S., & Soloman, J. (2008).** *Signs of life in the USA: Readings on popular culture for writers.* **Boston, MA: Bedford/St. Martin's.**

3. Two books by the same author

Be sure the entries are in sequential time order with earliest date first.

> **Maasik, S., & Soloman, J. (2004).** *California dreams and realities: Readings for critical thinkers and writers* **(3rd ed.). Boston, MA: Bedford/St. Martin's.**

> **Maasik, S., & Soloman, J. (2008).** *Signs of life in the USA: Readings on popular culture for writers.* **Boston, MA: Bedford/St. Martin's.**

4. Anthology or collection

Editor's Last name, Editor's Initial of first name. (Ed). (Year of publication). *Title of book*. Place of publication: Publisher.

> Smith, A. D., Smith, T. G., & Wright, K. (Eds.). (2007).
> *COMPbiblio: Leaders and influences in composition
> theory and practice.* Southlake, TX: Fountainhead.

5. Work within an anthology or collection

Author's Last name, Author's Initial of first name. (Year of publication). Title of work. In Editor's Name(s) (Ed.) *Title of anthology* (page numbers). Place of publication: Publisher.

> Tan, A. (2010). Mother tongue. In R. Bullock, M. D.
> Goggin, & F. Weinberg (Eds.). *The Norton field guide
> to writing* (pp. 564-70). New York, NY: Norton.

6. Article in a scholarly journal without DOI (digital object identifier)

Include the issue number if the journal is paginated by issue. If there is not a DOI available and the article was found online, give the URL of the journal home page.

Author's Last name, Author's Initial of first name. (Year of publication). Title of the article. *Journal Title, volume number* (issue number), pages. URL (if retrieved online).

> Holbrook, T. (2010). An ability traitor at work: A treasonous
> call to subvert writing from within. *Qualitative
> Inquiry, 16*(3), 171-183. Retrieved from E-Journals
> database.

7. Article in a scholarly journal with DOI (digital object identifier)

Author's Last name, Author's Initial of first name. (Year of publication). Title of the article. *Journal Title, volume number* (issue number), pages. doi:

> Franks, L. (2006). The play in language. *Child Signs, 73*(1),
> 3-17. doi:10.1770/69873629

8. Article in a newspaper

Use *p.* or *pp.* before the page numbers in references of newspapers.

Note: if the newspaper article appears on discontinuous pages, be sure to give all the page numbers, separating them with a comma (e.g., pp. A4, A10, A13-14).

Author's Last name, Author's Initial of first name. (Year of publication, Month and Date of publication). Title of article. *Newspaper Title*, pp. page numbers.

Genzlinger, N. (2010, April 6). Autism is another thing that families share. *The New York Times*, p. A4.

9. Article in a magazine

Author's Last name, Author's Initial of first name. (Year of publication, Month of publication). Title of article. *Magazine Title, volume number* (issue number), pages.

Note: only use day if magazine is published on a weekly or bi-weekly basis.

Musico, C. (2009, November). Sign 'em up! *CRM Magazine, 13*(11), 49.

10. Review

Be sure to identify the type of work being reviewed by noting if it is a book, film, television program, painting, song, or other creative work. If the work is a book, include the author name(s) after the book title, separated by a comma. If the work is a film, song, or other media, be sure to include the year of release after the title of the work, separated by a comma.

Reviewer's Last name, Reviewer's Initial of first name. (Year of publication, Month and Date of Publication). Title of review [Review of the work *Title of work*, by Author's Name]. *Magazine or Journal Title, volume number* (issue number), pp. page numbers. doi number (if available).

Turken, R. (2008, May 5). Life outside of the box. [Review of the film *Signs*, 2002]. *Leisure Times*, pp. A12.

11. Article in a reference book

Author's Last name, Author's Initial of first name. (Year of publication). Title of chapter or entry. In A. Editor (Ed). *Title of book* (pp. xx-xx). Location: Publisher.

Jones, A. (2003). Semiotics. In B. Smith, R. Lore, and T. Rex (Eds.). *Encyclopedia of signs* **(pp. 199-202). Boston, MA: Rutledge.**

12. Religious and classical works

In APA, classical religious works, such as the Bible and the Qur'an, and major classical works that originated in Latin or Greek, are not required to have entries in the References list but should include reference to the text within the sentence in the essay. Note: it is always a good idea to check with your instructor on this type of entry since there can be some variety across instructors and schools.

Formats for online sources

1. Web site

The documentation form for a Web site can also be used for online message, blog, or video posts.

Author's Last name, Author's Initial of first name (if author given). (Year, Month Day). *Title of page* [Description of form]. Retrieved from http://www.xxxx

United States Post Office (2010). *United States Post Office Services Locator* **[search engine]. Retrieved from http://usps.whitepages.com/post_office**

2. Article from a Web site, online newspaper, blog, or wiki (with author given)

Author's Last name, Author's Initial of first name. (Year, Month Day of publication). Title of article. *Name of Webpage/Journal/Newspaper*. Retrieved from http://www.xxxxxxx

Ebert, R. (2002, August 2). Signs. *Chicago Sun-Times.* **Retrieved from http://rogerebert.suntimes.com/**

3. Article from a Web site, online newspaper, blog, or wiki (with no author given)

Title of article. (Year, Month Day of publication). *Name of Web-page/Journal/Newspaper.* Retrieved from http://www. xxxxxxx

> **China's traditional dress: Qipao. (2001, October). *China Today*. Retrieved from http://chinatoday.com**

4. Online journal article

The reference for an online journal article is set up the same way as for a print one, including the DOI.

Author's Last name, Author's Initial of first name. (Year of publication). Title of the article. *Journal Title, volume number* (issue number), pages. doi:xxxxxxxxxxx

> **Franks, L. (2006). The play in language. *Child Signs*, *73*(1), 3-17. doi:10.1770/69873629**

If a DOI is not assigned to content you have retrieved online, use the home page URL for the journal or magazine in the reference (e.g., Retrieved from http://www.xxxxxx).

> **Austen, V. (2003). Writing spaces: Performance of the word. *Kairos.* Retrieved from http://kairos.com**

5. Article from an online service, such as General OneFile, LexisNexis, JSTOR, ERIC

When using APA, it is not necessary to include database information as long as you can include the publishing information required in a normal citation. Note: this is quite different from using MLA documentation, which requires full information about the database.

6. Article in an online reference work

Author's Last name, Author's Initial of first name. (Year of publication). Title of chapter or entry. In A. Editor (Ed). *Title of book.* Retrieved from http://xxxxxxxxxx

Jones, A. (2003). Semiotics. In B. Smith, R. Lore, and T. Rex (Eds.). *Encyclopedia of signs*. Retrieved from http://brown.edu/signs

Formats for other commonly used sources

1. Television or radio program (single episode)

Writer' Last name, Writer's Initial of first name. (Writer), & Director's Last name, Director's Initial of first name. (Director). (Year). Title of episode [Television/Radio series episode]. In Executive Producer's name (Executive Producer), *Title of show*. Place: Network.

Bell, J. (Writer), Carter, C. (Creator), & Manners, K. (Director). (2000). Signs and wonders [Television series episode]. In C. Carter (Executive Producer), *The X files.* New York, NY: FOX.

2. Sound recording

Writer's Last name, Writer's Initial of first name. (Copyright year). Title of song. [Recorded by Artist's name if different from writer]. On *Title of album* [Medium of recording]. Location: Label. (Date of recording if different from song copyright date).

Emmerson, L. (1970). Signs. [Recorded by Five Man Electrical Band]. On *Good-byes and butterflies* [LP]. New York, NY: Lionel Records.

Emmerson, L. (1970). Signs. [Recorded byTesla]. On *Five man acoustical jam* [CD]. New York, NY: Geffen. 1990.

3. Film

Producer's Last name, Producer's Initial of first name. (Producer), & Director's Last name, Director's Initial of first name. (Director). (Year). *Title of film* [Motion picture]. Country of Origin: Studio.

Kennedy, K. (Producer), & Shyamalan, M. N. (Director). (2002). *Signs* [film]. USA: Touchstone.

4. Painting, sculpture, or photograph

Artist's Last name, Artist's Initial of first name. (Year, Month Day). *Title of material*. [Description of material]. Name of collection (if available). Name of Repository, Location.

> **Gainsborough, T. (1745). *Conversation in a park*. [Oil painting on canvas]. Louvre, Paris, France.**

5. Personal interview

Unlike MLA documentation, personal interviews and other types of personal communication are not included in APA References lists. Be sure to cite personal communications in the text only.

6. Lecture, speech, address, or reading

Speaker's Last name, Speaker's Initial of first name. (Year, Month). Title of speech. *Event name*. Lecture conducted from Sponsor, Location.

> **Stephens, L. (2009, December). The signs of the times. *MLA annual convention*. Lecture conducted from Hilton Hotel Downtown, New York, NY.**

Sample References list using APA

Following is an example of how a completed References list would look at the end of your paper.

Your Last name 14

References

Emmerson, L. (1970). Signs. [Recorded by Five Man
  Electrical Band]. On *Good-byes and butterflies* [LP].
  New York, NY: Lionel Records.

Franks, L. (2006). The play in language. *Child Signs*, 73(1),
  3-17. doi:10.1770/69873629

Kennedy, K. (Producer), & Shyamalan, M. N. (Director).
  (2002). *Signs* [film]. USA: Touchstone.

Jones, A. (2003). Semiotics. In B. Smith, R. Lore, and T. Rex
  (Eds.). *Encyclopedia of signs*. Retrieved from
  http://brown.edu/signs

Lansky, D. (2005). *Signspotting*. Oakland, CA: Lonely
  Planet. Stephens, L. (2009, December). The signs
  of the times. *MLA annual convention*. Lecture
  conducted from Hilton Hotel Downtown, New York,
  NY.

Tan, A. (2010). Mother tongue. In R. Bullock, M. D.
  Goggin, & F. Weinberg (Eds.). *The Norton field guide
  to writing* (pp. 564-70). New York, NY: Norton.